IN

DIVINE

FRIENDSHIP

IN
DIVINE
FRIENDSHIP

*Letters of Counsel
and Reflection*

SWAMI KRIYANANDA

Interior Design by Tejindra Scott Tully
Cover Photo by Barbara Bingham
Cover Design by Renee Glenn
Produced by Crystal Clarity Publishers

Crystal Clarity Publishers
14618 Tyler Foote Road
Nevada City, CA 95959 USA

Tel: 800.424.1055 or 530.478.7600
clarity@crystalclarity.com
www.crystalclarity.com

Library of Congress Cataloging-in-Publication Data
Kriyananda, Swami.
 In Divine Friendship : letters of counsel and reflection / Swami Kriyananda.
  p. cm.
 ISBN 978-1-56589-225-5 (tradepaper, photos, index)
 1. Ananda Cooperative Village. 2. Kriyananda, Swami.—Correspondence. I. Title.

BP605.S38A525 2007
294.5'44--dc22

                                2007022738

Contents

Foreword

This book of letters by Swami Kriyananda is entitled "In Divine Friendship." What is a divine friend?

Imagine someone who never judges, who loves you despite your faults, who sees you in terms of your highest spiritual potential, and is totally committed to helping you realize that potential. Imagine someone who gives you strength and understanding, seeking nothing in return, who offers, but never imposes, his views. Imagine someone who is always forgiving, respectful, and loving, even under the most adverse circumstances.

This begins to describe Swami Kriyananda, as seen through the letters in this book.

A newspaper reporter once asked Swami Kriyananda why so many people love him. Kriyananda's answer was, "Perhaps it's because I love them." Love is the magnet that draws love, and love is the thread that connects the letters in this book, whether to students, friends, or total strangers.

Swami Kriyananda's life of service began in 1948 when he became a disciple of the great Indian yogi, Paramhansa Yogananda, author of the spiritual classic, *Autobiography of a Yogi*. Trained by Yogananda for a life of writing, editing, and lecturing, Kriyananda has given thousands of lectures in many countries, written over 85 books, and composed over 400 pieces of uplifting music. He is the founder of Ananda Sangha, a worldwide organization that disseminates Yogananda's teachings.

On many occasions, Yogananda strongly encouraged the establishment of "world brotherhood colonies," places where people could live simply, guided by spiritual ideals. Fulfilling his guru's vision, in 1968 Kriyananda founded Ananda Cooperative Village, which has expanded to eight communities and ashrams in the United States, Europe, and India. Letters covering the various stages in the development of the Ananda communities are included in this book.

Swami Kriyananda once described Paramhansa Yogananda as "wearing his wisdom without the slightest affectation, like a comfortable old jacket that one has been wearing for years."

The same can be said of Swami Kriyananda. Clearly and with deep insight, he explains in these letters how to live every aspect of life in attunement with the Divine. Ultimately, it is divine attunement that enables Kriyananda to offer God's love and friendship to all, and that will also enable other truth seekers, inspired by his example, to do the same.

Friends of Swami Kriyananda

~~~~~~~~

The nearly 250 letters in this book were taken from Swami Kriyananda's paper and computer files dating from the mid 1970s to the present, and are essentially as he wrote them, edited primarily to delete identifying information, digressions, and other non-essential material. Before publication, Kriyananda carefully reviewed each letter, and made only a few minor, clarifying changes.

Crystal Clarity Publishers

IN
DIVINE
FRIENDSHIP

"This is what I would like to see ever-more deeply in you: childlike trust in Divine Mother, devotion,

---

L O V E

---

openness to Her guidance and love, holding nothing back from Her because you are completely Hers."

Dear _____ :

If we feel God's love in someone's love for us, then that is right and good. I remember once in India telling the woman saint, Anandamoyi Ma, how much I and others in America loved her. Her reply was, "There is no love except God's love."

The worldly ego might take her reply as a put-down, but I understood it as a reminder that we can truly love others only to the degree that we do so consciously as instruments of God's love.

It is easy to feel love for those who are kind and good, and easier still if they love us. But the test of godly love is to be able to feel it also for those who hate us. And especially for those who are determined to destroy us. God says to us, "They are My children, too." In other words, "If you love Me, you must love them also, for they too are Mine." We must love not only them, but all the tests that God sends us.

Ultimately, the only important thing you can do in life is love God. The only fact that truly matters in life is that God loves you.

It is a simple fact that the more we try to do good, the more enemies we will have—along with those who sincerely love, appreciate, and support us. But even were everyone to turn against us, the supremely important fact of God's love will never change. The tests we face, therefore, are always blessings. If nothing else, they inspire us to keep that one divine priority fixed ever before our gaze. Everything else passes. Our relationship with God is eternal. He is our own, as no one else ever will or ever can be.

The solution to our worries is love, and more love—divine love, not egoic love (the ego's love is rooted in likes and dislikes). As the Bible says, "Perfect love casteth out fear."

"Blessed are the pure at heart, for they shall see God." When your love for Him is effortless and complete, you will have Him.

In divine friendship,

April 4, 1995

Dear _____ :

I understand you're on a retreat. That's wonderful! We all need to retreat now and then, not for recreation, but to *re-create* ourselves.

In thinking about love, it's important not to emphasize someone's personal love for you, or yourself as the receiver. What's important on retreat is to understand as deeply as possible God's love for you, and yours for God. He loves you far more than any human being ever could—far more than you could ever love yourself, except in Him. So don't be afraid to open yourself to that love completely, inviting it into all the dusty corners of your heart, and sweeping them clean.

On retreat, one thinks of God's love and of other eternal verities. But it is important also to translate that love onto this practical plane of existence. Here are two sayings from a new book of mine called, *Do It NOW!* that you might enjoy, for we all get our feelings hurt occasionally:

> Don't close your heart, when your feelings have been hurt. For contraction causes its own pain. How others behave toward you is like the weather: not under your control. But how *you* behave, and what your feelings are, need be determined by no one but yourself. To accept a hurt from anyone is to suffer twice.

> Be not afraid to love. Even if your love is unrequited, you will be the richer for having loved. Water that doesn't flow grows stagnant.

The more you feel God's love in your heart, the more important it is to channel that love to everyone. As I've written in *Do It NOW!*

> Wish the best for everybody, and, in the very act of blessing them, you yourself will be blessed. A stained-glass window, when the sunlight pours through it, is brighter and more beautiful itself than the light with which it graces a church.

God bless you,

April 4, 1995

Dear _____:

Retreats generally are supposed to be times of self-examination. The important points to remember on retreat are these: There is only one true goal in life: to please God; to come closer to Him; to love Him; to unite our souls to Him.

The way to know God is by inner stillness of heart. This stillness is attained by loving more fully, more calmly, more wholeheartedly, never by deadening the emotions or hardening our hearts against those who would harm us.

Nothing and no one truly belongs to us; we are His alone. Joy is ours when we accept fully that we are God's, that God's nature is joy, and that His nature is our nature, in our souls.

I've always loved a statement of St. Jean Vianney's: "If you knew how much God loves you, you would die for joy!"

In divine friendship,

Circa 1989

Dear _____:

Know that my love and blessings are with you.

It is difficult sometimes to understand what is happening when we look at life only from a "human" perspective. We can only trust that whatever comes is from Divine Mother. The more we love Her, the sweeter Her ways become—whatever they may be!

Do keep in touch. Let us know how you are doing and what your plans are.

In divine friendship,

December 5, 1990

Dear _____:

A letter like this one from your mother cannot, in charity, be ignored. You must respond to her with love. You yourself have, as you've admitted, much anger to work out. Love is the way to expiate that anger, and her letter gives you that opportunity. Be grateful for the chance.

Your parents made a mistake, and seem to be admitting it. While remaining strong in yourself, you must give them, too, the opportunity to correct the error—at their own pace, and according to their own understanding.

They brought you into this life, and gave you what love they could. For your part, you also chose this family. If they want now to prove themselves good parents to you, you must be to them a good daughter. The important thing only is not to allow them to impose their desires on your own chosen path to fulfillment. But they seem to have recognized this point.

Take this single step, _____. Don't expect to run the whole course in a day.

In Master's love,

June 18, 1991

Dear _____:

To define your sense of dignity and self-worth in *any* terms that affirm your ego is in itself, for a devotee, at least, a delusion. Let me put it this way: I'm a composer. Some people think I'm a good one. To the extent that *I* think I may be good, I might make this a basis for some sense of self-worth. If I did, however, I'd be like any other worldly person. My compositions would be ego-accomplishments. NO! I am *not* a composer! I'm a devotee. I've written music as part of my service to God.

A drama director visited Ananda recently, and told me, "You are the first playwright I've actually had a chance to talk with." I replied, "I'm not a playwright! I'm just someone who has written one or two plays." Do you see? The more we define ourselves in terms of external accomplishments, the more we limit ourselves!

Dear _____, rest your sense of self-worth on realities that are *intrinsically* worthwhile—above all, on soul-qualities, and on your deepest reality as a child of God.

What Ananda is about is loving God, and serving Him. Our hopes should rest on absorption in Him, and on ultimate freedom from our mere humanity.

Joy to you!

Nothing in this universe is ours | 7

January 18, 1975

Dear _____:

The best "method" that I know for unlocking any blockages of energy in the mind is to constantly offer one's self to Master and God. The more open one becomes to divine grace, the easier it becomes simply to lay one's inmost thoughts at His feet. His grace alone can make you whole.

This is not a passive process. Don't just wait for God to come and make everything right for you. Think of it as a constant, dynamic self-offering. Nothing in this universe, least of all your self and your little personality, is really yours. The less you allow yourself to remain attached to your problems, the less they will exist for you at all. And the way to become less involved is by meditation, prayer, and selfless service without any desire for the results of your own actions.

My love and prayers are with you. May Master bless you always.

In divine friendship,

Circa 1989

Dear _____:

I don't know the book, but infer that you've gained from it the message to love yourself. A good message for you, personally. Yet in presenting this message to others I think you must make it clear to people that it is their inner, soul essence that they must love, the God within them, and not their egos as such, lest they slip into a kind of spiritual smugness that is a great trap on the path.

We must *accept* ourselves as we are, but *love* only that in us which lifts us toward God. God loves us in spite of our mistakes and delusions, but that doesn't mean He loves our mistakes and delusions. If the teaching to love oneself is not presented in the right context, it can lead to a kind of spiritual mushiness rather than to that heroic strength and determination without which little progress can be made.

Best wishes to you.

Love,

To receive love one must first give love | 9

Late 1990s

Dear _____:

If you feel unhappy and lifeless it's because you need to give more of yourself. You want love. Of course! Everyone does. But love is obtained by learning first to give it. Love God in people, and be open and giving to all. In this way you will develop the magnetism to attract the right partner.

Music could be one way of doing it, but whatever you do should be entered into with the thought of giving, not of getting. I think it is time you committed yourself more deeply to God and to the spiritual search, in a giving, not a getting, way.

My love to you always,

November 24, 2000

Dear _____:

Please tell _____: The ship of life needs a rudder. Otherwise it will drift about without a clear purpose. That rudder is devotion. To guide a ship, the polestar has always been a reference point. That polestar is God. It would help her to put a lot of energy into singing Master's chant, "Polestar of My Life."

In divine friendship,

*Asked whether or not to
devote more energy to "fun"* | 11

2001

Dear _____:

I'm sorry for not getting to your letter sooner.

I do think it would be good to devote more energy—not to "fun," necessarily, but to devotion to Divine Mother. You and I face a similar problem: we have active and fertile brains. Love God ever more deeply. Do *japa*. Chant to God. In this way—yes, have fun! And do more "fun" things with _____.

God bless you both.

Love,

*After Ananda faced a difficult
spiritual test, a devotee expressed doubts* | 12

March 14, 1998

Dear _____:

Thank you for your sweet letter. That you could even write it shows me what I have sensed in you already, that you are growing spiritually. Develop ever more in sweetness, devotion, and self-giving to God.

The doubts you have experienced are natural. I myself have had to make an effort to dismiss them. "Why, Divine Mother?" was my question. But I refused to complain that She was wrong or unfair, or that She didn't love me. I *know* She wants only our best. And I *know* what we have at Ananda is a wonderful thing.

I also knew the behind-the-scenes truth of the matter, and I knew _____ was acting against all *dharma*. I was certain that, even if Master and Divine Mother had wanted for some reason to destroy Ananda, they would not have chosen as their instruments for this purpose liars, traitors, and, indeed, criminals. And so, I clung to God, and refused to lose faith.

Still, I am sure this has been a test of faith for many others. We look back, and see how many miracles God has done for us. Now, I think, is the time for us to stand up and say, "I love You, Lord, not for what You give me, but for the sheer joy of giving my life to You."

That, _____, is what I would like to see ever-more deeply in you: childlike trust in Divine Mother, devotion, openness to Her guidance and love, holding nothing back from Her because you are completely Hers. I don't suggest an outer change. Nor do I suggest change—only an ever-deeper devotion and trust in God.

In Master's love,

October 12, 1988

Dear _____:

You asked me for suggestions on how you might obtain God's guidance in your work. I meditated on it this morning, and these thoughts came to me:

Work to deepen your devotion, and a childlike openness to God. Use your mind less. Take the knowledge you've gained, and offer it up to the superconscious for your solutions rather than trying so much to *think* your way to your answers.

Don't push aside what you know, but instead offer it up to God for clarification, at the spiritual eye, praying to receive your answers from that level of consciousness. Concentrate in the heart chakra, especially, when waiting to receive your answer, and see then what comes.

May God and Gurus bless you always in your divine search.

Love,

*Helping someone relate to
the female aspect of God* | 14

February 4, 1975

Dear _____:

It seems self-evident that different aspects of God fulfill the different needs of different people. Consider the numerous manifestations of both male and female gods and goddesses in Hindu temples, each one representing certain combinations of divine qualities, enlivened by the stories that accompany each one.

In your case, it is better to think of Krishna, or Master, etc., and to concentrate on their lives as a means of inspiration, until the magnetism of your positive devotion to the male aspect displaces all negative, rejecting confusions about Divine Mother. When you have become single-pointedly positive in your search to know God, you will automatically begin to see the female aspect of God in a clearer light, and to realize that, far from denoting frailty, it expresses enormous strength in love and self-giving.

In my lessons I go into great detail about the spiritual basis of masculinity and femininity, and the nature of duality. We must become the best of both, integrating deep compassion with indomitable will power. But let it come at its own speed, and for now concentrate on deepening your devotion to the Father.

In divine friendship,

September 11, 1990

Dear _____:

Astral *samadhi* is not going into and roaming about in the astral world, but merging in the infinite energy of which the astral worlds are projections. It is a form of AUM *samadhi*. Causal *samadhi*, by contrast, is oneness with the Christ Consciousness.

Don't get all tangled up in definitions, however. Love God. That's what it's all about.

In divine friendship,

February 28, 1990

Dear _____:

Thank you for your letter. I think perhaps your problem is that you are too much in your mind.

When we love someone, or like him, or even respect him, there is surely no need to define those feelings. The need for definition normally arises when our feelings are equivocal, or indeed when we don't have any special feelings on the subject.

In the hope that your problem is the latter, I suggest you consult your heart, not your mind, on this matter.

I will pray for you.

In divine friendship,

Late 1980s

Dear _____:

I was interested in your dream. Yes, deepen your attunement with Master. It will help you to develop deeper faith in him. Surrender every little worry to him. He is pleased when we offer him everything. Ask always, "Is this what you would have me do?"

Feel him working through you, meditating through you, speaking to others through you. Serve him in everything you do. Ask him to guide you in all things, to discipline you if needed, and always to help you to feel his love for you.

Don't identify with your failings. Your aspiration is to reach the Infinite, and your sincere devotion will surely lead you there.

In divine friendship,

"Whatever skills you have,
feel that these are God's way
of manifesting through you.
He will use you to whatever extent
you invite Him to do so.

ADVICE &
ENCOURAGEMENT

Above all, pray always that
God's will be done. Then
leave the problem of success
or failure in His hands."

March 5, 2003

Dear _____:

Don't let yourself feel guilty about anything. If people knew all the things they'd done wrong over countless lifetimes, and allowed themselves to feel guilty about them all, they'd be unable to bear the burden of existence itself. But bear it they must, anyway!

As Sri Yukteswar said, "Forget the past. The vanished lives of all men are dark with many shames. But everything in future will improve if you are making the right spiritual effort now."

We can't ever really fail anyone but ourselves. And we can't fail ourselves, either, if we keep on steadfastly moving in the right direction: upward, toward God.

Love,

July 6, 1973

Dear _____:

Contentment is an attitude to be deliberately practiced. It is not simply a state of mind that comes to one once things are going well. That sort of happiness can be lost in a second, under the least setback. Contentment, however, if practiced determinedly, can remain with us under every circumstance.

Good company, too, is important. Without it, contentment may be too difficult to practice steadfastly. If you could mix with contented people, you would automatically begin to acquire their magnetism, and to grow in contentment yourself. That is why I have urged you to take your next vacation at Ananda. You would like it here, I'm sure.

With love in God and Gurus,

December 26, 2000

Dear _____ :

I do want you to grow spiritually through your service to God. My concern always is to keep you from letting your ego-consciousness interfere with your spiritual advancement. I'm less concerned with boosting your ego than with encouraging soul-consciousness in you. I'm well aware that a discouraged ego can hinder your progress; therefore I do my best to help you keep out of that trap. And I'm very happy to see you stabilizing in this regard.

Do I want you to do this "business"? I really don't know. I want you to succeed in it, and I'm not wholly sure you have a "business head." I think of it in terms of serving Master and Ananda, anyway, not advancing your own interests. That's always how I've viewed my own work.

How much am I for what you're doing? It all depends on how much it's helping you, spiritually. That's really my only criterion.

My love and best wishes always,

November 15, 1991

Dear _____ :

The best way to find out whether this is your path is simply to try it first, and see. Guidance rarely comes to us when we sit back and wait for it. So long as you take positive steps, God will guide you toward the further steps to take. But if you wait for guidance to present itself to you full-blown, it may never come.

The secret of attracting guidance is to raise one's level of energy. By moving forward in the best way we know, we generate a flow of energy that can draw God's guidance to us. This is true even when our initial understanding isn't as clear as we'd like. So long as we use common sense, keep an attitude of openness, and offer our best efforts up to God, our understanding will grow, in time.

You wrote of feeling the need to make a spiritual commitment. You are blessed to feel this way. If you are feeling inspired by Yogananda's teachings, why not commit yourself to them provisionally? Yogananda promised that anyone who was not his disciple, but who came to him sincerely seeking his own true path, would be led to it.

We must all seek God inside us, in meditation. But it is a mistake to suppose that we can find Him on our own. It is His way to come to us through human instruments, particularly through divinely awakened masters and their disciples.

Yogananda's vibration is very much alive here at Ananda. Since you've already felt to visit us, and to write to me, it seems natural for you to try deepening your connection here. If you feel inspired to go to another of Yogananda's disciples instead, that's fine, of course. But don't try to do it on your own. The spiritual path is just too challenging for that!

May God and the masters bless you with clarity and joy in your search.

In divine friendship,

Feel joy in your "nothingness" | 5

August 26, 1988

Dear _____:

I'm sorry to hear about your discouragement. It is the negative side of humility to feel inadequate, to doubt one's abilities. You have much humility, and the humbler we are, the better God can work through us. It is right and true to recognize one's own fallibility. God's is the only true strength and guidance. Only egotists glory in their own cleverness and ability. In so doing, they shut God out and, in the end, fail.

But there is another side to humility, too. To feel inadequate is one thing, but to feel badly about it, or to take too personally other people's criticisms, is possible only because, despite your humility, there is some ego-involvement present. Otherwise you would feel joy in your own noth-ingness and in God's "everythingness."

Give it all to Him. The more you do so, the more you will find Him using you in everything. I think He has given you these tests for you to learn these lessons.

In Master's love,

Advice on overcoming self-doubts | 6

June 1, 1999

Dear _____:

I thought I had given you my reactions to your _____. I'm so sorry. I thought it was lovely. I also had a slight hesitation about it, as I have about everything you do: a sense of just what you've described in your letter—your lack of self-confidence. I feel it as a desire to convince, and a need to draw support from others instead of just being yourself.

It sounds funny when you say that you don't want _____ to discover what an awful person you are. Of course, you mean it to sound funny. But you're not an awful person! You're a fine person, with a great deal to give others. You've no call to feel this lack of self-confidence.

However, I can understand your problem, because I've had it too. So maybe I can help you with it. I've been plagued, in the past, by self-doubt. And yet, strange to tell, I've *never* been nervous about speaking in public, which I've heard is one of the greatest fears people have. My "cure"—fortunately, before I even started—was to think, "Well, if I really am a fool there's no harm in people knowing it!" So I've just forgotten about myself and gone ahead with whatever needed to be done. I often thought, "I'm the *last* per-son who ought to be starting a community for Master! And yet, the job's there to be done, and there's no one else doing it, so—here goes!"

The whole secret lies in simply accepting that we, of ourselves, really can't do anything right, but that God through us can literally do anything!

Forget yourself. Simply accept that you aren't perfect. (You aren't awful, ei-ther. You're just human, and no human is perfect. And no human is awful, because we're all children of the same Father/Mother.) I repeat: Forget yourself, and ask God to use you as He will—badly, if you get in the way, but even so He can use you to whatever extent you let Him. Forget yourself, and leave the problem of success vs. failure in His hands. Do your best, with His power, and forget it.

Love,

Sometimes a compromise of quality,
though painful, is inevitable | 7

August 20, 2000

Dear _____:

The question of bottlenecks is an objective matter, and doesn't depend on anyone's attitudes about it. _____ will simply drop us if we don't deliver when we say we will.

There is always a part of us that desires perfection, but we must—I've certainly had to, though never happily, in my life—adjust to objective circumstances. Sometimes a compromise of quality, though painful, is inevitable. Delivery dates are very important. We can't afford to miss them, even if it means doing something second best, which none of us wants.

Love,

Devotee objected to Kriyananda sharing
statements in her letter, critical of | 8
him, with Ananda colony leaders

May 19, 2000

Dear _____:

I don't know what to say. If I've offended you, I am very sorry. Will it change me? I'm sorry to have to disappoint you, but I must be honest. No, it will not. When I have principles to share with my friends and fellow ministers, I don't hesitate. I feel it is good to share them. In that way, we all learn. I, too, learn. I try to keep names out of it.

If I had thought of your communication as confidential, I certainly would have kept it that way. Since it involved, as I recall, a criticism of me and of what I say publicly, I felt that it would be good to get feedback, if only for the sake of my own more effective teaching, which I am always eager to improve.

My interest now is to create harmony, and to help you. Harmony can come if we recognize that, though our ideas differ, we are friends anyway, and we both love the same truths, and both love God. This kind of harmony, I am ever seeking.

What your letter seems to be trying to do is make me feel guilty. I don't think guilt can be a basis for any sort of harmony, and surely not the basis of any real friendship, which is what I'd like in this case.

You have my sincere best wishes and spiritual friendship.

In divine friendship,

Asked whether a monastic lifestyle could facilitate artistic endeavors | 9

Circa 1973

Dear _____:

I think you are right to give your time to your creative work and yoga. You have a talent, and ought to express it. The path of creativity, and also the path to God, are lonely paths, but at the same time much more fulfilling than human involvements—especially now that you've had your satisfactions, as well as frustrations, from the latter.

It really seems to me that human partnership, and all the energy that would demand of you, would now have the effect of pulling you down, where at one time it may have been a necessary release. You feel inwardly that you have something else to accomplish, and I think your real frustration now would lie in not having the freedom and the time to accomplish it. Indeed, despite what the world says, it is amazing how much time is completely wasted in inter-personal relationships!

Do visit us sometime. Perhaps you'd even like to live here, where you'd find friends who would add to your spiritual and creative energy, instead of draining it by drawing it to themselves.

In divine friendship,

*To a devotee Ananda was helping
secure parole from prison* | 10

June 24, 2003

Dear _____ *:*

I want first to thank you for your kind thoughtfulness in sending me that present. I was very touched.

Second, I want to suggest an attitude I think would help you in dealing with your present situation—which I hope isn't as hopeless as it looks at present.

Thirdly, I wanted to plead with you for _____, who has been deeply hurt by your anger toward her. She has been a true friend to you, and wants the best for you. There's a limit, however, to how much she can do as she has *many* other calls on her time. Nevertheless, she's been extremely anxious on your behalf. The latest word she gave me, just a couple of days ago, is that the *pro bono* lawyer does want to help you.

However, I still want to say that the wisest attitude would be to rely on God, not on any outer person or event. God is the real power in the universe. If He doesn't come through for you, your wisest attitude will be to try to adjust your thinking to the possibility of being where you are for your whole life. Not pleasant, but if it happens that way it can only be karmic. What I've found in my life is that when I really adopted that attitude, suddenly everything worked out for me as I'd wanted, and quickly.

I wish you all the best. And I pray sincerely that you will be able to come out soon!

Love in Master,

(*Eventually this person was paroled.*)

September 21, 1998

Dear _____:

You asked for my suggestions on how you should respond to _____'s letter.

You might write a brief note thanking him for the friendship and concern that prompted him to write as he did. Where you yourself are concerned, say that these are things you sincerely want to work on in yourself: that it is not easy to change oneself, but that we are all living here primarily for that very purpose.

On a more general note, you might say that this is one of the wonderful advantages of living in a spiritual community: that we get repeated opportunities to see ourselves through others' supportive but sincere eyes. This is divine friendship, and it is something one rarely encounters in the world, where everyone seems to want only to justify his own actions and character.

Where _____ himself is concerned, yes, the truth often IS spoken in anger, but as Master said, anger leaves a residue of disharmonious vibrations which in themselves are deleterious.

Citing Master's admonition, add that you hope his anger leaves him, as you yourself feel only friendship and gratitude toward him. Tell him that you hope also that his outburst will serve as a reminder in his work with others *not* to lose his temper with them, but to speak always with their welfare, as well as that of Ananda, in mind.

Your letter should smooth things between the two of you and preserve _____'s good will and friendship.

Love,

October 3, 1987

Dear _____:

I am sad about your situation. You and your husband are in my prayers.

I cannot understand the advice to cut all ties with the spiritual path. It's true that Brother _____ knows you both, and may well be aware of things in your husband that don't come to me through your letter. I would have thought, however, that while the advice not to meditate may well have been perfectly sound, some more physical service for God would therefore have become all the more vitally necessary. Surely God is the answer to all our problems. The issue is only how we approach Him.

Couldn't your husband have been encouraged to work on the grounds at the Lake Shrine? Or, if his condition is such that it would have demanded too much energy to supervise him, couldn't he have been encouraged to work for God and Gurus—that is, in the thought of them—in your own garden? Surely it was a mistake to cut him, and you, off from the path. I must admit there is much here that I don't understand.

If indeed your husband is possessed, isn't there something to be done about it? Master said that chanting AUM in the right ear insistently, with deep faith and concentration, is one way of driving out astral entities. Another thing to practice is to make large circles of light around the body, joining the hands in front and then behind, while chanting AUM-TAT-SAT; then to trace out AUM on one's pillow three times with the forefinger before going to sleep.

In all of these teachings there is the constant rejoinder to cling more than ever to God—not as an escape (which is why, in certain cases, it is better not to meditate), but with faith. If we can't cling to God, to whom in God's name *can* we cling? It is only the presence of higher vibrations that can drive out lower ones.

Please write again and let me hear how you and your husband are doing.

In divine friendship,

Late 1980s

Dear _____:

Without more complete information, it seems that your friend needs to strengthen his will power and to get more closely in touch with the Divine Power within himself. Service, and a giving outlook and attitude, could help him very much to overcome this problem.

From your description of it, what he has experienced does not sound wholesome. Whether it comes from the subconscious or from some astral entity is difficult to say at this point, but in either case the above advice may prove helpful.

With prayers and best wishes,

Try not to mix with those who can tempt you | 14

January 28, 1974

Dear _____:

Because of your mother's deteriorating health condition, I think you ought to help by being with her for now, giving her your love and spiritual support.

I strongly suggest that you not mix with friends who can tempt you into old ways of life that you have hoped to leave behind forever. Even out of love for them, you should leave them for now, for you will be their truest friend if you can develop the strength in yourself to affect them on a higher level.

The yoga postures are helpful, but not nearly so much as meditation and devotional communion with God. I urge you to learn how to meditate and to practice meditation at least an hour and a half every day. In addition to that, be of service to others, particularly at this time to your mother, feeling that it is God you are serving, not man, and also that it is His power that you are using in your service.

In divine friendship,

February 26, 2001

Dear _____ :

I hope you'll be able to do something with the suggestions I made. I recognize the problems you'll have, especially the fact that, because they do represent a compromise, they won't in themselves lead people even to think in terms of attaining high spiritual states. But then, how many achieve such states anyway? The important thing, first, is to get them to include God and spirituality in their lives, and spiritual *aspiration*.

If the different churches could at least unite in this understanding, very much would be accomplished. And my sense, for the South, is that from there this understanding could spread, as it never will, adequately, if it lets itself get bogged down in religious dogmas.

A mass rejection of the atheism among governmental and educational leaders, and of opportunistic modern law practice itself, is essential if America is effectively to claim its true role of leadership in the world— a role of service, not domination, which is, I believe, its divine destiny. Yoga and Yogananda's teachings are too refined to accomplish such a sweeping development, but filtered through something like what I recommended, the insights they inspire can accomplish wonders.

So you see, _____ , I really have deep hopes for what you can do. Remember, *People are more important than things*. You do need buildings to house activities, but it is people, not buildings, that will accomplish these high objectives. Their minds, and above all their hearts, must be affected. You can do it, with God's grace and with inner guidance. You have the talent and the intuition. You need very much, now, to redirect your thinking from things to PEOPLE. Where you live, however, the pickings will be few to non-existent. You need a broader audience. I think you'll find it best through the medium of radio.

As I said, only two things will effect such a change: One, inspiration; and Two, a push upward from below, in the form of urgency for change. The second is something over which you and I have no control, but I feel it is coming—perhaps, first, in the form of a real economic depression. This, if and when it comes, can be turned into a great blessing. The suggestions I've made will be needed, as a means of directing people's minds in a more positive direction.

As for the first—the need for inspiration—what I felt in the South was a certain spiritual complacency—even lethargy. Can people feel inspired to rise above the level of being merely good neighbors and begin actively seeking God, and serving Him in others? Not so long as they aspire to nothing higher than a good life, instead of a divinely guided one. I think it will be difficult to inspire people to higher aspirations until that complacency is shattered.

There is more spiritual openness in the West for the primary reason that there is also more tension and inner dissatisfaction. Greed exists everywhere, but I think in the South there is less consciousness of that soul-disease. This is good, obviously, in a human sense, but inasmuch as the disease of ignorance exists anyway, the awareness of it can be a great incentive.

Your need now is to see *everyone* as your family. Most of the people I met during my visit there were your family members and their friends. A good thing, of course; good that they're interested in good things. But remember the words of Jesus Christ: "Who is my mother and father and brethren but those who love God?" (I haven't got the quote exactly, but that is its message.) *Reach out* to others. You have the ability, and God wants to give you His grace to do so.

Love,

To a truth seeker whose visit to Ananda renewed her faith | 16

May 7, 1990

Dear _____:

Thank you for sharing your experiences with me. I am pleased to hear how these experiences have reaffirmed your faith in God and Christ. I try to serve this same Christ and I hope that this work of Ananda is helping others' faith to be deepened also. I pray that I may be ever open to His guidance.

Without in any way detracting from the validity of your teacher's experience of Christ, I would say it often happens that when one gets a glimpse of the Divine, he assumes it is the one and only true glimpse, and that other revelations are wrong. This is a sign of spiritual immaturity, for, as I wrote in a song of mine called "What Is Love?", "Not a church binds Him as its own, not a creed makes Him fully known, foolish we if we limit him, every atom is His throne."

It was not your teacher's destiny to find what he was seeking in his own country. This does not mean that others have not found it. Each one must follow his own path. But the goal is infinity itself.

If Yogananda was influenced by a deceptive spirit, then, applying the test Jesus himself gave us, we would have to say that the results of that deception must have been demonstrated in Yogananda's life. Jesus said, "By their fruits ye shall know them."

The fruits of the divine life are selfless love, humility, and all divine qualities. These Yogananda manifested in his life to a greater degree than I have ever seen in anyone else. I do not want to enter a controversy on this point, but only to help you keep your mind open, for a narrow mind cannot accommodate the vast ocean of divine love. Yet I am happy for you that you have found a path that satisfies you and inspires you to deeper faith.

In divine friendship,

A Roman Catholic expressed interest in moving to Ananda | 17

April 1, 2002

Dear _____:

I've been thinking and meditating on your question, which has come up before. It seems to me it might be better for you to live *outside* Ananda and think of us as your friends, rather than live *within* Ananda and struggle to reconcile your beliefs with Master's. I was hoping your visit to Ananda Village would resolve your questions on reincarnation, but you have the same problems with this doctrine as you had before, and raise another big difference in our belief systems: the Eucharist.

I'll be happy to discuss these issues of dogma with you when I see you, but I seriously suspect they won't be resolved quickly or easily. To me, the issues are clear, and I have no problem confronting both of them openly and sincerely. But habits of thinking are a powerful anchor. I'm afraid other doubts would arise, in time.

I myself am unhesitating in expressing my views, and I really fear I might offend you with some of them. I wouldn't want to at all, but in my own home—at Ananda Village, that is to say—I won't be so careful as I would be when lecturing to the public. At Ananda, I *expect* everyone to be on the same wavelength as I, and I don't weigh my words so carefully—don't even *want* to have to weigh them in the same way as I would during a public lecture.

I'm perfectly likely to speak of Master's incarnation as Arjuna, or as William the Conqueror, or of my own as Henry I. Chatty stuff, for us, but a bit of a conversation stopper for someone who can't accept reincarnation as even a possibility. Moreover, my sense of humor is all too likely to tip the scales for someone who feels he has a contrary belief to defend.

For your own peace of mind, I'd say you were safer where you are, much though I reacted positively to your wish to join us. The door, however, is open. I am only pointing out the difficulties in *your* mind, not in our acceptance of you.

In divine friendship,

Advice to a woman with an abusive relative | 18

Dear _____:

Your question is a complex one, and it is harder not being able to actually talk to you about it. I do not feel I can deal with the psychological problems of your brother, especially as they are so deep-seated and the situation has gone on for so long.

What I can do, and what I feel is more important, is to give you spiritual advice which I hope will help you stay calm and centered. There is little you or anyone can do for your brother until he seeks help and puts out the effort to help himself. What you *can* and must do is to help yourself. Be strong—like the saints who were not affected by being tortured or put in concentration camps except by becoming more joyful.

Ensure that you and your daughter are physically safe from your brother. Once you have ensured that you are physically safe why is there any need for fear and anxiety? It is only making you unhappy. *And* it is demonstrating to your brother that his actions have an effect upon you. If he cannot get the attention he craves in the form of affection, then your fear is almost as satisfying to him.

Do not give him this privilege! Practice the yoga techniques and feel God's reassurance and calmness during meditation. See this as a lesson for you to develop courage and even-mindedness. In your meditation pray for your brother and forgive him. Then you are free.

I don't know how much of this you have done already, but I would suggest that, out of love not hate, you be very firm with your brother. Ignore him completely. Have no communication with him. Demonstrate that he has no effect on you.

Enlist the aid of the police if necessary to discourage him from staying near your house, but do not get involved yourself. If, at the same time, *others* in his life would offer him love and attention and help, this *may* divert his attention from you.

I hope this is of some help. I am praying for you and may God bless you.

In divine friendship,

Is abortion ever appropriate? | 19

Late 1980s

Dear _____:

The taking of life is a broader issue than just the legal one. Human law may recognize a higher law, but it cannot alter it. The only mitigating factor I can think of in taking an embryo's life is if the mother's life is seriously threatened.

In the case you've described, I would think abortion was indeed possible within the divine law. But even so, it would be a difficult matter to decide.

This is, I realize, a very sensitive social issue nowadays. I am hesitant to plunge into it with seeming callousness, particularly where I myself am not at all affected. Nevertheless, conscience bids me speak truthfully when I am asked. The soul is already present in the forming foetus, and is there, Master said, from the moment of conception. Taking the life of a growing creature cannot, except in extreme circumstances—to which I would be inclined to include rape—be condoned, either morally or spiritually.

For those who have already had abortions, it is important not to feel a weight of guilt. There was surely not a *will* to kill involved, and that, certainly, is the main thing. We make many mistakes in life. Our duty is to love all the more deeply. The sins—which are only errors of judgment—of countless incarnations will be washed away forever by God's grace, when we find Him.

In divine friendship,

To a person discouraged by certain Ananda Village guidelines | 20

Circa 1990

Dear _____:

I'm so sorry you took our conversation the way you have. Truly, I want you to find the right situation for yourself, one in which you can be happy and at peace, and can continue your search for God. What I asked of you was what we ask of everyone. Surely, if you look at it impartially, you will see that it is what we *have* to ask everyone.

Indeed, _____, your very rebellion at doing what I asked of you indicates the serious difficulty you would be likely to encounter in living here: the ability to fit in with a large community of people, most of them much younger than you; people who already have their own self-definition, clarity of purpose, and a definite momentum of their own.

Your discouragement over my requirement, which I expressed to you with love and which was, I think, based not only on normal Ananda requirements but also on common sense, suggests that you would not find it easy to fit in with those requirements which are normal to any community, and particularly to one of our size.

It makes me think that the best thing for you might be to go in with one or more people who are buying land near to Ananda. I imagine it would be possible in this way to have a situation that would cost you very little to settle in and to live. In this way, you could work with the community and gradually build a relationship on many levels that would help you to create your own degree of involvement. Where this might lead in future is anyone's guess.

_____, the way to win in any situation is to show courage and to begin at the natural point of entry. If one believes in himself, he eventually finds for himself the niche he has earned. No one should seek anything for himself that he hasn't rightfully earned.

_____, you have my love and support. Pray deeply that you receive the guidance and the opportunity you crave to live ever closer to Master and God.

In divine friendship,

A God-given responsibility | 21

Late 1980s

Dear _____:

I have done my best to make _____ see sense. I did agree with her about her wish to try homeopathy, but I said that if it doesn't bring about a change quickly, she *must* go through with the advice of Peter and other doctors.

You might remind her of what I said, and urge her, now that two months have passed (a reasonable test period in a case as critical as hers), to get herself tested again. Her body is a responsibility, given her by God. If she fails to take reasonable care of it, she will be held accountable in her next life. Doctors have, admittedly, much to learn about the body, but they know much also, and in serious cases like this should not be ignored.

In divine friendship,

December 31, 1988

Dear _____:

I think there may be something in you that makes it difficult to cope with anyone having authority over you. You have an independent nature, and while you love Ananda, and are loved by all of us in return, I think your own fulfillment demands that, at this time, you work independently—as you have been doing.

I hope this separation from us will not be permanent, for indeed it is a virtue to be able to work cooperatively with others. It would help round you out as a person. For this time, however, and given, among other things, your age, and your need to discover your own potentials, do be on your own. I see you visiting us, but having your own space.

_____, you always have my friendship and support. I pray above all for your continued, deepening attunement with God. Do visit us as often as possible. I hope that in future we'll be able to work more closely together. You will always, in spirit, be a part of our Ananda family.

In Master's love,

Circa 1990

Dear _____:

I am sorry to hear that you are upset. I like what you made and the energy you put into it. And I like you. When I gave you my friendship it was forever. Your anger with me doesn't affect my feelings toward you.

But what you've created is very large and doesn't fit in my house. What would you have had me do with it? The money I hoped to get from its sale would have helped pay for new video equipment, through which I still hope to benefit thousands. It wasn't for personal gain.

You have been meditating some years now. This anger is unbecoming in a devotee. It's not that I hold it against you. We all have our moments when we fail to live up to the ideals we hold up for ourselves. Still, for your own happiness I hope you will take this outburst as a reminder to yourself to be more generous in your sentiments, and less attached to the fruits of your labor, as Krishna counsels in the *Bhagavad Gita*.

Because of the disharmony now surrounding this gift, I would not want to sell it anymore even if I were offered a substantial price for it. Nor would I want it in my keeping. I have asked _____ to return it to you. I hope you will accept it with my love.

You have my best wishes and my friendship always. Please give my best also to your husband. And please remember, finally, who it was who brought you together. It never helps to turn against the instruments of blessing in our lives.

In divine friendship,

Advice on meeting life's trials | 24

July 18, 1990

Dear _____:

I've often found that understanding comes to me not so often through ideas, counsel, etc., as through being with the right kinds of people, and doing the right kinds of things. Mixing with people who are negative, or who see life too much in terms of problems, tends to influence one to see things in negative terms, and to view problems as fixed realities on life's path.

On the other hand, when we mix with people who are basically positive— not because they live in a dream world, but because they meet life's challenges with courage—that association tends to make us strong in ourselves: to become "solution conscious" rather than "problem conscious." The company of strong people influences us to discover ways to surmount our own problems.

Doing the right things means, among other things, finding work in which we can be creative, in which we can give of ourselves, in which we can be serviceful or useful to others. It involves trying to be helpful rather than trying to be helped. Perhaps this sounds trite, but I've found that it works.

How does one love? One simple—though I admit, not easy—answer is to think more of others, less of oneself. Another way is to do things for others, and not to wait for them to do things for you. Another is, give them what you want from them in return: love, encouragement, support.

In divine friendship,

October 1, 1999

Dear _____:

I was interested in what you wrote about my song, "Life Flows On."

I think I felt somehow that you didn't like the song. I didn't want to embarrass you, but it seemed to me right for you to express your true feelings and not be diplomatic about them.

As I recall, my delight was in your expressing them, fairly and not unkindly. This was, to me, a breakthrough for you in expressing friendship. I was happy for that reason. (What did the song matter?)

Love,

May 17, 1990

Dear _____:

Thank you for your letter. I'm so sorry things have turned out as they have, and pray that in the end this story will prove a glorious one for you in your growth toward perfect understanding.

Self-reliance is an important quality. Many people, alas, have allowed this wonderful teaching of both Emerson and Thoreau to reinforce their own egos. That application of their teaching, unfortunately, simply does not work. Not to depend too much on the opinions of others is good, provided one's resolution is to stand firmly by Truth. It's not good, however, if it means being simply stubbornly committed to one's own opinions. Self-reliance must be balanced by humility before that Infinite Reality of which we are all a part.

Life has put you in a position where now you must face this lesson. Let us hope you will learn it well. If you do, as it seems you are earnestly disposed to do, then we must view your present trial as a great blessing, even though the trial itself is a hard one.

Our prayers are with you, _____, that you receive the highest grace through this experience, and with as little pain as possible.

_____, I deeply pray that you will stand firm by your resolution to be humble, and to accept God's will in this matter, as in all things in your life. If you do, that which you find painful today will bring you great joy tomorrow. Any rejection, moreover, that you feel today you will recognize tomorrow as the basis for an ever deeper friendship in God.

May God bless you always.

In divine friendship,

Be only a "fellow seeker" | 27

Mid 1990s

Dear _____:

Don't seek to be a teacher, but seek, rather, to help people spiritually, with a sense of sharing with them.

You write that they haven't been listening to you. That is because you haven't manifested the magnetism to *attract* them to what you say. In trying to be a teacher, you've awakened the thought in their minds, "Who are *you* to tell *me*?" Instead, serve people humbly, according to what you perceive to be their present needs and understanding.

I myself have, if you like, been a "teacher" for over forty-five years. Never in all this time have I thought of myself as teaching anyone. I've always seen myself as a fellow seeker, blessed in turn when anyone accepts whatever I've felt guided to say.

May I earnestly suggest you get a copy of Paramhansa Yogananda's newest book, *The Rubaiyat of Omar Khayyam Explained*? It is a *great* work, and explains many of the dilemmas you are facing.

I will pray for you.

In divine friendship,

January 8, 1976

Dear _____:

Thank you for sending me the transcript of that "reading." I appreciate your letting us know about this material. I must say, however, that Master didn't recommend going to mediums. In fact, he recommended definitely against it. It can too often, he said, be a real trap. I urge you not to get involved in such things. For while it is true that good things sometimes do come through such channels, that good is usually mixed up with a great deal that is not valid, and is not helpful at all. The question remains, how to tell the difference? The mere fact of being in the astral world doesn't make souls omniscient!

As for the specific threat of destruction to Ananda, I can only say that I truly don't expect such to happen. On the other hand, if it be God's will, then there is nothing we can do to prevent it. We are doing our best to serve God as He wills. The rest is in His hands.

But to get some perspective on the matter, it is important to realize that, of the predictions made in this manner, the majority—the *vast* majority—have proven false. Someday, of course, the earthquakes may come, but even Edgar Cayce spoke only of changes to the coastline, not of the whole state being destroyed. Since California is, at this time, the most spiritual part of America it is difficult to imagine that the entire area will be wiped out.

God, truly, is our only protection in any case. It seems far better to trust in Him, and to try to follow His guidance, derived through meditation and prayer, rather than to get sidetracked in the questionable truths of astral beings who purportedly speak to us through mediums.

You seem to have a fairly good understanding of the limits of this kind of experience. I would repeat again, however, that Master recommended that we not get involved in such matters.

My best wishes to you and your family.

In divine friendship,

The best way to change others | 29

June 9, 1989

Dear _____:

Master had a great reverence for life and for all of creation, for he saw all things as expressions of God. He was very mindful of the little details in life, and trained us to live simply, with divine respect for others.

It is also important, however, not to try to be another person's teacher, unless he asks you to accept that role. The best way to change others is through example and by sincere love. If you can practice simplicity and humility, letting others feel your love for them and your respect, you will have a better chance of helping them to change.

In divine friendship,

Man's common destiny | 30

January 30, 1992

Dear _____:

I was touched by your sincerity, and I'm glad you found my book helpful.

In answer to your question about Buddhism, whereas the truth is ever one, the Masters present it at different times and in different places with different emphases, depending on the needs of the people they are teaching. During the time of Buddha, people had come to an overly personal expectation of being helped by the gods through Vedic ceremonies, known as *karmakand*. They wanted the gods to do all their work for them, without proper effort on their own part. Therefore it was that Buddha didn't speak of God. He was by no means an atheist, however. The proof that his teachings are true is that those who follow them faithfully eventually discover the very same truths that are discovered by the followers of other true spiritual paths.

You asked whether it is truly possible to feel God's grace and guidance in our lives. Absolutely yes! Many signs of God's love are given to everyone who seeks Him with devotion. In time, moreover, when we have purified our hearts of every desire except the longing for Him, God gives us the supreme gift: Himself. This blessed state comes to each soul, in time: It is man's common destiny.

The love you feel for God is a precious gift. It is the most important ingredient in spiritual progress. You are fortunate indeed, therefore, to possess it! If you haven't felt God's response to your prayers, perhaps it is because you haven't learned yet how to seek Him in quite the right way. For, though it is by God's grace that we grow, we need to learn how to *cooperate* with that grace. God and the Masters work on us from within. For, as Jesus put it, "The kingdom of God is within you."

The spiritual teachings show us how to "cooperate"—with truth, with others, with God's will. Wherever you are in your own development, I'm sure you would benefit from contact with those who may be further along in the spiritual search than you are. Why don't you investigate what we can offer you at Ananda? Since it was to me that you wrote, living here seems like a natural possibility to explore. True teaching is "vibrational" much more than just factual; it is generally much more easily imparted in person.

May God and the Masters bless you in your divine search.

In divine friendship,

August 3, 2001

Dear _____:

Chitta is the feeling aspect of consciousness. It also underlies all consciousness, inasmuch as consciousness IS *feeling* awareness. Therefore Master wrote in the chapter on cosmic consciousness in *Autobiography of a Yogi*, "I cognized the center of this empyrean as a point of intuitive perception in my heart."

Consciousness has various aspects in human manifestation, separated as you know (*mon, buddhi, ahankar, chitta*), but its all-embracing reality is *feeling awareness*. Therefore *chitta* comes at the end, not so much to sum up as to underline. To sum up suggests separate things being added together. Cosmic *chitta* is one underlying reality, of which mind (the human ability to perceive), intellect (the human ability to discriminate), *ahankara* (ego, the limited, human perception of the one, infinite Self), and *chitta* (the human manifestation of cosmic feeling which, united to ego, says, "I like, I don't like"), of which all of these are manifestations.

Yes, likes and dislikes are the most obvious waves of *chitta*, on a feeling or emotional level. So also are attachments and aversions, and a whole gamut of other human feelings (most of them related, of course, to the first of these—likes and dislikes). It is in their emotional form that they become binding, and in their emotional form that they become separate and distinct from *buddhi, ahankar*, etc. Otherwise, as pure *chitta* they underlie and embrace everything. Hence Master's words, "I cognized the center of this empyrean...."

Pure *chitta* doesn't divide. It's the human manifestation of *chitta* that does so.

I hope this clarifies.

Love,

"*Master said that whatever we criticize in others, we will have to experience personally ourselves, either in this life or in some future incarnation.*

JUDGMENTAL ATTITUDES

To judge others is to invite judgment in return—not only from others, but on the part of Divine Law."

Dear _____ :

On the path to God, right attitude is the most important thing, not what you do or say but the attitude you bring to it. This is something Yogananda always emphasized.

Mr. Jacot, in an episode I cited in *The Path*, stirred up many emotions by the way he defended Master when an unscrupulous member of the SRF church in Hollywood attempted a "take-over." Master later thanked Mr. Jacot for having saved the day. After expressing his gratitude, however, he added this gentle admonition: "It is not good, regardless of one's intentions, to create wrong vibrations through anger and harsh words. The good that you have accomplished would have been greater had you employed peaceful means."

I went on in the next paragraph to explain: "Negativity, from whatever motive, creates its own momentum. Unfortunately Mr. Jacot failed, even after Master's admonishment, to see the need for curbing righteous anger in a good cause. Thus he gradually developed a judgmental mood that ultimately separated him from the work."

Master also said that whatever we criticize in others, we will have to experience personally ourselves, either in this life or in some future incarnation. To judge others is to invite judgment in return—not only from others, but on the part of Divine Law.

"Blessed are the merciful," Jesus said, "for they shall receive mercy." Implicit in this statement is its corollary, that the *un*merciful shall be treated without mercy. And yet, Divine Law *is* merciful in the end, for it teaches and guides us, as fast or as slowly as we choose, on the pathway to liberation. Judgmental people, however, are not concerned with the transcendence of those they scorn: They want only for those people to be hurt or destroyed.

Here is how the karmic law works: It is a question of magnetic attraction. Qualities on which you focus in others, you will attract in return. If you concentrate on goodness, you will attract goodness. But if you concentrate on evil, you *cannot but* attract evil to yourself. An obsession with the real or imagined impurity of others must infallibly, in the end, result in your developing the same impurity, yourself.

The point here is not whether your judgment is valid, but only that the judgment itself creates its own magnetism. You might be certain that a reputed saint was actually a sinner. Regardless of the validity of that certainty, if you allowed it to become a vortex of condemnation it would generate a magnetism that would draw energy inward, eventually, in judgment upon yourself.

Does this mean we should blindly ignore evil if we find ourselves exposed to it? By no means! To ignore evils that are thrust at us is, if only passively, to endorse them. If you really believe a situation to be seriously wrong, then you owe it to yourself, and to those involved, to do what you can to improve matters, or else to distance yourself. In such a case, the important thing would be not to let yourself be drawn into a downward spiral of negativity in yourself. It would be important, in other words, not to react angrily or in other ways disharmoniously.

Dharmically it would be best to uphold before others a higher vision, to invite them to a better way of living or of looking at things. If you found your listeners blind to your good advice, then the only right thing to do would be to leave Ananda quietly, blessing all here even in their ignorance. To create an emotional stir even in a spirit of righteousness would be to involve yourself karmically in the very negativity you condemn—rightly or wrongly—in others.

There is another aspect to this matter of judgment. Master said, "Whenever you see wrong in the world, remember, it's wrong with *you*." Our very criticism of others—I'm not referring to that impartial observation which is a necessary part of discrimination—is not only an indication of qualities that we'll inevitably attract, someday, to ourselves: It is also *one of the surest indicators* of faults we already have in ourselves.

I pray that you grow daily in devotion.

In divine friendship,

May 17, 1998

Dear _____:

Loyalty should never be equated with agreement. Loyalty means, rather, an underlying love and support regardless of disagreements, even when you disagree emphatically. It means putting love ahead of any disagreements. It means trusting others' good will and good intentions, regardless of their mistakes.

When you make a mistake—and we all make them—the desire to straighten the matter out would demonstrate an affirmation of loyalty. A mark of friendship is to assume good will on the other person's part, especially his good will toward oneself, and his openness to resolving any disagreements.

An attitude of judgmental criticism would come under the general heading of lack of loyalty to the extent that it had personal feeling behind it. We might be offended enough by what someone does to feel the need to reproach him. The important thing would be never to disapprove of him as a person, to want only the best for him always, and to remain his friend even if he withdraws his friendship.

In Master's love,

December 22, 1994

Dear _____:

I quite agree with you: It is necessary to maintain the highest standards in our lives and in our work. At this point, however, we seem to part ways. Why do you speak of "reduced expectations"? Why do you speak of "forgiveness"?

One of the greatest problems people create in their lives is the expectations they hold of others. Expectations, in this case, are the equivalent of judgment. And one of the greatest presumptions in human nature is the thought that we can grant or withhold our forgiveness from others for things they haven't even done to us, personally.

Taking Jim Jones as an example—he himself, some day, will recognize his error, come to grips with it, and change. Part of his self-transformation will surely involve drawing those same souls he betrayed, or others acting in their place as symbols of his karma, to a right understanding.

Forgiveness simply doesn't enter the picture. God loves Jim Jones despite anything Jim did. Someday, Jim will come to love God's presence wholly in himself. Meanwhile, let us bless, not condemn with unforgiving thoughts, the errors of a fellow wanderer that his soul may return to the light.

Jim Jones's actions, however, are not the issue here, so let us take something closer to home. While I was working at the Dock Street Theater in Charleston, South Carolina, early in 1948, I was part of a barbershop quartet. The other men in the group were always making mistakes, and accusing one another of having made them.

I managed to be the influence for peace and harmony in the group by claiming all the errors for myself. When others spoke to me of how disharmonious we were as a group, I didn't object. I *identified* with the group, you see, as a means of helping it. My way has always been, not to "divide and conquer," but to *unite and heal.*

I don't think we should "demand perfection" of anyone. If we feel inspired by anyone, let us act according to that inspiration rather than to any limited definitions of what we think *ought* to be.

If we don't feel a certain teacher can inspire us anymore, then let us seek elsewhere, but without judgment, without condemnation. Respect them for who they are, and if they are trying sincerely to grow, support them. Give them a chance to grow in their own way, with the God-given right we all have to do our humble best in life.

What concerns me most deeply about your letter is that it reflects an attitude that I have seen creep repeatedly into the churches, where self-righteousness *seems* to many people the way of truth, and therefore becomes the ruling philosophy of the congregation.

Meanwhile, charity flies out the window, and what you have left is no longer a church but a mausoleum. The remaining, loveless members are right, right, right all the way down the aisle, only to end up in a crypt, spiritually dead, beneath the church floor.

I would not want such an attitude to creep into Ananda, and I am aware of the ease with which it could do so. Please think about it. I will pray for you.

In divine friendship,

Taking ourselves lightly | 4

October 3, 1999

Dear _____:

To judge anyone else is, in a sense, to judge yourself. To judge yourself is, in the same sense, to judge everyone else.

It will help you if you try to develop a God's-eye view of things—to see others as divine sparks that are trying to merge back into the Infinite Fire, instead of leaping out of the fire as many sparks do. Accept people not for themselves, but as parts of that infinite whole.

There will then be no sense of judgment, but only an acceptance of them as they are, and of seeing them, with love, as they might be. Love them as a divine friend, and do what you can, even if only mentally, to help them to know who they really are: expressions, like yourself, of the Infinite Lord. By loving others, you will overcome the tendency to judge them, which means, to compare yourself with them. They will become actually *more* lovable to you for their very eccentricities!

This is a capacity you often show in yourself, where you yourself are not touched. It would be well to learn to view yourself with that same lovable tolerance and good humor. You are, in fact, a fine person. You need only to learn to take yourself more lightly.

I have a T-shirt I bought at East West in Mountain View, which I often wear at night. It says: "Angels can fly because they take themselves lightly."

Love,

January 2, 1977

Dear _____:

When I invited you to come and live at Ananda, my primary concern was to provide you with a happy environment, among devotees who loved you. Your sweet way of speaking had led me to believe that you were a woman of compassionate concern for the welfare of others.

I confess I was quite unprepared for the unsympathetic way you reacted to circumstances of which you disapproved. You quoted Master as your justification, saying what a stern disciplinarian he was. But Master himself said, "I scold only those who listen. I won't scold those who don't." The hallmark of his nature was infinite patience, tolerance, and compassion. He never condemned those who were weak or misguided, any more than Christ did. Wherever Master saw the slightest hope, he encouraged people in the paths of righteousness. He never judged them.

He also said that the tendency to judge others attracts similar judgment to oneself. "Blessed are the merciful," said Jesus Christ, "for they shall receive mercy."

I encourage our members to live according to the highest spiritual principles, and to understand that there is no fulfillment possible to anyone outside of God. But I encourage, I lead: I never drive. In this way I help people, and that is what Master told me to do. Once, when I myself acted judgmentally toward someone whom I felt not to be acting according to true spiritual principles, Master scolded me saying, "If I were so uncompromising, few would be left here" (at Mt. Washington). It was by love, not by judgment, that he won us and inspired us to change.

I don't consider it my place to advise you, so I'm not going to try, though there is much that I might say. However, for your own spiritual welfare I beg you to consider whether it is not rather the divine way to bless than to condemn. We attract to ourselves what we look for in others. Is it not possible that the rejection and betrayal you have received from others in this life are rooted in deep-seated attitudes in yourself?

In Master,

October 11, 2006

Dear _____:

I am impressed that, not knowing me at all, you have been able to find me so full of faults. I suggest, inasmuch as the subject of my inadequacies seems to interest you, that you make an effort actually to get to know me. It may be that, after that attempt, you may find you've only scratched the surface, and that in fact I am even more riddled with faults than you now imagine.

In any case, please know that you have my good wishes.

Swami Kriyananda

October 26, 2003

Dear _____:

I've often puzzled why you so often wrote me that you admired my work, but didn't like me. "All right," I thought, "so she doesn't like me. Many people don't. But why does she feel a need to keep *telling* me so?"

And even now, you write that you've come to like me, but want me to know that what you like about me is what flows through me, rather than liking me for myself. The truth is, I'm perfectly happy with this idea. I don't really worry about my personality; I want only to be a channel for Master, so I quite agree with you.

But I wonder why you feel a need to keep telling me so? I'm assuming it must be something in you—possibly a projection onto me of a tendency in yourself to be judgmental? I don't want even to suggest this in a critical way, because I see from what else you've written that you have been handling this, and well.

In divine friendship,

"It has taken many hands to make the miracle of Ananda—Master's most of all.

THANK YOU

Thank you for the part you are playing. God bless you."

October 21, 2000

Dear _____:

I have read your paper, and want to thank you for it with deep sincerity and humility. Really, reading it was for me a moving experience. I'm amazed also at the massive research you've done, and the creative thought you've applied to that research. I thank you above all for what you've done to draw attention not so much to my book as to a truth so widely and so greatly needed today.

You have also done, in the service of this need, what I myself could never have done: you've given it a basis in scholarly knowledge and authority, tying it in to the thoughts of others through the ages. My strength, but also my lack, is that what I write comes from inside myself. It is a great advantage to pair that with other minds, and to test it against what they, too, have written. For human knowledge grows by accumulation.

You'll be interested to hear, in light of your commentators' emphasis on the importance of music, that at Ananda people have been drawn to join the community even more through our music than through our teachings. Books and teachings give them the ideas, but the music has made them *feel* the importance of the teachings. In fact, last May a choir of about 55 members from several of our communities came to Italy and did a tour of six cities, singing my oratorio, *Christ Lives.* Everywhere they went, they received standing ovations.

I am so grateful for your work. If this system is to be heard, it will need energy (and training) like yours to push it along. I don't ask you to promote it. I only ask you to be who you are, and to "keep up the good work."

Unless you object, I will send your manuscript to our schools and colonies. But if it will come out in book form, that will be wonderful. Perhaps you can let me know?

With very best wishes.—And, congratulations!

In divine friendship,

February 8, 1974

Dear _____:

Thank you for your sweet letter. I appreciate your support in the matter of _____'s unkind remarks.

I confess I was hurt when I first got his letter, for I had never given him anything but my sincere affection. But when I discovered how many copies he'd sent to people, my hurt dissolved in merriment. Such buffoonery surely deserved only applause. In fact, I sent him a dollar donation towards his mailing costs.

Yet I must tell you I feel deep kindness for _____. What sort of friendship would it be that couldn't ride the waves of a friend's behavior, or that was withdrawn when others treated one wrongly? Don't all of us make mistakes from time to time? Indeed, if we can't love our friends in spite of their mistakes, I really don't see how we can expect to have any friends at all! And if we can't put up with imperfections in our friends, by what right do we expect them to value us, imperfect as we are?

_____ is basically a good man. Jealousy and pride are normal human weaknesses. Truly, I feel more kindness for him now than before, if only because he needs it more when he is in error than when he is going along well. He may treat me as he pleases; that is his business, not mine. But my business is to continue to be his true friend. He can't affect my feeling for him, or my loving wish for his highest good.

And if his letter—basically invalid as it is—should turn a few people against me, why, I would consider that only good fun! The divine drama would get a little boring, don't you think, without a little comedy? For what do people's opinions matter, whether good or bad? I'm not seeking God to please them!

Love,

September 7, 1998

Dear _____:

Thank you for your letter, and for letting me know about this group you've found yourself leading! I'm glad to hear about it. It certainly sounds as if it's filling a real need, and one that will only grow, of course, as our present members get older.

What Master brought to the world will revolutionize every institution and habit of thought we grew up with. America's peculiar worship of youth will surely be prominent among these. Of course, what's really worthy of respect isn't age per se, but the wisdom that develops along with it (or does, at least, when people live their lives well).

Americans these days, unfortunately, are much likelier to admire athletic stars than those who've won life's more important battles. I expect, though, that as respect for wisdom grows, the elderly will be invited to fulfill quite a different role in our culture.

Thank you also for your words of friendship. It has taken many hands to make the miracle of Ananda—Master's most of all. Thank you for the part you're playing. God bless you.

In divine friendship,

October 26, 2003

Dear Vimala:

Thank you for sending me your book. I want to start off by saying, Congratulations! It is really a superb job—intelligent, insightful, and *Dwapara*. I'd like to see us use it in our schools. It is in line with what I feel needs to happen these days.

Many years ago I looked briefly into graphology, and was not particularly impressed. For one very important thing, it didn't tell one where to take the subject. You have done so. If handwriting can be used to improve oneself, it can be a wonderful tool. It isn't everything, of course, but what is? It emphasizes the personality, when we are trying to transcend the personality. Still, it *is* important, and what you've done is by far the best I've seen on the subject.

I congratulate you again on a great job. God bless you always.

In divine friendship,

To Swami Chidananda, who sent money
after Ananda's temple was destroyed by fire | 5

September 7, 1970

Revered Swamiji and Beloved Friend:

How generous of you to send us a donation towards our new temple. I accept it, as you wish, in your great Master's name [Swami Sivananda of Rishikesh], and in that of my beloved Guruji. The check itself was most liberal, but most of all we are deeply touched that you would help us at all, knowing as we do the financial strains that must be placed upon you during your travels.

Immediately after the fire I was fortunate to find another, and a better, harmonium, and purchased it immediately. As you wish, I shall consider your loving gift as applying retroactively to that purchase.

The new temple is almost completed. It is larger than the first, and will be much more attractive. The first was only 3/8ths of a sphere, and looked too squat, though it was the best we could do at the time. This one will be, as we wanted the first one to be, a full hemisphere. Best of all, perhaps (in the light of our sad experience), it will be fireproof. With God's grace, the money for the new structure has already been raised.

Swamiji, let me take this opportunity again to thank you for the inspiration we all received from your visit here. Your presence was a blessing on our humble venture, and on the hearts of all the people living here.

I am happy to say, too, that your remarks in the garden on the subject of neatness as an aspect of reverence accomplished in a few moments what months of pleading had not accomplished.

It is my increasing hope to be able to spend a few years in seclusion. I do not know whether it will be here or in India. Let us see what Mother wills. I may get to India towards the end of this year. If I do, I shall certainly come to see you.

With loving regards from everyone,

"I'm deeply sorry for the betrayers" | 6

January 1, 1999

Dear _____:

Thank you so much for your letter. I greatly appreciated it. I'm deeply sorry for the betrayers. What they've done, really, is betray their own higher natures, in which I did believe. There is always pain when one gives pure love, only to have it flung back at one contemptuously. But the greatest pain, still, is seeing their *self*-betrayal.

In divine friendship,

About a painting of Yogananda given to | 7
Kriyananda by an experienced artist

January 13, 1976

Dear _____:

I'm very sorry for not responding sooner to your kind offer.

But in fact I find myself caught on the horns of a dilemma. I want, on the one hand, to let you know how sincerely I appreciate your kindness. But, on the other hand, while admiring the painting's very real artistic merit, I'm forced to admit that the painting doesn't quite "do it" for me, who knew Master personally.

It is a good painting, but not a good one of him. The artist couldn't know that, of course. She has tried to be faithful to a photograph, and has, I think according to her own purposes, succeeded well enough to satisfy most people. But how could I, in all sincerity, accept it to show my appreciation of you, while knowing that I probably wouldn't hang the painting in the kind of spot it deserves, if it be considered purely on its artistic merits?

I think I must refuse, reluctantly, and suggest that maybe some SRF center, (perhaps in Richmond or Sacramento) would be more happy with the painting, while my own happiness in receiving it would be centered more in the kindness of your gift to me as a friend.

In divine friendship,

To a musician who sent a recording of his performance | 8

December 27, 1998

Dear _____:

Today I had the time to listen with greater care to your recording. I want you to know I think it is exquisite! Thank you so much not only for doing it, but for doing it with such deep sensitivity.

The parts you feel might have been better are the eternal concern of every sincere artist, whether musician, singer, or writer. I still remember Longinus in his essay, "On the Sublime." He said (I'm paraphrasing) that the greatest works cannot but have minor technical flaws, because an excessive concern with the achievement of formal perfection prevents the mind from soaring in skies of inspiration.

Indeed, excessive "perfectionism" indicates a pedestrian mind. The arms of Krishna, at Jagannath temple in Puri, are truncated on purpose to symbolize the truth that the Infinite can never be captured perfectly in form.

Love,

December 26, 1988

Dear Ones:

I want to thank all of you for your many demonstrations of divine friendship this Christmas season. I am grateful of course for your presents, but also for your kind and happy smiles, for the love in your eyes, and for the joy I feel in your devotion to God, Christ, and gurus.

To every one of you I would like to say the same things: Thank you for your gift, and for your love, and above all for the love of God that I felt shining through you. The actual nature of each gift is secondary to the deeper, less tangible reality of your friendship.

In divine friendship,

"I think that in your longing for
a romantic relationship,
your heart is actually longing
for much more than that.

MARRIAGE &
RENUNCIATION

I'm not saying, don't seek a wife,
or that you should enter a
monastery. But I _am_ saying,
seek a loving relationship
above all with God—
with the Divine Mother."

April 30, 1980

Dear _____:

It is a mistake to think that you will ever find the perfect mate. Life, outwardly, cannot be other than compromise between the ideal and reality. This is true in *every* walk of life, even in the ashrams of saints, for the world is limited, relative, and otherwise conditioned in countless ways.

Seek perfection, therefore, within yourself. The more you depend on outer circumstances to give you perfection, the more you will find disappointment.

Remember, too, that your path to perfection depends not only on inner growth, but on the *application* of that inner growth to outer circumstances. In other words, a relationship that seems lacking in personal fulfillment may be a great spiritual blessing for the opportunity it gives one to be a channel for divine love and service to help the other person. "It is more blessed to give than to receive." Service and sacrifice, not outward fulfillment, are the essence of spiritual development.

In divine friendship,

June 23, 2000

Dear _____:

People nowadays use the word "relationships" mostly as a synonym for "romantic relationships." Needless to say, there are many other kinds of relationships in the world, and not only human, either.

In the broadest sense, the word *relationships* refers to *all* outer relationships the ego has with *maya,* or delusion, and includes *all* outer relationships between one ego and another: the relationship not only with friends, but also with casual strangers, with those who hate us or even seek our destruction; with family and neighbors; even with animals. It also refers to a person's feeling of relationship with the universe and everything in it.

Lifting the word, *relationship*, out of the category of romantic involvements enables us to see that the word refers also to vast and exciting spiritual discoveries: the realization that throughout all existence, a relationship *already* exists. As the Irish poet A.E. said (I'm forced to paraphrase here), "The least movement of my finger has an effect on the most distant star." We are united not only with one another—friend and foe equally, though in different ways—but also with all that IS.

We are also united with the Spirit. As Meister Eckhart said, "I move my hand, and Christ moves who *is* my hand." He was saying that divine union, on that level of reality, exists already. And so it did, at least in his case.

For most people, however, *relationship* implies two separate entities seeking and exploring an underlying oneness that still needs to be affirmed. This is true even between self-defined enemies.

In superconsciousness, and in God-realization, *relationship* is not something to seek or to be created, but only something to be realized on ever-deeper levels. The unity exists already. The relationship enjoyed in that unity, like a great saint delighting in the worship of God, is not a search but a re-affirmation, and, finally, a rediscovery that can be enjoyed "ever-newly" through all eternity.

In that context, what is romantic love? Remember, the only real lover is God. There simply IS no love, outside of Him (or Her, the Divine Mother). It doesn't exist. Thus, romantic love is actually a delusion. It promises everything, and gives little—indeed, almost nothing, and the little it does give melts away in time, like snowflakes on a hot day.

Human love is fleeting and disappointing. It is a kind of emotional release— UNLESS: unless it is self-giving, not grasping; unless it seeks fulfillment in the joy of another, not selfishly in one's own self. It is fulfilling when it is sought, not by making demands, but in inner freedom. It is fulfilling when it is based primarily on soul-friendship, not on bodily, emotional, or intellectual demands. And it is true only when it is completely unconditional.

Can such love be a path to transformation? Only to the extent that it inspires selflessness, kindness, generosity, loyalty, and a self-expansion that includes another person's happiness, then that of increasing numbers of other people's happiness, in one's own. In this sense only has this always been an important teaching in Hinduism. The Hindu scriptures say that the wife and husband should love one another, not only for each other's sake, but for the sake of God who dwells within them both.

Can I give examples from my own life and/or from those I have counseled (or known in my life), as to how relationships and the issues that come up in them can be worked with and lead to higher clarity and knowledge of the Self? Yes, indeed!

Intimate relationships, especially, force us to face ourselves. Instead of blaming anyone else, we should think, "What does this inter-personal problem tell me about how I can change and improve myself?" Never blame the other person. And don't blame yourself, either. Blame, you see, is useless. Look on every difficulty as an opportunity—not for changing the other person, but for self-improvement. As for examples, I suppose a thousand could come to mind, but the brief sentences in this paragraph are a condensation of all of them, and are more real to me than any specific episode could possibly be.

Ultimately, all the same, these all relate to improving the personality, which is nothing but a mask for the Self. As aids to knowledge of the Self, they serve only to the extent that they teach us to stop thinking of ourselves, to stop *wanting* for ourselves, and to realize that all relationships are reminders of that One Self of which all of us are inextricably a part.

The danger in all relationships, spiritually speaking, is that they hold present experiences up so close that we are tempted to confuse them with reality. The benefit of relationships, spiritually speaking, is that the more we can learn to maintain our hearts' equanimity in the face of every test (and relationship tests are among the greatest that people experience), the more we can remain, as Paramhansa Yogananda often put it, "unshaken amid the crash of breaking worlds."

Remember, the basic reality of the universe, the fundamental reality of all existence, is duality. For everything there is, without exception, an opposite. The more we allow ourselves to be elated by joyful emotions, the more we are bound to attract, and to be susceptible to, emotions of suffering. The one follows the other like the phases of the moon. In any relationship, fulfillment will come not in momentary "highs," but only in calm giving from one's inner Self to all.

I have covered these matters in my book, *Expansive Marriage*, which is not, as I'm afraid some people may expect, a manual on "wife swapping," but a book on soul-expansion, and on self-giving and self-sharing with one's spouse and with all others. [The book is now called *Self-Expansion Through Marriage*.] I've also covered them to some extent, though more indirectly, in my new book, *Awaken to Superconsciousness*.

I hope the above answers will prove useful.

In divine friendship,

Cautions against a too emotional relationship | 3

Circa 1990

Dear _____:

I have been happy to see you looking so well spiritually. I would like to see you go on growing in the direction of non-attachment, centeredness inwardly, and especially devotion to God. Outward relationships are secondary in importance to our inner relationship with Him.

From the other, outward aspect of love, I can only suggest that any relationship you form should be conducive to inner calmness and growth. A too-emotional relationship can only disturb your inner attunement. I think that perhaps that was what wasn't working in your relationship with _____. Put God first, and your duty to Him, and as Jesus said, all things else shall be added unto you.

God bless you this holy season.

Love,

Spiritual reasons for sexual moderation | 4

September 14, 1974

Dear _____:

As to your question about sex: The thing to realize is that nothing in God's creation is wrong in itself. There is often a choice, however, between good, better, and best. Walking in the woods can be inspiring, but if one did that to the exclusion of meditation he would be forsaking a greater inspiration for a lesser.

Sex is undeniably one of the strongest instincts of human nature. Because of its very strength, however, it can take precedence over finer feelings and perceptions, making it more difficult to develop such refinement. Moreover, sexuality makes great demands on one's energy. Just imagine: From that act begins the process whereby new life is born on earth. It is not a casual diversion for the body's energies, like playing tennis, but involves a major sacrifice. The pleasure involved is put there by nature to make sure creatures will be willing to make the sacrifice necessary to propagate the species.

In the sex act itself, to be sure, a man's energy is much more drawn upon than a woman's (100 times more, Master said; woman's sacrifice, of course, comes during the subsequent process of pregnancy and child birth), but woman, too, loses subtle energy through sex. Mind you, I'm speaking primarily of a subtle energy that worldly people never miss. But the more one advances spiritually, the more he really can feel the loss.

Now, pitted against this loss is the fact that the sexual impulse is so strong in human nature that for most people, especially couples who live together, to try rigidly to exclude sex from their lives can amount to at least as great an energy drain. Many are the couples I've seen on this path who go through utter misery because of their inability to control a perfectly normal impulse. Worse still, they treat the sex instinct as something base, something to be ashamed of, instead of a holy force before which one ought to feel reverence—and until one does, I think it may not even be possible to overcome it.

Sri Yukteswar said that when sex is in a normal, healthy state, one's appetite for it will be infrequent. This is important—that one realize that excessive indulgence is debilitating, especially spiritually. Infrequent enjoyment (moderation, in other words) is permitted, and should be an act of joy and love, never of shame, if one is ever to get out of this lower joy into a higher joy.

And that is the next thing to understand, namely, that there are higher joys before which sex becomes a mere distraction, and no longer an emotional necessity.

Do, therefore, whatever feeds your inner joy, ever seeking a subtler and subtler joy in the Self, and even at the time of worldly enjoyment, relate that joy inwardly to the joy of the Self. Joy is the highroad to true morality.

In divine friendship,

For a married man concerning the sex impulse | 5

May 27, 1999

Dear _____:

Let me see what I can suggest. Basically, I think you've been saying the right things. Regarding sex, abstinence would be highly beneficial. But not merely outward abstinence: inner transmutation.

A technique taught by Lahiri Mahasaya is as follows: Place a little ice and water in an ice bag. Crushed ice might be better, if he has the means available of crushing it. Hold the bag on the closed tip of the penis for ten minutes, letting the coolness encourage an inward drawing of the energy to the spine. After a time, feel the coolness moving up the spine to the head, cooling the brain. If he has been circumcised, then in order to protect the sensitive head he should cover it with a cloth. He should be told also to take the name of Lahiri Mahasaya during this practice. He can do it morning and evening.

Since he is married, complete abstinence may not be possible or even feasible. In this case, moderation is essential. Even during intercourse, some withdrawal of energy can be practiced. He can do so by not allowing himself to be drawn *emotionally* downward into the act.

Lahiri Mahasaya taught a further technique: during intercourse, he said, one should hold the mind at the point between the eyebrows, feeling the sexual stimulation going upward, rather than downward and outward. He further suggested holding that position for a long time (an hour, even) while remaining focused at the Christ center, and not allowing ejaculation to occur. This, he said, is a way of conquering desire altogether. This method, however, is difficult, and should never be practiced merely with the excuse of transmuting the energy.

I hope this helps.

Love,

Circa 1985

Dear _____:

The dilemma you pose is a serious one—one, however, to which I see no solution as yet. We have a community; the only way we can have such a community is for it to be one composed primarily of householders. Celibacy is desirable on the path, but it is not practicable in an absolute sense for most householders. The ideal suggested by Lahiri Mahasaya was moderation, with abstinence in time as a goal. On the whole I think this works best, among other reasons because it is more in tune with actual realities.

As you have said, our strongest devotees seem on the whole to be those who are married. This is one actual reality, and one that we may as well try to understand in order to know what God wants of us at this time, and in this village. That which is in harmony with the divine plan flourishes; that which goes against the divine plan withers and, eventually, dies.

I have certainly seen many celibate men and women who do not seem to be flourishing spiritually, though others of course do thrive in a single state. But I think the two important things to achieve are inner self-control and non-attachment, rather than mere outward abstinence. These two mental states I find are strong here—stronger than I have seen in many monasteries. When one sees our Ananda members alongside the monks and nuns in Assisi, Italy, one cannot but be struck by the spiritual light in Ananda eyes in contrast to the relatively dull look in those of most, perhaps, of those outward renunciates.

I would never gainsay the statements of great Masters like Sri Ramakrishna. The kind of complete renunciation he suggests, however, seems to me capable of flourishing only in the soil of a balanced society, and not in the soil of the spiritual confusion that surrounds us today. Our job now, as I see it, is to concentrate on bringing spiritual awareness back into society as a whole, and not on withdrawing from the general spiritual rout in order to find salvation selfishly for ourselves alone.

This, I believe, is why at this time monasteries throughout the world are practically decimated, and, some of them, empty, some of the greatest of them reduced in numbers from thriving hundreds to a mere handful of tired old men shaking their heads sadly at the sinfulness of this age. In fact, the spiritual power seems for the time to have been passed on to those people who seek a divine life in the world.

So what should you do? I would seek God ever more earnestly, more deeply, and not worry about anything else. Thus, whatever He wants for you He will give you in His own time, and in His own way. Especially for one who is new on the path, an intimate outward relationship can prove time consuming and extremely distracting. A single life is still ideal for one who wants to dedicate all his thoughts to God. Seek Him above all, therefore, and let Him guide you as He will.

In divine friendship,

On working with an unwilling spouse | 7

June 22, 1979

Dear _____:

I think that what you have been reading on renunciation in marriage assumes that both partners are on the path and are willing. There is a balance in your personal situation. With greater patience, you may find it for yourself.

Try to see your husband as a manifestation of God. Serve him with this attitude. You might visualize him, in meditation, surrounded by light. Sooner or later he will be more attracted to the subtler aspects of your relationship, as he experiences this divine energy directed toward him—instead of, as he now thinks, its being directed too much elsewhere.

Bring God into every action in your life. In this way, you will bridge the separation that is now growing. You will be able to see your relationship together as a way of serving God. Your husband, moreover, will see your spiritual efforts as strengthening to your relationship, rather than undermining it. Renunciation means giving up all our attachments, and all our selfish attitudes. It doesn't mean giving up our responsibilities in serious relationships.

Try these ideas, anyway, if they feel right to you. Please let me know the results.

In divine friendship,

July 25, 1994

Dear _____:

I have prayed and meditated on your letter, and shall do my best to answer it.

I think that in your longing for a romantic relationship, your heart is actually longing for much more than that. It seems to me that at the essence of your desire for a romantic relationship is your soul's longing for its relationship with God.

I'm not saying, don't seek a wife, or that you should enter a monastery. But I *am* saying, seek a loving relationship above all with God—with the Divine Mother.

From your letter it seems that there has been certain dryness in your search for God, that it has been too intellectual. Swami Sri Yukteswar, the great saint of wisdom, wrote in his book, *The Holy Science*, that the first thing one must develop on the spiritual path is the heart's love, and that without that love, one cannot advance a single step on the path.

Don't go too much by thought. It's not a saint's thoughts that make him outstanding. It's his *perceptions*. But all this will unfold as your heart's qualities develop more.

Another thing that will help you very much is *satsang*—good company. It would be a good thing to visit Ananda sometimes.

In divine friendship,

On why couples at Ananda live together before marriage and don't practice celibacy | 9

February 18, 2003

Dear _____:

I too am uncomfortable with some of these decisions. I decided years ago that to win people to higher truths I had to go with what they understood as right for them in the context of today's society. A leader can only lead; he must never try to *drive*. I can discuss these matters with you sometime. I'm too busy now to go into them as deeply as they require. My hope is that, with our teachings, they will be inspired to discipline themselves and to try always to go in the right direction.

Basically, my policy has been one of non-intervention, rather than one of approval. I *have* found, fortunately, that many couples, treated with leniency and friendship, come of their own accord to the path of loyal commitment in marriage. In itself, moreover, marriage in America hasn't proved to be a truly sacred institution. Leniency, rather than judgment, has won many to a serious commitment. Otherwise, the sin of over-indulgence in sex is quite as possible within marriage as outside of it. Loyalty and self-control are the ideals, not (at this time in our society's development) the legal formality of a marriage document. I hope and believe that society's present state of confusion will grow calmer with time, and that people will return of their own accord to traditional ways.

I'm glad to say that Ananda people are purer for this approach than many communities where the negative rules are sternly enforced. I refuse to honor sexuality of any kind as a way of life, but I feel that people must be allowed to grow naturally and sincerely toward a goal they have, I hope, accepted in simply joining Ananda.

Joy to you!

A true devotee | 10

April 27, 1999

Dear _____ :

I am sad about _____ no longer wanting to be part of Ananda. I know that her husband would like to be with us, but we must respect his desire to be loyal to his wife. That respect, however, is qualified by the fact that a true devotee lets NOTHING stand between him and God, and between him and his chosen path.

Love,

March 23, 1989

Dear _____:

The question of renunciation and divorce is not easy to resolve. The essence of renunciation is giving up the sense of "I" and "mine." In this sense, Ananda members, whether married or single, *are* renunciates. Sex is only part of the story, but even here they are encouraged to train themselves gradually to transmute their sexual energy. Few devotees, whether married or single, have reached the point of becoming *completely* chaste—that is to say, in thought as well as in deed.

In this sense, none, even monastics, are complete renunciates until they have transcended their natural appetites both outwardly and inwardly. At the same time, however, one is justified in calling himself a renunciate if such transcendence is the true goal of all his aspirations.

I don't see why one should be faulted for a divorce, if it was his partner who left him, and who gave him (or her) no choice in the matter.

There have been more divorces at Ananda than I would have liked, but I must say that, as long as people are trying sincerely to progress on the path, we must respect them for doing what we at least hope is their best. In any case, people have a right to make their own mistakes, and to learn from them and grow from them.

In divine friendship,

To a woman who had recently
faced a serious crisis in her marriage | 12

October 21, 2002

Dear _____:

Thank you for writing. This episode has been painful to all of us. But I remember something my father said once, "After a war, many things have to be forgiven if people are to get on with their lives." This is true of countless crises in human life. I'm glad to see in you the right attitude: Bless, and move on. I really hope, and also believe, that all will work out well in your life and in _____'s, and in your life together. I pray for both of you.

Who knows where these delusions come from? The important thing is to recognize them as such, and to refuse to dwell on them any further. Remember our Ananda Sangha marriage vow: "We will forgive one another always."

You mentioned numbness, which is a common reaction to deep hurt. I went through that, many years ago, and decided I'd only lose twice by not loving. "I'm happier when I love," I realized, "and unhappy when I don't love, and while I'd rather be unhappy than numb, I choose to love regardless of how I've been and am being treated." Thus, a major tragedy in my life became one of my greatest blessings.

God bless you for hanging in there, and for showing the willingness to work with _____ rather than apart from or against him. Now if he will do the same, all will be smooth sailing once again. I deeply pray that it will.

Love,

Asked why a relationship had failed | 13

1990s

Dear _____:

I am sorry things did not work out. Unfortunately, you draw disappointment to yourself by your very eagerness. Learn non-attachment, by giving yourself more wholly to God in your heart. You will see then that the more you are detached, the more the world will run after you. But if you pursue it too eagerly, it will only turn its back on you.

This is particularly true of women, who are not attracted to weakness in men, and who see weakness in excessive dependence on their company. You must become strong in yourself; otherwise they will continue to see you as a boy, not a man.

In Master's love,

June 14, 2000

Dear _____:

Remember the chant, "No birth, no death, no caste have I; father, mother have I none." The words would be equally true if you sang them as follows: "Son or daughter have I none!"

They are God's children, not yours. Perhaps God wants you to break your attachment to them—not to love them the less, but to love them in God and not as your own. Be free in your heart! Then love anyway, for in impersonal love you ARE free!

In Master's love,

Asked how to overcome a | 15
strong attachment to her son

October 3, 2006

Dear _____:

Ultimately, you will have to release your son to God. He has only come through you. He has his own destiny to work out. It would be lovely if he could be on the spiritual path, but even that is his to work out.

Yes, I will pray for you, and also for him.

In divine friendship,

Can separation be a good thing? | 16

February 17, 1976

Dear _____:

Master said that there are times when it is right and necessary to separate from your spouse. At this time I think this separation may be good for you. Through your meditations you will be able to understand further yourself what is best to do. Being alone will also give you more time to meditate and gain a clear perspective on the whole situation.

My prayers and blessings are with you always.

In Master's love,

January 16, 2003

Dear _____:

God doesn't treat those who love Him in quite the same soft way He treats others—more softly than many of them realize! For instance, the devotee may wonder, "Why cannot I, too, have the human love others seem to have?" But God may take that normal fulfillment away from devotees, while giving it to others. Why? Because He wants them to go deeper: to love Him alone.

Turn more to Him, _____. Don't ask for anything else. He will give you what you need, and when you need it.

Love,

*"You've given your life for
many years to something very
good—good for you, good
for many others; good for your
own progress toward God.*

STRONG MEDICINE

*You stand in danger of
throwing it all away—and
for what? Do those people
love you? Do they even
care about you? They care
only about themselves!"*

To a devotee wanting to start a
theater festival at Ananda Village based
on the offerings of major world religions   1

October 7, 1998

Dear _____:

Thank you for writing. You've told me about a new idea, but haven't asked for feedback. I'm therefore a bit shy about giving any. Still, I suppose a letter gets written in at least the hope of a response. So here goes:

The enthusiasm you express for this new idea tends to crowd actual realities into the background. I am grateful for your enthusiasm, and recognize it as a great asset both to yourself and to others. Still, I must be truthful and say that I don't share it for this particular project, for the following reason: What you are speaking of promoting is theater pieces not on the Ways of *Awakening*, but on the Ways of *Belief*—the very thing that separates religions rather than drawing them together.

Have you read my book, *The Hindu Way of Awakening?* It is just the eclectic mixture you've favored that I've tried to correct and bring to a deeper level of understanding.

But the thing goes deeper. To invite churches or other religious groups to present their ideas in this vitally important matter, when they haven't even begun to absorb the unity underlying those ideas, is to court confusion of the worst kind. The potential problems would be limited by the fact that few, if any, would be ready to participate meaningfully in such a project, new to them as it would be, but even so it would put us out there as backing what really is almost the opposite of what I've tried to do through that book: eclecticism, not unity.

We're talking of something deep here—not theater, not showmanship, not involving crowds of people, not widespread publicity. The idea of a festival is not only premature, but not the right approach at all to this very serious subject. If my book were to begin its journey into people's minds on this level, it would dampen its potential for reaching the serious audience for whom it is intended.

The essential unity of religions is close to my heart, too. But what you've proposed would not further that unity. It would only—if it worked, which in fact I doubt it would—fan people's curiosity and eagerness for intellectual knowledge.

So: No, I don't like the idea.

That much said, I'm still grateful for your enthusiasm and therefore hesitate to say anything to squelch it. But I must be truthful, and the truth is that such a festival just wouldn't have my endorsement.

In Master's love,

January 3, 1992

Dear _____:

Your letter touched me deeply. I am so sorry you have felt unloved. For, of course, love is what everyone in the world wants, and needs. I am also deeply sorry that you were not treated more gently at Ananda.

I'm sorry also that I was unable to see you before you left Ananda. My health was very bad at the time and I had to conserve every ounce of my strength. I *did* want to see you. It grieved me to disappoint you.

I am going to direct my words now, not to your emotional needs, but to certain blocks in you that have prevented you from fulfilling those needs. I hope you will take the rest of this letter in the spirit with which I write it, which is with love and a sincere desire for your welfare.

After all, any time any of us suffers in life, our greatest need is to discriminate and see what it is *in ourselves* that has attracted such suffering to us. We may be able to change the way a certain few others treat us. When, however, it comes to changing the behavior of numerous others, the obvious thing is to try to change those aspects in ourselves which seem to be attracting this repeated treatment.

If, as an illustration, someone has the unpleasant habit of sprinkling us with water whenever we must pass under his window, we will naturally do what we can to break him of this objectionable practice. When it comes to something more universal, however, like the rainfall, the only sensible thing to do is use an umbrella.

What I'm saying doesn't exculpate any of us at Ananda from your charges. If I, or others here, have behaved unlovingly towards you, it behooves us to change our behavior. For even if this unlovingness were directed only towards you, it would indicate a test that we had failed to pass.

I could even leave matters there, with an acceptance of blame and a plea for forgiveness. I might well do so, if I didn't feel your sincere desire for love and understanding. If I can give you true understanding, as opposed to mere acceptance, I believe I will show friendship for you on a much deeper level. That, therefore, is what I feel I should do.

One of the problems we all face in life is the fact that each of us stands to a great extent *behind* the scenes in the theatrical pieces we present to others on life's stage. We don't get to see ourselves from the point of view of the audience.

You probably are not aware of the image you project to others. It is one— forgive me for being frank; I really am trying to help you—of criticism, fault-finding, judgment, and lack of willingness to commit yourself to anyone.

You write me that you've always wanted love. Well, the way to draw love from others is to love *them*—not in return but first, and freely. It isn't enough merely to love them secretly in the depths of one's being. One must express that love outwardly, too, by serving them, and by giving to them. The greatest gift one should concentrate on giving them is happiness.

You say that you did give of yourself to various people here. Well, if you gave, and they failed to show proper gratitude in return, that is their loss far more than yours. They deserve your compassion, therefore, not your condemnation.

To develop that kind of magnetism which draws love from others, we must love them first unconditionally, even when they hurt us. For, mind you, the law of life is very exact. When we give love, even if that love is misunderstood by certain others, it *must* return to us—eventually, a hundred-fold—if not from those people then through other channels.

Our job, then, is to love, no matter how others treat us. If we do so, we cannot but receive love in return—if not from those to whom we have expressed, then from countless others. There is no way for this law to be controverted.

I have observed another law of life, equally ineluctable: The more we think in terms of our own needs and desires, the more pain we feel; but the more we forget ourselves in the thought of others' needs, the greater the happiness we ourselves experience inside.

Your thoughts, for as long as I've known you, have shown themselves to be directed inward, toward your own needs, not outward toward what you might give to others. I know this goes directly counter to what you've written about the many services you've rendered others. Well, none of us is purely one thing or another—purely selfish, for example, or purely unselfish. I don't question the kindnesses you've done others.

Ask yourself, however: Why is it that the lingering impression other people have of you is one of self-involvement, of self-preoccupation? Even those who have worked with you seem prone to think of you as some-one who wants to prove the merits of his system over other systems, rather than as one who wants generously to help them to unfold their own inner talents.

I think it all comes from a feeling of deep insecurity in yourself. You feel shy of expressing love to others, or generosity, or concern, for fear of being rejected by them.

The trouble is that insecurity is self-perpetuating: By withholding the expression of your heart's natural love for them, you make *them* feel in-secure in your presence: unsure of what you really think of them; doubt-ful whether, behind the aura of aloofness that you project, you are not merely judging them unkindly, no matter what they might do to show you friendship.

This must be what _____ meant when he described you as he did. That was an unfortunate thing to say, and an even more unfortunate thing for anyone to have repeated, whether to you or anyone else. Yet _____ is truly one of the least judgmental people I know. If, then, he said such a thing, it can only have been with reference to the tendency many have observed in you: to want something from them without giving to them in return.

The way out of the trap of emotional insecurity is to be impersonal in the love we give others. We must learn to love them not for themselves, individually, but because we love God, and God's manifestation in them. Again, the trick here also is to stop thinking of the impression you make on others, and to concentrate on *their* emotional needs, and on how you might be able to help them to fulfill those needs.

My college friend, Rod Brown, told me that he had been preoccupied in high school with what others thought of him. His mother wisely told him once, "Rod, they're too much concerned with what you think of them to devote so much energy to what they think of you!"

In fact, the person who makes the best impression on others is that generous soul who succeeds in reassuring others that *they* have made a good impression on him! This may all seem very human and ego-boosting, but not only does it work: It also helps to diminish the grip one's own ego exerts on his mind.

I do believe you feel you are doing people a service in suggesting ways for them to improve themselves, or to improve the ways they do things. Up to a point, I'm sure that, if they really do desire to do better (as they ought to desire, especially if they are devotees, and thus devoted to finding ultimate perfection in God), they will be grateful to you for any good suggestions you might offer.

In any suggestion one makes for the betterment of others, however, there is always the possibility of conveying the impression that one considers one's own wisdom to be superior. Even when there is no such suspicion conveyed, there is always a danger of appearing presumptuous for having stepped in with ideas of one's own in matters where, it may be fairly safely assumed, the conscientious person, at least, has given long and serious thought and has determined on what, for him, is the best course of action.

The builder who, for a variety of reasons, decides to build with wood and stucco in preference to stone, is not edified by the critic who stops by and tells him it would have been better to build in stone. The least his critic might have done (the builder will think to himself) would have been to ask him *why* he had chosen wood and stucco in preference to stone.

I'm dealing here with deep-seated aspects of your nature. I know you can't change them overnight, even if you think my suggestions are good. But I ask you, for your own sake: Do try. Once you succeed in changing yourself in these respects, even to a minor degree, you'll find an amazing change in the way others treat you. For what we receive from others is, always, a reflection of what we first project outward, towards them.

I pray that you will not take offense at my words. They are offered to you from a sincere desire to help you find the happiness and kindness that you so much want in life, and to which you, as a child of God, are forever entitled.

In Master's love,

Discusses a devotee who needs
to learn to stand on his own two feet | 3

February 27, 2000

Dear _____ :

Ananda is in no position financially at this time to start a new community, whether at _____ or anywhere else. My idea in suggesting to _____ that he might want to start something on his own was not that it be sponsored by Ananda, which would mean making Ananda financially liable. Ananda will be happy to bless him in his undertaking, but that blessing cannot be extended to financial or other kinds of practical assistance. He will have to do it all on his own, as I did in founding Ananda.

He hasn't shown this sense of financial responsibility in the past, which means Ananda might actually find itself stuck with a huge burden of debt by the time he's done with his project. We can't handle such a responsibility for him, and must make it clear to him from the start that we cannot and will not. It is his risk entirely, not Ananda's.

If he can show himself responsible *all the way*, as he hasn't in the past, it will be a big victory for him and will win our wholehearted approval.

Meanwhile, however, for him to think of Ananda as a cushion in case of failure would be foolish for us to encourage, and impossible for us to sanction.

So, no, we cannot let him take our name until he's proved himself. The same goes for the school name. I was wrong to agree with him on this point, but in fact I didn't agree—I only tried to give him suggestions for future possibilities in his work, not to offer him specific directives.

Truthfully, I don't see that he'll be able to pull this off. He has fed off of Ananda's energy for a long time, but it is time now that he showed himself, and us, that he can do the things he wants to on his own; truly on his own. He is a grown man. It makes me uncomfortable to see so many people feeling they need to support him. To me, this means he draws on them for support. I'd like him to show that he can really stand on his own feet, without people feeling they need to "go to bat" for him.

To be even franker, I'm not convinced that he even *wants* to do things in attunement with Master, with me, and with Ananda. He is not an underdog, and it doesn't do justice to his own dignity as a man when people cast him in that role.

In divine friendship,

To two devotees leaving Ananda in order to feel Yogananda's guidance on their own	4

August 7, 2000

Dear _____ and _____:

I received your letter, and must admit to being disappointed. You want to withdraw from Ananda so you can feel "Master's guidance." Friends, it won't come to you that way. I know. His "guidance" will take the form of showing less interest in you. You'll pray to him, and he will smile on you for doing so. But that will be all. In matters like this, you must make up your own minds. When you turn your faces toward the light, you'll receive it. But when you turn them here, there, and elsewhere, what you'll get increasingly is mere glimpses.

Master wants warriors. Heroes. *Martyrs*! Would he welcome those who wanted to find him only in meditation? Yes, I'm sure he would. But you are not

Ram Gopal Muzumdars! You have children to raise; a family *dharma* to work out; youth; energy; the finances to be of help to others. Do you think you might be able to build something on your own—another Ananda perhaps? It takes ENERGY to do any kind of work in this world, but especially a work involving other people. Have *you* that kind of energy? Face it, life has been kind to you, but you are living on past good karma; you have not generated the kind of karma that leads to real outer success. I've been worried to see both of you more and more simply drifting, spiritually.

There are two things Master has given you: Kriya Yoga, and his ideal—one he literally *pleaded* with people to embrace—of "World Brotherhood Colonies." You, _____ , have been doing Kriya, but Master summoned you to another calling, and this is one you've been neglecting for years.

Do you think Master has sent us the tests of recent years to make us question what we are doing in serving him? We've emerged from every test stronger both in ourselves and in our outer calling. Our faith in God, too, has been immeasurably strengthened.

I had a dream of Master the other night. He showered great love on me. I asked him then, "Will Ananda and SRF ever become one?" Unequivocally and powerfully he replied, "No!" We have another mission. It is not a sidetrack: It is *central* to what he came to bring.

Ananda is, I feel, one of the most important things happening in the world today. I've said it for years. The results already prove me right, though much, much more needs to be done. You could be, and have aspired to be, part of this divine drama. Do you think our line of masters will pat you on the back for backing out and "rethinking" everything? Well, they may do so if re-thinking leads you anywhere in the end, but I've seldom seen this process end up doing so. All it has meant in most cases has been time out, and time lost.

Well, I will not say more. I am your friend, and it has been and is my joy to consider you my friends. But I don't think I'd be a true friend if I let you go your own way without telling you what I know in my heart to be right and best for you.

In divine friendship,

April 19, 2000

Dear _____:

In any line of work one can't expect constant wins. What one loses, however, if one reacts unhappily, is that people hesitate even to offer suggestions. In time, they begin seeking help elsewhere, even if they like your ideas better than someone else's. After all, who wants to face a possible upset when one is only trying to get a job done?

I suggest you always ask yourself: Why am I at Ananda? To find God, right? Does it further that purpose to have others always *like* what you come up with? Can't you see that your distress over their reactions, and not your actual work, is what makes them so often skirt around you rather than work with you? Who wants to upset you? No one! Their natural reaction will be to avoid you, even for your sake.

I had this situation arise in Rome two weeks ago, on my arrival from America. I'd just flown in all the way from Seattle. My body wasn't well, and I was exhausted. Even pushing that trolley with those heavy suitcases on it was exhausting. I couldn't go to the bathroom, because it was unsafe to leave the trolley anywhere. I haven't learned how to use the public telephones in Italy, so I asked people to help me, but was too exhausted to ask in such a way as to invite their interest in helping me. They refused. Finally, for 50,000 Lire, (about $25.00), I got a man to phone Assisi for me. (It was too difficult, with that heavy trolley, to go looking for change, and 50,000 was the smallest bill I had.)

The office told me Mark and Kirtani were on their way. Perhaps, I thought, the rain was delaying them. So I waited. And waited. Finally, after nearly three hours I saw the same man and got him to phone again for me, so I could tell them in the office that I'd decided to take a taxi to Assisi. "Oh," they cried, "they were planning to be there at 12:30."

For some reason they'd been told my plane was coming in at 1:00 p.m. instead of at 9:00 a.m., which was when it had always been scheduled to arrive and when it did, in fact, arrive. The office then told me there was a message waiting for me at the Delta counter. Well, pushing that heavy cart to the elevator, going upstairs, then pushing it the length of that long concourse to the Delta counter, was actually quite an undertaking. I managed it, however, and waited in line until I got my message. It read, "Please call the Assisi office." That was all!

So then—the long trip downstairs again. My trolley tipped over, and I was struggling with those heavy bags when, fortunately, a young man saw my difficulty and came over and helped me.

I must admit, I was a little tempted to get discouraged. I was too exhausted to feel merry about it, as normally I would have. But I decided there was just no use in feeling sorry for myself. I told myself, "No one would do this to me deliberately. It's just my karma." Mark and Kirtani did arrive at 12:30, and the drama ended at last.

My point here, however, is that what we need to do in life is seek reactions that *work* for us, reactions that are *useful*. The only person who suffers when we allow negative thoughts to intrude is ourselves. And who wants to suffer?

The world is *not* out to get you. If, however, you keep feeling misjudged and unappreciated, people will leave you to yourself, for your peace of mind as much as for theirs. They'll suffer in doing so, but who wants disharmony if he can avoid it? And you will suffer even more. *Why?* It's all completely unnecessary!

If you were out in the world, working among worldly people, they'd trample all over you. Some of them would even *enjoy* hurting you. Some of them would just push you aside to get what they want done. And even good people would try to work around you rather than with you. You'd find yourself avoided by everyone, except those very few who might be willing to take the time and the trouble to help you to grow spiritually.

Ananda people are much better even than most good worldly people, whose priority still is ego-satisfaction. Ananda people have open hearts. Many of them are real friends to you. Why should *any* of them "have it in" for you? They don't! You have it in for yourself.

When others don't like some idea you come up with, don't look on it as a failure. It's your discouragement that is your failure—a spiritual failure. For you are at Ananda to grow spiritually! The first thing is to develop a right attitude. What you do in your work is of minor importance. What you do in your work on yourself is of major importance, and is the only thing God wants of you.

Be stronger in yourself. Absolutely refuse to feel sorry for yourself. The truth is, whatever attitude you put out will be a magnet that draws back to yourself situations that reflect your expectation. If the attitude is negative, the "echo" will be negative also. If it is positive, everything will turn positive for you. It is *you* who create your own universe!

Remember, finally, that people like working with others who like working with them. It's all that simple! Try to learn this truth! It will be the cornerstone of anything you build of your own happiness and fulfillment.

Love,

About a certain Ananda meditation group leader | 6

July 29, 2000

Dear _____:

Let me begin with his statements about the results he claims to have received from that other Kriya. He claims, first, that the other Kriya works better than the one we've received from Master, and teach others; and, second, that Master "diluted" this technique for American consumption.

1. Does his Kriya work better? I have given Kriya initiation now for fifty-one years in America, Europe, and India, and to countless thousands of people. Not once have I heard from anyone that some other "Kriya" works better than Master's. Master told me himself that he was grooming me to take his message out to the world, and—as he himself put it—to do a "great work." He surely would have let me know if what I'd received from him was only a dilution of the real Kriya technique.

2. People's imagination can do many things, especially if their minds are arrogant and prone to exalt their own position in the eyes of God. _____'s statement that he (and "many others") receive more from this new Kriya he has received is certainly an example of arrogance, inflated by the power

of imagination. I do not say he is misguided, for the only test we have of the value of Kriya is whether or not it actually works.

This test must also be applied, however, to the persons themselves, who practice them. If it has made them less humble, rather than more so; less charitable, and not more so; less magnetic, instead of more so, we must assume from the evidence that they are fooling themselves. This is in fact a common enough mistake on the spiritual path. (Therefore it was, incidentally, that Patanjali proposed a number of objective tests for the validity of subjective spiritual experiences.)

I have never met anyone else who claimed that the teacher he speaks of guided them more correctly than Master. I have not seen actual examples of spiritual radiance in the eyes of those who followed those teachings. In my fifty-one years of teaching, _____ is the first person I know of to say that he's on to something better than Master's Kriya. His premise seems to be founded on sand.

Did Master "dilute" Lahiri Mahasaya's—and Babaji's—Kriya technique? Did he teach Kriya differently in India from the way he taught it in America? No! I state this denial as an unequivocal fact. I took advantage of several opportunities to check out the differences that have been claimed between Master's Kriya and that of other lines from Lahiri Mahasaya. Some differences do exist, but they are superficial. *All* of the actual differences convinced me only that Master was bringing people into Kriya more gradually. He brought them to the full technique, however, as they showed themselves ready for it.

_____ claims that "many people" have received better results from what they have learned from this other teacher. Do you believe it? I don't. For one thing, I have seen nothing in _____ or in the others to convince me that they are soaring spiritually.

I should make clear, however, that I've no interest in persuading them to change their practices! Master always said that the proof of Kriya lies in its results. If _____ and others think they get more results in following this other way, I don't think we should allow our discussion of the matter to descend to a level of dogma. Let them go their way. In taking initiation elsewhere they have already separated themselves from our line of gurus, and are less likely to receive their blessings.

However, I think they should be given a chance to express themselves on this point, for possibly only _____ and one or two others feel as he has expressed himself. Let anyone who desires another path go with the spiritual ray he chooses. That is everyone's privilege. If, however, not all of them are in agreement with _____, then they should have the freedom to tell us so, and not allow him to dictate their own future.

We can all remain friends; it doesn't matter to us where their loyalties lie, so long as they are loyal first of all to God. But it is inappropriate for us to continue giving them energy, if this energy is neither understood nor properly received.

In Master,

To a devotee in Australia not invited to *an Ananda colony leaders' meeting*	7

March 28, 1999

Dear _____:

I was glad to get your recent letter. I hope all keeps going better for you.

Yes, we're having a colony leaders' meeting here [in Assisi] in May. It isn't for center leaders, only for leaders of our colonies in America and in Italy. Yours isn't a colony work in Australia, so you wouldn't normally be invited at this time. It will be a meeting to discuss Ananda's future directions.

I'd love to think of your work there as part of Ananda's present outreach. Why don't I? Basically, because you've said frankly you want to do it your way and not listen to my or to our guidance unless it agrees with what *you* feel. I've nothing against that attitude, but I've simply suggested to our leaders in America that, given that attitude, they serve you in whatever terms *you* ask for, but not treat you as wanting our guidance. You've expressed hurt, anger, and resentment of what I and others have written you. I don't mind that you want to do things your way, which must mean, surely, that you want to *go* your own way. I've told our leaders in America to give you what energy you want, but not to impose their thoughts on you for the simple reason that you don't seem to want them.

If you tell us you want to work with us, we'll gladly work with you. But if you tell us, as you have, that you don't want to do what we suggest, we'll respectfully give you whatever it is you do seem to want, but not more. This is your decision, not ours. Working with us, however, must mean *with*, not apart from, what Ananda is doing. We've told you what we think would be best for you and for our work there, and you haven't accepted it. Our thought, therefore, is by no means to abandon or exclude you, but to let you tell us just what you do want from us.

Inviting you to a colony leaders' retreat, even if you had a colony there, wouldn't have been appropriate under these circumstances. Ours will be a meeting of disciples who *want* to work together. We are not opposed to what you are doing. I want you to know that. Moreover, as you know also, we are very happy to have _____ come here as well as to the Expanding Light, even though he and _____ have broken away from us (though perhaps less so he, now, according to your recent letter).

Any positive energy you want to give us, we'll accept joyfully. Please, however, don't give us resentment and anger. It is unwarranted. We hold no negative feelings toward you.

I haven't been sending you the videos I've made for America, because I haven't felt you'd want or appreciate them. When you go to America this time you might make a point of watching them and telling me whether they interest you.

My love and friendship are always with you both.

In Master,

To a devotee who wanted to have a "dialogue" with people trying to destroy Ananda | 8

November 17, 2001

Dear _____:

No one is going to tell you what to do. However, in matters like these, it isn't reason that rules. One thinks to reason things out carefully. Meanwhile, however, *maya* takes control.

Please believe me, for I've seen this drama play itself out many, many times in my life. I myself might have left the path, many years ago, if I hadn't *acted*, simply, with love for God, instead of trying to reason my way to clarity. Master himself told me that's how things would have worked out. The matter runs deeper than reason. Divine Mother won't allow those to stay at Ananda whose hearts are divided on such issues.

I say these things not to try to force you in any way, but because I love you. What saved me was the awareness that Master loved me, and that I loved him. Clarity came later. I love you, _____. Ask yourself this simple question: Do those people love you? Do they even care about you? They care only about themselves!

Most important, ask yourself, Do I want to be like them?

Asha wrote a plea to people to speak up on Ananda's and on my behalf. It was a good letter, and there have been many good responses to it. I am happy for those people's letters above all for what it signifies for them. The best thing for you right now is to take the time to write such a letter yourself. I've never liked the word "proactive": It seems to me rather a non-word. But it fits in this case. Don't just think about these things: ACT!

Believe me, I know what I'm saying. I know the signs. I know you. Don't just smile benignly and say, "Well, I'll think about it." You've given your life for many years to something very good—good for you, good for many others; good for your own progress toward God. You stand in danger of throwing it all away—and for what? You very likely will say, "You're taking it all too seriously." Am I? You'll see, if you don't take it at least as seriously.

With love in Master,

Be divine warriors! | 9

June 30, 2001

Dear _____:

I'm writing now especially to ask all of you who are involved in the music and publications: Please, don't allow yourselves to channel negative energies.

These tests aren't personal. I think they are part of an attempt to do harm on the part of conscious, negative energies. Please do your extra best to be loving and harmonious toward one another: positive and loving. I know that is how you all feel in your hearts. Give extra emphasis to that divine feeling now. *Radiate* love and harmony. And don't blame yourselves, nor anyone else, for anything no matter what the seeming reason.

The pains a few of you are undergoing are a passing thing. Love God. And love God in one another. The energy you radiate outward to others will determine what you become in yourself.

Negativity cannot win, in the end. Be divine warriors! Work, however, in harmony and love: together in a spirit of love. This is the only way. Don't let personal difficulties block your broader vision.

With much love in Master,

"Once you have decided
which path is truly your own,
then you should sink deeply
into one way—not becoming
narrow-minded, but rather

YOGIC
TECHNIQUES

in order to achieve that one-
pointedness of concentration
which alone makes depth
in meditation and
inner awareness possible."

*A man who received Kriya initiation from
Kriyananda asked permission to teach Kriya to a
friend. Here Kriyananda addresses both of them* | 1

October 23, 1973

Dear Ones:

I should be very happy for you, _____, to get Kriya Yoga initiation; however, you would need the proper preparation for it. This would include
taking the lessons from Self-Realization Fellowship in Los Angeles [no
longer a requirement at Ananda], and, if possible (though not necessary),
also my *14 Lessons in Yoga* [now called *The Art and Science of Raja Yoga*].
You would need to practice the Hong-Sau technique of concentration for
some period of time and embrace our particular discipline.

There are many different paths to God. When one first enters the spiritual
path it is right and proper for him to study many ways, and compare. But
once he has done the comparing, and has decided which path is truly his
own, then he should sink deeply into one way—not becoming narrow-
minded, but rather in order to achieve that one-pointedness of concentration which alone makes depth in meditation and inner awareness possible.
For this reason, initiation, when one takes it, is more than simply learning
a technique. It is embracing the path of discipleship to a guru, or, as in
our case, to a line of gurus.

I would want you to know more about our path and our Guru's teachings
before you took the step of Kriya Yoga initiation. For you to take Kriya
now would not be fair to you. You would not get results, and would soon
stop your practice in disappointment.

So, teach her the Hong-Sau technique, and tell her how she can take the
lessons. And help her in any other way that you can.

So glad to see you, _____, wanting to help her with your spiritual knowledge. And I am so glad that you, _____, are responding so well. For
truly the only important thing in life is to know our own Selves, the God
within us.

In divine friendship,

Circa 1975

Dear _____:

I would be interested to hear how many Kriyas you were doing when you experienced so much difficulty. Awakening of kundalini is the path to enlightenment, not a horrendous experience. However, the awakening of forces for which one is not ready can be bad. Therefore, I would like to know what exactly you were doing.

I remember your intensity, and that there was a great deal of tension involved also in that intensity. I believe your greatest difficulty lay in this attitude, rather than in your practices. Nonetheless, I have always been impressed and touched by your sincerity, and would like to see you come out of what I consider to be a misunderstanding of an important point on the path.

I am, however, very pleased that you are still following the path earnestly. May Master bless you.

In divine friendship,

May 21, 1993

Dear _____:

Here are a few suggestions.

As much as possible, don't talk to others about this experience. Keep it very private. And try not to let others observe it.

Be completely relaxed, physically, to lessen the expression of this experience through your body. Try to expand your awareness and to feel that the experience is taking place beyond the confines of your body.

Don't take it too seriously, either. These things happen on the path. Keep your concentration at the point between the eyebrows, more than in the heart. Live more in your aura, less in the body. Accept that soul-consciousness *is* different from body-consciousness, and don't be afraid.

So as not to be so sensitive to other people's vibrations, direct your energy into a giving, rather than a receiving, mode. Pray for them, secretly. Mentally bless them, so that you act as a channel for the divine energy.

It is natural that you should be more conscious than ordinarily, at this time, of the inner battle between light and darkness, which we all must fight. Don't let the battle become stressful, for in the stress you may find yourself pulled down, or, alternatively, find that the experience goes to your ego. Surrender yourself to God and Guru, and let them guide you. Be relaxed and have faith.

In Master's love,

A person with mentally demanding work
asked how to quiet the mind for meditation | 4

July 7, 1998

Dear _____:

I think you'll find my book *Awaken to Superconsciousness* helpful. It's got plenty of food for thought and experimentation. See what you feel drawn to.

One thought does come to me: Have you done much chanting? One of the challenges of being in so mentally involving a profession as yours is that, when it comes time to meditate, it's hard to shut off the flow of words, which continue to flood the brain. I've found chanting to be very helpful in quieting and interiorizing the mind. I just put out a CD of some chants of Yogananda that I recorded, which you might find helpful. There are, of course, many other such recordings available, from us and from others as well.

Music, among all the arts, affects us in a particularly powerful way, as it is a direct manifestation of the AUM vibration. (A painting, by contrast, communicates only via reflected light to the viewer.) Music is effective not only in quieting the mind, but also in filling one with a devotional hunger to go deep in meditation, setting all other thoughts resolutely aside. Without that heartfelt yearning, deep meditation just isn't possible. Chanting helps greatly to awaken devotion, and so also can other kinds of uplifted music. Another album I've just put out I've called *Some of My Favorites*. With a title like that, how could I not recommend it to you?!

Thank you for writing. If I can be of any further help to you with your meditation, or otherwise, please do let me know. My blessings and best wishes to you.

In divine friendship,

Evolve in a relaxed way | 5

November 21, 1973

Dear _____:

The difficulties that you describe are the result not of the techniques themselves but of the vigor with which you have been going at them. As Master said, one mustn't try too hard, but evolve in a relaxed way, naturally, gradually.

Devotion is a very, very important counter-balance to the mental effort put forth in Raja Yoga.

In divine friendship,

Asked about the Hring Kling *mantra* | 6

February 16, 1988

Dear _____:

The *Hring Kling* mantra is a *bij* (beej) mantra, which is to say it is a mantra of power, rather than of meaning. *Hring* vibrates with the heart; *kling* is to destroy its impurities. You could give it a loose translation: "Destroying my heart's impurities, I prostrate myself at the feet of the Lord."

Properly speaking, one does not chant *bij* mantras. One speaks them. I wrote a melody because I wanted to sing it, but I know it was unorthodox of me to do so.

Love,

April 30, 1980

Dear _____ :

I'm not sure I can answer your questions satisfactorily, though I will try. There is on the spiritual path a whole world to be gone through before reaching superconsciousness: I mean, the world of the subconscious. It is possible to go straight through it to the superconscious level, but many people see "visions" and experience a great variety of phenomena that are imaginary rather than real, and much spiritual literature is devoted to helping people to learn how to tell the difference.

For example, a person will see Jesus Christ in meditation: How is he to know whether Jesus has actually come to him, or whether he only imagined the visit? The imagination can be very keen. In my book, *The Path*, you may recall (if you have read it) the story of the man who told Master that he experienced cosmic consciousness, but Master proved to him that it was only his highly developed powers of visualization that had led him to think so.

How can one tell the difference? I won't go into this subject in depth here— it's long and involved—but the most important point of all is the *effect* it has. One who has really seen Jesus Christ in meditation will be changed by the experience, and changed much more dramatically than he would be by the slight changes that can be effected by the imagination alone.

I do not believe that superconscious experiences can be induced by hypnotic suggestion. Superconscious realities exist on a higher level; they act *upon* the conscious and subconscious; they are not acted upon by these lower states. This is not to say that imagined experiences are wrong or harmful. Master was not in favor of hypnosis, but I am sure he would not have objected to getting someone to visualize the spiritual eye, etc. Such visualization can help to awaken the soul's memory of the deeper reality. Nonetheless, the visualization should not be confused with that reality.

Yes, there are similarities between hypnosis and yogic trance, as in fact there are similarities between sleep, or drunkenness, and *samadhi*. But the seeker is wise to accept the warnings of the masters that these similarities are superficial, and ought not to be explored by one who truly wants to awaken from the sleep of delusion.

In divine friendship,

December 12, 1982

Dear _____:

First, let me tell you that I am praying deeply for you that you see this situation clearly.

When one receives visions and voices, such as you have experienced, it becomes very difficult to distinguish how real they are. I cannot tell just how real your own experiences have been, but I do have certain doubts concerning them. My strong advice to you is that you not give them too much attention.

There are many subtle forces seeking to influence people. Some of those forces are evil. Some of them may be disembodied souls who are just confused, selfish, or petty. And sometimes a part of our own mind tries to fool us, by telling us what our ego would like to hear. Voices and visions do come on the spiritual path, but we shouldn't think of them as goals in themselves. Nor should we pursue them too seriously. In any case, try to be absolutely sure of their divine origin.

It is a lot more helpful simply to develop our devotion and love for God, and our attunement with Him and with those who serve Him sincerely. When we seek devotion and humility, we are not tempted by the powers and spiritual attainments that are more fascinating to the ego than to the soul.

We can lose our spiritual powers very easily, if they mislead us into spiritual pride. A much more lasting and useful spiritual goal is to develop love and devotion for God, and the ability to manifest love every day in our lives. This is the way of the masters.

In divine friendship,

July 16, 1982

Dear _____:

Yes, the danger from yoga practice is as you say—namely, that it can make one self-centered, if he thinks only of developing himself. It can also be harmful if one practices violent breathing exercises, which can awaken energies before the body is ready to receive them.

There is another aspect to yoga, however, that makes it a much safer path than the better-known path of mystical love and prayer. In the West, many saints have suffered in their bodies from the inflow of divine grace. No, they weren't destroyed by grace, and their suffering gradually became transmuted into perfect attunement with the Divine Flow. They might have been spared much physical suffering, however. What happened to them, especially as grace first began to operate in their bodies, was like turning water on at the faucet before straightening out the hose. A strong flow of water can straighten out the hose, true, but how much better if we take the time to straighten it ourselves. The lashing back and forth which ensues as the water straightens the hose can create a degree of havoc.

So it is that the practice of yoga involves not only awakening energies, but also, even more specifically, opening up the channel of the spine so that the flow of grace can enter the body unimpeded. Not knowing what was happening, Western mystics and saints have often suffered physically, at least until finally the purification process ended. We don't find that sort of thing happening nearly so much among yogis.

In fact, then, yoga is very much the safer path. It is important, however, not to do the more violent exercises one finds available in books, and from certain organizations.

Would God allow a person to be destroyed by these energies? I cannot imagine Him doing so and know of no case to justify such a doubt. As Krishna says in the *Bhagavad Gita*: "O Arjuna, know this for certain: My devotee is never lost!"

In divine friendship,

May 13, 2001

Dear _____:

I assume you teach *Savasana* with the hands turned upward, as I always did. My explanation for doing so was that that position induces in the mind a more open, receptive attitude than when the hands are turned down. Recently, however, I've come upon another reason for keeping them turned upward. This one is purely mechanical. When the hands are upward, the lungs receive more air. Try it; you'll see it's true.

This may also be why Master had us turn the hands upward at the junction of the thighs and the abdomen during meditation.

Love,

January 20, 1982

Dear _____:

Meditation, in the purest sense, is not thinking of anything. It is a state of consciousness. Instead of thinking, therefore, we concentrate on a simple practice, like the Hong Sau technique. In this way our minds become calmer. After practicing a technique for a while, just enjoy the fruits of your efforts for at least a quarter of an hour (the longer, the better), trying not to let stray thoughts intrude. This state itself is meditation.

Sometimes, when you sit to meditate, this state may not come. With some people, it may seldom come. These results of meditation are not nearly so important as your efforts to grow closer to God. To an extent, your efforts will determine the result. God's grace, however, is a factor also. If you do your part in showing Him your devotion and sincerity, He will do His by blessing you in some way.

Rather than trying to visualize, you might want to just feel Master's presence and offer your devotion to Him, while doing the techniques.

When you focus your awareness on a technique, and when you feel God's presence in meditation, this is a different experience from "thinking about" something. Mundane thoughts do come up during meditation. Instead of being too concerned about them, be aware that the thought is there, bless it, and offer it up to Master.

Every person's experience of meditation is different. You felt insecure about your efforts, but I don't think you are doing badly. Just relax and enjoy the experience.

Joy to you,

On Yogananda's Energization Exercises | 12

July 29, 2003

Dear _____:

You've written about the Energization Exercises and developing the will power. Yes, *of course* the Energization Exercises help to develop the will power. Master defined the will as "Desire plus energy directed toward fulfillment."

An *awareness* of the energy, which the Exercises help to develop, is an important aspect of using will power.

In divine friendship,

On whether certain inverted yoga poses are harmful, as claimed by some "experts" | 13

July 18, 1990

Dear _____:

I'm tempted to lump the objections of those "experts" with the medical opinion of a century ago that it is harmful to bathe every day. In any given number of "experts," one will always find a wide variety of opinions. Presently, there is so much publicity against sunbathing that one might conclude that it was dangerous even to go out of doors. People carry little "facts" to absurd lengths. In fact, sunbathing is good if it is done in moderation. Your physician's advice, too, is good: Do the pose comfortably and without strain.

It's an important rule of yoga not to force anything. I've often emphasized the need to stretch only slightly, *if at all*, beyond the point of comfort. Some people, instead, adhere to the Rolfing principle, "No pain, no gain." This is a highly questionable doctrine even in massage, and certainly is not the rule in doing the yoga postures.

The rule with those particular poses (*Halasana*, etc.) is to balance them by following them with their opposite positions (*Bhujangasana*, in this case).

Hatha Yoga has survived for thousands of years. It is not a new fad, but a tried and proven system. What you are doing with the inverted poses is perfectly correct.

I hope this answers your questions. If you have more, please don't hesitate to write.

In divine friendship,

Kriyananda answers questions about yoga's *growing popularity among celebrities* | 14

October 22, 2000

Dear _____:

I've written answers after each of the reporter's questions.

Question:

Why do you think yoga is so intriguing to many Hollywood celebrities, that is, why do you think so many of them are getting interested in it?

Answer:

I think that living in a world of fiction helps to develop in those people who are more aware a sensitivity to alternate realities. Of course, the physical aspects of yoga are attractive to people whose livelihood depends on their looking young and physically fit, which they can accomplish through Hatha Yoga, but the inward, truer aspects are most attractive to those whose minds are open and are not enclosed in habit-created patterns of thought. Certainly the movie profession invites new ways of looking at things.

Question:

How is yoga of particular importance (for everyone) in today's electronic, stressful world?

Answer:

You've paired two things that needn't of their own nature be paired. So here, in fact, there are two questions in one.

The first is, "How is yoga of particular importance in today's electronic world?" And the answer is that yoga makes us more aware of ourselves as bodies of *energy*, not merely of material substance. The more aware one becomes that one is energy, the greater control one has in one's own life.

By increasing the flow of energy to the body, one can maintain good health, and overcome illness and other physical setbacks in record time.

By increasing the flow of energy in one's work, one can be more successful in everything one attempts, and can greatly shorten the time for achieving it. With great energy, indeed, one can do in a few minutes what others may require weeks or months to accomplish.

By increasing the flow of energy to other people, one can vastly increase and deepen the love and friendship between oneself and them, and also affect them for the good in their own lives.

By increasing the flow of energy in one's life, one finds abundant happiness, insight, and wisdom in guiding one's affairs.

As for the question of stress, yoga helps one to become calmer, more centered in oneself (in a good way—that is to say, it produces the opposite of *self*-centeredness), it puts one more in control of oneself and one's own life, and helps one to resolve problems with much greater ease.

So, _____, I hope this helps. Best wishes also to the reporter.

Love,

[A devotee wrote, "Master said the metaphysical cause of illness is the battle between the upward and downward currents in the spine. Since Kriya harmonizes and neutralizes these currents, it should bring about good health. Is this true?"]

March 20, 2002

Dear _____:

Yes. Lahiri Mahasaya recommended Kriya for *everything*. And you've said it rightly.

Love,

"If you are really seeking God, don't worry about who is a poorna (full) avatar, or who is even an avatar at all.

AVATAR

Many saints who are far less than avatars are perfectly competent to take you to God, and that is what the spiritual path is all about."

January 31, 1978

Dear _____:

One can be enlightened before he becomes a *siddha*. A *siddha*, by Master's definition, is a fully liberated being. One is a *jivan mukta*, or enlightened master, with the need, still, to work out some past karma, before he becomes a *siddha*.

Masters are not all equal in outward expression, but all are equal in God. *Avatars*, moreover, are more than *siddhas*. An *avatar* is a "descended" master: one who, after attaining full liberation, comes back to earth for the salvation of many. More divine power flows through an *avatar*, but greatness must in any case be judged primarily by what people do. All masters are equal in God, for example, but all, even *avatars*, may be judged outwardly at least in terms of their missions. This has nothing to do with their inner stature.

According to my understanding, Jesus and Lahiri Mahasaya were both *avatars*, and were therefore equal in spiritual realization.

I believe that the followers of the different paths to God will one day live in greater harmony than they do today. It depends on the spiritual development of the world as a whole. Religion truly, of course, is not to blame. It is only man, with his human limitations, who sees differences even among teachings that preach basic oneness.

I send my blessings and best wishes to you.

In divine friendship,

June 10, 1987

Dear _____:

The consciousness of the Master is not influenced by delusion, but he may not be aware on a conscious level of many of the currents of contemporary philosophical thought. I have been amazed, however, at how perfectly Yogananda addressed and resolved in his life and teachings issues which I very much doubt he had ever studied.

For example, I was recently reading some of the great controversies in Christian theology, and realized that Yogananda, more than any writer before him, shed light on these issues, even though he himself was no scholar.

The issues you touched on in your letter are superficial. I hope you don't mind my saying so. I would suggest that you tune in to what Yogananda has to say, rather than trying to block him on an intellectual level.

Rather than ask him to attune to your thoughts, your growth would be much greater if you were to try to attune yourself to his infinite wisdom, a wisdom not influenced by passing fads, because it is eternal.

In divine friendship,

Circa 1999

Dear _____:

I am not in the game of comparing saints. As Sri Yukteswar said once to a devotee, "Why make comparisons? This is how God is playing through you and through me."

I have my own mother. She was, in her way, a great woman, but I would not say that she was the greatest possible mother. It doesn't interest me to inquire into the matter. The plain fact is, she was mine. It would have been foolish for me to go looking for a better mother. Master, similarly, is my spiritual mother. I believe he was as great a master as any, but the important thing to me is that he is my Master. This is quite sufficient for me.

Please ask yourself, "What is this spiritual search all about that I'm on?" Certainly, it isn't some spiritual World Series to determine which team is the best! No true master is, or can ever be, greater than any other. Their relative greatness can be judged only in a worldly sense, according to the outer roles they play. But I once met a great master in India who, so Master had told me, was fully liberated; yet his sainthood was unknown even in his own village. He had almost no disciples. I said to him, "You have so much to give. Why don't you have more people following you?" His reply was, "God has done what He wants to with this body."

The modern mind—especially the modern American mind—thinks that bigger is better. Why should this be so? There is no rivalry in God. In Him, all is one; the differences are superficial. If you are really seeking God, don't worry about who is a *poorna* (full) *avatar*, or who is even an *avatar* at all. Many saints who are far less than *avatars* are perfectly competent to take you to God, and that is what the spiritual path is all about.

I myself consider Master to be the *avatar* of this age because I see that his life, mission, and teachings address so many of humanity's actual needs at this time—especially from a standpoint of energy, which is the hallmark of these times we live in. But my devotion to him has nothing to do with this belief. I am perfectly willing that someone else fill that role, if this be God's will. In a sense, I would even prefer it, simply because the beauty of my Guru's life was so much what he was, as a person, and as a spirit with which I commune in meditation.

Great outward roles can be a distraction from that divine intimacy. I try to help fulfill what I believe he wanted of me for the completion of his mission, but I am content if my understanding of his role should be exaggerated. What does it really matter? It would mean I haven't fully understood the significance of his mission, but it would not mean I have overestimated his divine greatness. Nor would it mean he couldn't give me what I came to him to receive: Self-realization. He is my spiritual mother.

Outward missions are of secondary importance in the spiritual search. Whatever plan God has for this world is His business. The important thing, for me, is to come closer to Him.

I bow with devotion to God's manifestation in all His saints. But I follow my own Guru. That he is my Guru is quite enough for me.

In divine friendship,

March 23, 1989

Dear _____:

How do you manage to equate Yogananda's accounts of Babaji with your parents' stories of Santa Claus? I assume your parents never claimed to have seen Santa Claus, or to have known anyone else to have seen him. Moreover, stories of Santa Claus are not told to children in order to "fool" them. Myths are often beneficial and, in their influence on people, are often truer than mere facts.

The difference between Babaji and Santa Claus is that all of our masters *do* claim to have seen him. Disciples I know personally also claim to have seen him. I myself have had experiences of him, though I have never yet been blessed to behold him in vision. The evidence is strong enough, surely, to inspire you to conduct your own tests in the matter, rather than announcing so boldly to others your unseasoned judgment that he is a myth.

And what does it matter whether or not Babaji does cut his toenails? If he does, he does, and if he doesn't, he doesn't. From some of the things one reads in Yogananda's autobiography, Babaji's body may be subtler than our normal physical bodies, though capable of grosser manifestation. Sri Yukteswar, for instance, failed to see him standing "behind the sunbeams." But such details are, I think, not pertinent to the sincere devotee.

When I met Yogananda, I had many doubts that I determined to "put on a shelf" for the time being, since I was in no position to resolve them. In time, they were resolved indeed. The most important lesson I learned, however, was that doubt itself is a spiritual disease, and that the only cure for it is divine love.

I pray that you grow daily in devotion.

In divine friendship,

[A devotee wrote, "St. Francis and Therese Neumann say they had visions of Christ's birth and that he didn't have a physical birth, but manifested as light. Were these true visions? What about other avatars, *like Krishna and Yogananda?"]*

October 31, 2001

Dear ———:

My first reaction upon reading your question was, *"Who knows?"* I certainly couldn't say for sure. Since that's not all that enlightening an answer, though, why don't I at least share a few thoughts that suggest themselves. Your question is interesting in that it's easy to get pulled off into an unreasonable extreme one way or the other if one doesn't appreciate the truth on both sides.

I'm sure that those visions reported by St. Francis and Therese Neumann were true. Just what were they saying, though? Master once told us, "I see all of you as images of light. Everything—these trees, bushes, the grass you are standing on—all are made of that light. You have no idea how beautiful everything is!" He was describing a reality deeper than the physical one we could see. He wasn't saying, though, that the material world we beheld didn't exist: simply that it isn't what it appears to be.

I can't be certain of these things, as I said, but my best understanding is that the visions you mentioned are likely to have been similar in nature. Seen with inner vision, of course, Christ's birth certainly *did* appear quite different from that of an ordinary person. It was that deeper reality which drew the wise men to the manger.

But this isn't to say that the birth didn't have a physical reality much the same as other births. The great ones make a point of acting out in their own lives most of the outward drama through which the rest of us have no choice but to pass. Like Christ on the cross, they could do otherwise, but they choose not to. It's in condescending to live out these scenes that they make the example of their lives real and meaningful to us, and encourage us with the thought that, as they have overcome, so can we.

Master had a vision once in which the Divine Mother told him, "I have suckled thee through the breasts of many mothers. This time, She who suckled thee was I, Myself." His mother, then, was no ordinary woman! And yet Master never suggested to us that his birth, viewed from the physical point of view, wasn't in full accordance with natural law as God has established it.

I've heard that when they were making the movie, "Gandhi," a group of Gandhi's followers insisted vehemently that it would be sacrilegious to portray him in any way other than as a beam of light! This is the sort of silliness one wants to avoid. Stated that way, of course, it looks ridiculous. But it's easier than you might think to fall into errors of this sort. Even the Gnostics, wise as many of them were, appear to have erred along these lines in denying any physical reality to Christ's suffering on the cross.

I hope that's of some help, at least.

Love,

About a book that compared Yogananda unfavorably to Ramana Maharshi | 6

April 14, 1975

Dear _____:

I am familiar with the book you quote from. In fact, I have a copy of it myself. Master's humility was so great that he often asked saints questions as though he himself were a seeker. He did not have to ask for the Maharishi's advice. He had himself attained a higher state, for that saint, great as he was, still has—Master told me—some karma to work out from the past. Still, I should add that even a *jivan mukta*, as he was, is God-realized already, and in that sense has already reached the pinnacle of achievement. In God, all are one.

Master himself said that a great master works quantitatively as well as qualitatively. The quantitative good that he does is through his general teachings. The qualitative is not only directly to intimate disciples, but also working from within souls of sincere seekers everywhere. Such teaching is not "instruction en masse." Of course, it should be noted that where Master's teachings are extremely diverse, the Maharishi's are practically unvarying. The real individual instruction of the devotee, which he certainly gave to his disciples, was the infusion into the soul of inspiration within, of divine power to progress spiritually.

This is the real teaching of the guru, and seems to have been misunderstood by the translator on that occasion, or by the less evolved disciples around that great guru. Otherwise, quite obviously the saints all say the same basic truths. None of them say, for instance, that we should be dishonest or untruthful. Certain basic teachings are universal the world over.

True saints, beholding God in all, bow to the divine qualities they see expressed in one another.

In divine friendship,

Asked if Yogananda gave his unconditional love to all disciples	7

October 31, 2003

Dear _____:

Of course he gives his unconditional love to everyone, but I think there was also a deeper kind of bond: a promise to follow through to the end, with the disciples he took on. Strange, that I never looked into this when I was there. I just couldn't say to someone, "He gave *me* his unconditional love. Did he give it to you, *too*?" And then, if the answer was yes, to go on canvassing others!

Still, from what he said about Smith, in answer to someone's question, ("When will he be back?" "Never. He was never in.") and also from Abie George insisting that it was something *very special* when Master told a disciple, "I give you my unconditional love," I've assumed that this was an extraordinary bond, not a universal one.

As for sincere followers of this path, including of course, you, I do think you should know that you are *in*, and *accepted*, and have every right to believe it isn't just your presumption that you are *his own*, and that therefore his love for you is unconditional. But there are any number of people who don't feel that way in their hearts, but who think, rather, "Oh well, if this doesn't work I can always go elsewhere and try something else." But even some of them would really be Master's children in the sense that he'll never let go of them until they're out of this mess.

I hope this answers you.

Love,

"I visualize myself speaking
directly _with_ the reader—
not _at_ him, or _to_ him.

WRITING

I try to put myself in his mind
and understand things from his
point of view, with the idea of
helping him to understand what
I'm trying to say to him."

October 12, 1999

Dear _____:

It might be helpful, since we're on the subject of writing, and since you yourself show real talent in this direction, if I shared one or two more thoughts on this subject. I mentioned the importance of trying to maintain an awareness of different people's interests, biases, and doubts. Of course, one can't address such a broad field deliberately without bogging down hopelessly in the intellect. One must above all be centered within, where there is a natural understanding, or at least an awareness, of the human condition in its vast variety. This can't come from study; it must come from within.

And then, it is important to pay attention to style. The rhythm of a sentence, especially, but also the color, or sound, of each word is what helps people to sink into a thought and make it their own. It takes a certain will power to hang onto one's original inspiration while going through all this process of refinement, but without that inspiration the work itself will come out sounding dead. Most writing, unfortunately, *is* dead; most people's consciousness is in fact, as Jesus put it colorfully, dead also! Every word, every rhythm, every sound has to count. It's not easy to do, when one is writing deep truths.

I say this partly because, in your own poems, which are beautiful and inspired, there is sometimes a line that could be expressed more rhythmically to enhance, not sacrifice, its meaning. The final and most important ingredient in good writing, however, is *inspiration*. No rule is worth it, if it interferes with inspiration.

I recall how, years ago, I made a two-week *intensive* study of grammar. It was good to know, but I found that for quite some time afterward my writing was stilted. It wasn't until I'd digested that knowledge that I could write again, and much better both for knowing the rules and knowing when it would be better to break them. (For the rules of grammar are only aids to clarity, not fixed laws in themselves.)

English is a wonderful language to write in. Take a Romance language like French or Italian: You need to have composed a sentence in your mind, at least to some extent, before you even begin it, if only because an adjective must agree in gender with the noun you'll use later. English also has four times as many words as any other language: a fantastic legacy! There are so many ways of saying the same thing. Even this fact must be brought under the control of inspiration; otherwise the mind gets hopelessly bogged down in uncertainties, such as, "What is the best way to express this thought?" Usually there *is* no "best way." There is only the "right way" to express it here and now. Ultimately, this awareness has to come from within; it can't come from outward searching. That is why I rarely use a thesaurus.

Another thing about English is its genius for brevity. Other languages almost force you to write circuitously. A French friend of mind told me, "You simply can't write French the way you speak it. You have to follow the conventions." That means, for example, using the past perfect (is that the name for it?), like "*Il fut*," which no one ever uses when speaking. I wonder, however, if this is merely convention and thus something one can throw overboard if one wants to be clear rather than pompous. People in Italy have commented on my Italian style, which they enjoy and can follow better, but which is really just a departure from their conventional intellectual elaborateness. Still, the inflections themselves are an obstacle to an attractive, engaging, and uplifting rhythm.

Well, enough of this! I just thought you might find these few thoughts, based on fifty years of hard (though wonderful) experience, a help to you in your own writing.

Joy to you!

In divine friendship,

October 12, 1999

Dear _____:

I had a couple of further thoughts on the subject of writing that might prove helpful to you, and that I might also share with others I know who write.

First, I find it helpful to form a clear, even a visual, image of what I'm trying to say. Thus, when I use the illustration of the waves, I form a clear picture of them in my mind so that I feel I'm actually seeing them as a concrete, not an abstract, reality. I find for one thing that this helps me to find the right adjectives for the image. For another, it helps me even rhythmically to fix the image clearly in the reader's mind.

Secondly, I visualize myself speaking directly *with* the reader—not *at* him, or *to* him. I see him clearly in my mind's eye, as neither masculine nor feminine, but simply human, and a friend. I try to put myself in his mind and understand things from his point of view, with the idea of helping him to understand what I'm trying to say to him. Thus, my style itself is conversational rather than didactic, but I don't try to use *his* style. Rather, I speak to him from my heart, which means respecting who he is and neither writing down to him nor writing, as many writers seem to do, merely to persuade myself. Most writing, in fact, seems rather a monologue than a dialogue.

I've found in public speaking, also, that an important help is to ask God beforehand, "What do *these people* need to hear?" rather than, "What do I want to say?" In that way, though I have to speak from my own under-standing and not try merely to popularize my ideas, I can make them real to the present circumstances rather than express only ideas that I've worked out beforehand. I find it helpful, for this reason, not to prepare my talks in advance. The same is true for my writing. I try to go with the flow, rather than work out too carefully in advance what I intend to say.

As for your comments on *Hope for a Better World*, your suggestion was a good idea, but the point I'm making goes beyond that and I don't think it would be helped by giving an exhaustive picture of all possible atti-tudes. I prefer to make a point, then pass on. In this, I'm very unlike the German philosophers, who like to pound their ideas, like nails, into the wall of whatever building they're constructing. What I try to do is write seminally, so that others can come along and expand on the ideas. In that way, I involve them rather than—again like the Germans—beating them into submission.

In divine friendship,

[God Is for Everyone *is a rewrite of Paramhansa Yogananda's first book,*
The Science of Religion, *which was based on Yogananda's outline and ghost
written by one of his disciples. Kriyananda rewrote the book in 2003 to
make it more faithful to Yogananda's original intent.]*

May 25, 2003

Dear _____:

I wanted to write and thank you for your deeply touching comments on
the music. Thank you. I've been so immersed in my work on the book, it
has been hard for me to do anything else.

Your comment on chapter seven was a bit of a damper, considering how
hard I had to work on it. But I wouldn't want you to be anything but
sincere. The thing is, an editor needs to tune into the writer's *style*, if he
has one. Many writers don't have one, I know, but I think it's fairly evident that I'm one of those who are very style-conscious. Clarifications of
meaning are one thing; changes of style, something else.

An editor may not *like* the writer's style, but it's her job to go along with
it anyway. College students probably haven't reached the point yet in their
development where they have any particular style, but someone of my age
is not likely to change his carefully developed ways. The way I see it, my
style is either acceptable or I need to give up writing itself. It's too late to
change my ways.

When I write, I have a feeling in my mind of the rhythm I want for a sentence. Then I try to select words to fit that rhythm—always looking for
the correct meaning, of course: that is most important of all. But I try as
much as possible to write poetically, simply because it suits my fancy.

I am facing a difficulty with the present book, because it isn't *my* book.
I'm writing it in Master's name. I'm aware that his style isn't my style, but
I don't try to imitate his style because I don't believe he paid much attention to it when writing prose. I do try to express his *consciousness*, and in
that I hope I do justice to him.

I am severely limited, however. I can't bring in stories from my own experiences of life—a thing I like to do, normally. I can't bring in stories from *his* life, post 1920, for that is when this book first appeared. I can't bring in my own memories of him, which is what I like especially to do. I can't bring in scientific discoveries or events in history that post-date 1920. And I have to try to be true to his actual knowledge up to that time. I've only cited an actual Bible passage one time (it was in this seventh chapter). I've tried to bring in as much as possible references to Indian tradition, with which he'd have been more familiar at that time than with Western tradition. I've done my best, but it has been a bit like playing tennis in a straitjacket.

Some of your suggestions haven't taken into account these self-imposed limitations. A few, that don't involve questions of style, I accept gratefully.

And again, thank you for your sweet, touching, and (I do feel) true comments on the music. I don't take them personally. The music was given me. It isn't my own.

Love,

There's an inspiration "up there" | 4
waiting to be expressed

January 25, 2002

Dear _____:

A thought occurred to me that you might find a good suggestion. Seeing the care I put into the editing process, it may well seem that I am relying mostly on reason for it. In fact, I find I don't puzzle things through mentally so much as feel them. I'm not sure how to explain it, but when I see something that doesn't quite make sense, I ask mentally what needs doing rather than attack it wholly with logic, even though the problem is essentially one of logic.

Another thing I do is try always to hold onto my first inspiration. It would be very easy to lose touch with that inspiration while struggling through the thickets of reasoning, but what I do is hold back sufficiently from the process, inwardly, not to break that contact. What it seems to take most of all is will power. I think it's at this point that most writers and composers break down. You can sense they've had an initial intuition, but in the process of working it all out they've lost touch with it. A good example is the song, *Brother Sun, Sister Moon*, which starts off beautifully but soon peters out. It's as if Donovan had a true intuition, but then, to finish the song, started thinking, "Now, where would I like to go from here?" thereby letting his ego intrude into the picture.

Does any of this make sense? For me, I've found it very helpful. There's always an inspiration "up there" waiting to be expressed, if we don't succumb to the temptation to take over. This thought has been particularly helpful to me in writing music, the rules of which I don't really know well.

In divine friendship,

April 9, 2003

Dear _____:

Here, finally, is chapter eight [of *God Is for Everyone*]. This one, too, was *finished*—or so I thought—before I left for Goa. It has taken a lot of work also, though not so much as chapter seven. I do think you'll like it.

Master's teachings themselves impose a severe discipline. They allow no sloppy thinking, and in their very call to clarity they ruthlessly expose any attempt merely to *get by* with the self-assurance, "Surely the reader will understand what I've tried to convey." (How often I've found myself tempted to do just that!)

Yet clarity demands also that a truth not be *over-stated*. That fine balance can be achieved only by careful working and re-working.

It has been a wonderful adventure. Well, three more chapters to go. I doubt I'll be able to finish them before my visit to the States. I'll try, though. I look forward to seeing you all soon.

Love,

Devotee wrote that certain
statements about the Catholic Church in
God Is for Everyone *needed to be qualified*

6

January 24, 2003

Dear _____:

I never quite know how to react to your comments on my writing. I appreciate your sincerity, and am of course glad you like the book. But our approaches are so different. Yours is that of the pedagogue. Mine is very openly to get people to ACT! I can imagine Patrick Henry's statement, "As for me, give me liberty or give me death," being edited down to say something like: "Now, I don't know if you'll agree with me, and I realize there are many ways to approach the subject, but from my personal point of view I'd rather be free than have to coexist with a system of which I didn't fully approve."

No one would have taken that statement and *acted* on it! They'd have said, "All right, that's his opinion. And what is *your* opinion, Mr. Brown?"

Master said, "Jesus Christ was crucified once, but his teachings have been crucified every day since then for two thousand years!" *Of course* not everybody has crucified them! *Of course* there have been mitigating factors. *Of course* there have been sincere people in the church! *Of course* many of those, even, who changed the meaning of his teachings did so in all sincerity. Etc., etc.

I'm not writing as a pedagogue. I'm writing to get *action*. I try to be fair, but I don't want to bend so far backward in that attempt that I fall flat on the ground. I have studied a great deal specifically on this question of organization vs. the individual. I lived through it personally for many years. I lived in a Catholic monastery for six months. I studied Roman Catholic Church history in depth, far more, I am certain, than 99% of Catholics, and far more even than most priests. I tried to give space to religious organizations in the search for truth. I tried to be fair.

But I also felt a strong need to offset the hypnosis put out by church organizations, particularly by the Catholic Church, to tell people they need to belong. The individual needs a voice, and I've given him that. I could not have been more even-handed without having no view of my own. But I am not simply a reporter. Nor am I a pedagogue. I'm trying to change *lives*.

I hope you understand. I am impressed by how far you've come in your thinking, and in your sincere efforts to understand the truth.

Love,

A writer/editor suggested changes for Kriyananda's Secrets *books* | 7

December 11, 1992

Dear _____:

I'm touched that you would take the time to help with suggestions for the *Secrets* books.

The suggestions you've made would be fine for straight text—say, for a magazine article. These *Secrets* are in a different category, a rather peculiar one, perhaps. They aren't straight prose. In fact, they are almost a sort of poetry, and to some extent at least must be read as poetry. I worked hard to infuse into the rhythm of each sentence the vibrations I wanted for the secret concerned. My purpose was to write each thought in such a way as to make it enter the subconscious mind. Sometimes, to achieve this end, I resorted to unusual choices of words and word sequences.

Your changes, while quite legitimate editorially speaking, affected those vibrations and subtly changed them. For this reason I've left the text as it was, except for a comma that was a typo. In other types of writing I might well have been happy to accept all your suggestions.

Thank you.

In divine friendship,

To a devotee offering a possible addition to Kriyananda's book, Hope for a Better World! | 8

August 3, 2001

Dear _____:

Thank you for your comments. As for your personal reaction, the door must be left open for these without saying them all. Otherwise one gets into what the German philosophers love to do: plug every hole, but befog the overall trend. It's lecturing to an audience and responding so specifically to a question that everyone else is left mystified.

I try to answer questions in such a way that everyone is helped, not just the person I'm answering. If I can't universalize the answer in that way, I prefer to skirt around the issue. It isn't fair to the whole audience.

Love,

To Devi Mukherjee, a brother disciple and life-long friend, on his editing of Devi's book Shaped by Saints | 9

[The book describes Mukherjee's spiritual journey, which culminated in his becoming a disciple of Paramhansa Yogananda and a monk at Yogoda Satsanga Society [Self-Realization Fellowship (SRF)] in India in 1955.]

May 17, 2000

Dear Devi:

First let me give you my overall impression of your manuscript. It is a beautiful book, Devi. More than beautiful: It is filled with joy, inspiration, and wisdom. Many, many people will read it, and will, I am certain, find guidance and help from it.

Devi, Durga's particular concern was that what you'd written about Binay Dubey might sound negative, and might therefore lower the tone of the book. As I read what you'd written, however, and understood how important it was to you to include that account, I saw that what was needed was not its removal, as Durga had thought, but a longer explanation. In addition, however, I found the whole book so inspiring and beautiful that I put everything aside to devote my full time to working on it and making it into a book that people would be able to read and enjoy without the obstacle of unsophisticated English. At the same time, I feared to inject my own vibrations into the language, since this is your book, not mine.

Then the solution came to me: to attune myself to your consciousness, rather than to your language. This inspiration worked, for I could feel myself sharing in your experiences as if through your mind and eyes. Knowing you personally has been a help to me in this process, but your consciousness as I read was very vivid in my mind. The whole book reads as if you'd written it, in fact, though the wording is different from what yours would have been. I could feel your humor, your devotion, and your enthusiasm in everything you'd written. I simply "tuned in" to you. I should add that Durga, too, added enormously to what you'd done, especially to clarify it. What helped both of us most of all, however, was the fact that this really is a *marvelous* book!

The only part where I departed from my attempt to tune in to your consciousness was toward the end, where I went into the philosophy of music and Indian versus Western attitudes. This had to be my own addition, not your thoughts, but I made it clear in the manuscript that this section came from me, by having you say so, so that people would not be confused by the difference of vibrations.

I thought that the things you said about Dubey needed to be said, and I also explained those things further. I never realized how harmful he had been. In fact, I began to doubt the rightness of the decision that was taken about Atmananda. The fact that all of you loved him so deeply and sincerely was an important consideration for me. Another important consideration was the fact that one accusation against him had been that he used money from America to construct houses in his own name; yet when he was out of YSS [Yogoda Satsanga Society], he was left without money, when ownership of all those houses should have made him rich. Someone, I decided, had to have been lying. What a tragedy!

SRF has much to answer for, I'm afraid. And the pain that you and others experienced at the hands of Dubey: I could believe all of it, for I remembered how he talked, saying he would force everyone to come under his control. In fact, my greatest reason for leaving Calcutta and going to New Delhi was that I simply couldn't stand being around him any more, listening to his negative diatribes against all those people.

Well, that sorrow is under the bridge now. But I didn't feel that it would be right not to continue your thoughts to their own logical conclusion, rather than omit them. What I have tried to do is make your account of him less personal, basing it more on principles.

Devi, God bless you for this wonderful book! I hope you like what I have done with it. Judging from the manuscript, I think it will come out in printed form to about 115 pages, which will be thick enough for a spine, so the book can be placed on a shelf in bookstores, with the title readable. I am sure we shall print it ourselves, and we will try to find a publisher for it also in India. This may well give you a good source of income.

At first I wanted to put only your name on the title page. As I worked on the book, however, I realized that it would be obvious to the reader that you could not have written it yourself in its present form: the English is too correct. So I decided to insert after your name something that is often done in such cases: "*With* Durga and Kriyananda." In this way, if readers visit you in the expectation of finding you fluent in English, they won't be too shocked!

I hope you like the title, *Shaped by Saints*. This is just what the book is all about.

Everyone who has read it, while I've worked on it, has been thrilled by it. They say it sounds completely like you, except for that part near the end, which I've mentioned. I only finished the book this very afternoon, and hasten to send it off to you.

In our Masters,

Responds to comments on his book,
Crises in Modern Thought[*] | 10

Early 1990s

Dear _____:

Please forgive me for not answering your kind and thoughtful letter sooner than this.

Thank you for correcting me on the question of the terms, relativism vs. relativity. You are of course quite right. I'll try to change the text accordingly before the next printing—assuming there *is* a next printing, which

---

[*]Later revised and renamed, *Out of the Labyrinth*.

I hope there is, since twenty-six years of study and thought went into the writing of this book. I feel its conclusions are desperately needed today.

As for the first chapters, they were the hardest part, and represent my best try I'm afraid. I couldn't possibly go into all that matter again. It took a great amount of will power to stay with a study that was, in fact, wholly uncongenial to my own tastes and inclinations. My own "expertise," if you want to call it that, comes from forty years of commitment to the teachings of *Vedanta*, during which time I have labored to apply their clear vision to the universal problems of modern life.

I know what you mean about wishing I'd made the point more strongly that modern physics is no longer materialistic. Not being a physicist myself, I'm not sure how strong I can fairly make my statements on its present-day positions, but I felt the argument would in any case be strengthened by understatement, where the reader supplies his own affirmations on the point. Throughout the book, indeed in all my writings, I lean toward understating positions in which I myself believe quite passionately.

Thank you again for your thoughtful letter. I wish we could meet, but since we live far apart it is not likely. Even when I go to Europe, which is fairly frequently, it is more often to the continent, whereas I get the impression that your connections are more in England. In any case, I look forward to reading your books.

With best wishes,
Sincerely yours,

   (J. Donald Walters)

Responds to comments on his book
The Artist as a Channel* | 11

December 19, 1988

Dear _____ :

I was grateful that you took the time to comment at such length on my book, *The Artist as a Channel*. I might say that this book represents a

---

*Later revised and renamed, *Art as a Hidden Message*.

sort of revelation, as I considered it at the time, that I had when I was eighteen. I am now sixty-two, and it has taken me all these years to be able to formulate in words, and of course to refine, the essential insight I had then.

Central to that insight was the realization that the arts are, as I have written in my book, a human phenomenon, and must claim their validity on the basis of what is valid from a human, not merely an "artistic," point of view. The "revelation" then went on to show me what it means to be valid in human terms—an insight by which, subsequently, I have guided my whole life with an ever-increasing sense of inner fulfillment.

I made the point at the outset of the book that "art," in the sense I meant it, referred to all the arts and not only to the visual arts. I myself am an artist, though more in music composition than in sculpting or painting.

I know what you mean by the disadvantage of the title, *The Artist as a Channel*. The book doesn't in any way refer to channeling in the popular contemporary sense. On the other hand, I hope the book will still be around when this fad fades away. In fact, I understand it is already fading. Meanwhile, the advantages of the title struck me as outweighing the disadvantages, for the very reasons you advanced. I hope I am right. If a better title occurs to me I may change it, but books always lose a certain momentum in the stores when their titles are changed.

I try to make the point in the book that *meaning*, artistically speaking, has nothing to do with verbally expressed meaning. I also say that abstract art *can* be deeply meaningful—to the heart and the spirit if not to the mind. In this sense, Moslem architecture is among the most meaningful with which I am familiar. It stirs the soul. If those pipes in Hawaii do it for anyone, all I can say is they don't do it for me. I'm certainly not the last word in judging such things. What my book deals with is principles, primarily. These principles stand, I think, even if one or another example fails.

On the subject of the masculine pronoun, yours is the second complaint I've had. But as you yourself point out, it is cumbersome to write he/she, etc. My suspicion is that we'll all go back to the traditional use of the masculine pronoun to express not men only, but an impersonal reality that includes both men and women. Certainly I don't *think* of men when I use it. I'm forced, rather, to think "men and women" when I say he/she, etc.

I've had occasion to learn nine languages, and to have studied three others. In all of these languages, with the possible exception of Indonesian (which I don't remember well enough now to cite), the masculine pronoun is the linguistic way for referring generally to both sexes. It seems a natural thing to do, and as I say, it is the opposite of sexist. It is the contrived alternative which forces one to think of sexual differences.

Anyway, here, too, I prefer not to go with the fad of the moment, but to follow the longer rhythms. If the language ends up honoring the alternative you prefer, then I'll go along. I'm not trying to create language, only to use it.

You wrote, quoting me, "Artists themselves, even the greatest of them, have been more concerned with describing technical matters . . . than with discussing the relationship between any of these outward factors and human consciousness." The operative word here is "describing". I go to lengths in my book to show how they did indeed establish a relationship between these factors and consciousness. I think the point may have been too obvious to them to invite discussion. At any rate, if you are familiar with *statements* by them to the contrary you are better read than I, a possibility which I grant cheerfully.

However, from your answer I think you thought I was taking them to task for not *defining* art in terms of consciousness. I used another word. I'm well aware that Botticelli, for instance, defined his art clearly enough *to himself* to make him a great artist. It is the bad artists who haven't a clear idea of what they are trying to do. And it is the mediocre artists who accept the definitions of others regarding what they should be doing. Again, I have written of principles, of directions. My hope is that my book covers this ground.

Thank you so much for writing. I hope some day to have the pleasure of meeting you.

Sincerely,

(*J. Donald Walters*)

August 22, 2002

Dear _____:

It is a big help having Peter Schuppe send me the page proofs. Reading it in that format enables me to see things I'm more likely to miss on the long lines of the typing page. This time, though, it really *is* final!

What I've done, of course, is work from the published book. This will be the *fourth* edition in a year! A bit of a record. I'll spare you (and myself!) the gory details of why and how.

The main thing is, there was a certain urgency in getting it out, and deadlines. I couldn't devote the time I gradually came to realize this book needs. What I see I've done is take on the "big guns" of Western thought! I've *had* to do it impressively. Most of the subject matter, being dry, I've had to work at making interesting and entertaining, and also irrefutable. It isn't my usual "stomping ground," so I've had to work on it all the harder.

But I've realized increasingly that this is an important book, and deserves the best I can give it.

Love,

August 26, 2002

Dear _____:

I like your article. Thanks for sending it.

As for your question, yes, I find lecturing and writing surprisingly different media. In lecturing one can convey a more direct sense of *experience*. In writing, one can be more exact in what one says, but it is much more difficult to convey that sense of experience. The trick in editing a talk is to bring a sense of immediacy into the written word.

I had an interesting experience in this regard while writing *The Path*. I'd nearly decided to leave out that story of Doctor and Mildred Lewis with Master—the "Sub gum duff" story. I had the literal transcript of Doctor's relating of the story. But when he told it in person he did something one always does when speaking: used gestures, tone of voice, pauses, etc. Things you simply can't convey in writing. Although the story itself, as he had told it, was hilarious, in writing it came out flat and a bit disappointing.

Then it occurred to me to try to inject into his words at least a *sense* of his spoken communication. It was a challenge. For instance, in telling it he said, "And Mrs. Lewis, she . . ." accompanied by a facial expression of exasperation. What I did, and I think it worked, was write, "She turned for help to the wall."

Thanks for writing.

Advice on writing about a controversial subject | 14

August 1, 2001

Dear _____:

Anyway, I've been saying from the start: Don't be combative. Just stick with the facts. They are quite damning enough. Rhetoric, on the other hand, will offend people and leave us open to legal attack. To refer to something as a "47-year fraud" is rhetorical and combative.

Love,

Advice on how to promote books | 15

May 16, 2000

Dear _____:

Read my little book, *Secrets of Winning People*. It's very important to put yourself in your reader's shoes: to think, not, What do I want to say, but

What does he need to hear; what will interest him; what will wake him up to his need for this book?

Think of yourself as talking not only to him, but *with* him. It's communication. It's interest in *him* as a person, to which any interest in *me* as the writer must be relevant.

Love,

In response to a long list of corrections | 16

September 29, 2002

Dear _____:

I'm afraid you've misunderstood my intentions in sending you manuscripts. I wondered in the past why you'd made all those suggestions. Your letter made it clear. I haven't thought of a *team* of people helping me with my writing. All I've done is share what I've done with a few friends, out of my own exuberance. A long list of corrections gives me the impression, after I've driven myself to exhaustion finishing something, "Thanks, and here's what's *wrong* with it."

In fact, my writing is very much from within myself; one might say, it's an act between me and Master. I don't write by committee. If someone makes a suggestion, I consider it, but to send a manuscript to so many people with the main purpose of inviting their corrections would not only result in further exhaustion, for me, but would force me to adopt an attitude toward writing as though it were a matter of putting the pieces of a jigsaw puzzle together. I couldn't imagine writing like that.

After more than sixty years of writing, I'm pretty comfortable with what I do, generally. In such a field, perfection isn't possible because the standards vary so much. My main purpose is to get my thoughts and *vibrations* across. Some of your suggestions are good. Others are okay, but change the vibrations. I'll go over them carefully, and use what pleases me, but this month with the trial my mind won't be much on these things.

Thanks anyway, and love,

March 1998

Dear _____:

I must accept that our temperaments are different. My own outlook on life itself has always irritated some people, who believe that I toss off generalities liberally and without serious thought. In fact, I myself am impatient of generalities and will often challenge them.

What I strive to catch is the essence of things. When I wrote *Your Sun Sign as a Spiritual Guide*, for instance, I meditated on people in each sign and tried to capture the essence that bound them together. It would be easy to point out exceptions to my presentation; there are countless numbers of them. Nevertheless, what I've written is in fact something essential, and many people (including astrologers) have said that it's the clearest exposition of the characteristics of each sign they have ever read.

The same with *The Hindu Way of Awakening*. I am perfectly aware that there are many exceptions to anything I say. I myself could point to quite a few. Nevertheless, in essence I know I am right, and it is of that essence that I'm writing. If I am wrong in this, then my whole life has been a mistake, for that is how I see things, how I work, and how I try always to explain truth.

I don't want to offend anyone; I just want to express the essential truth as I see it, and above all to help people to see something that your letter suggests you don't want to join me in: to me, the crystal clear fact that truth is one and universal, and that the fundamental life view of all scriptures cannot be in conflict, else there is no real truth. This is the fundamental theme of the book, by which I hope to help give religion itself the respect of people once again, which it has lost.

Thank you for writing. God bless you.

In Master's love,

March 1998

Dear _____:

Reflecting further on our exchange of letters, I realize that your resistance to my book is inevitable. We simply think differently.

It is your nature to ponder the pros and cons of every subject. It is mine to condense the issues in an essential understanding. You have, I think, an aversion to generalities. To me, no truth can be stated except in generalities. To you it looks as if I merely, in almost cavalier fashion, jumped to my conclusions. I know I arrive at them only after deep thought and meditation, usually for years, taking countless pros and cons into consideration but finally offering them up to intuitive insight.

I know they look unseasoned to one of your outlook. It makes you uneasy to see me make statements without a lot of facts to back them up. For me, I can't think that way. What I do, rather, is condense those facts, which I've long considered, into sweeping conclusions. I can't think in any other way. You, too, can't think in any other way. It is for reasons like this that writers often feud. And I have no desire to feud with you.

So let us just leave things as they stand, agreeing to disagree on fundamental points of writing and thinking, but remaining friends, I hope, as human beings. I am doing the best job of which I am capable on this book, and I recognize that some people won't like it. The statements I make in it are not meant to offend, but they express clearly what I do, quite sincerely, believe to be true.

I've made one of the changes you suggested. But when you wrote of "many, many" points on which, evidently, you feel I've been too cavalier, I have to say that, no, I am being incisive, and true to my own understanding, and if in this clarity I offend I simply must accept it.

Nevertheless, I don't want you to think I oppose your way of reasoning, even though it isn't mine. Your way is your way, and it is good, because you are good. I wouldn't have you change it.

In Master's love,

Dear _____ :

I studied writing poetry for a semester under the English poet, W. H. Auden. I particularly remember two lines from a poem of his titled, "Letter to a Wound":

> *No cloud-like hand can hold him—*
> *Restraint by women.*

It always bothered me a little to read that second line, which merely explains the line before it. Poetry, it seems to me, ought not to offer such literal "footnotes" to its own images. To do so suggests muddy thinking to my mind—which is to say, lack of clear inspiration. Far better, I should think, would it have been rather to write something like:

> *No cloud-like hand can hold him*
> *with feminine entreaty.*

I forget what he actually wrote after that. The poem itself is a cipher. Someone who knew Auden as a friend once told me the poem was meant to be incomprehensible; Auden let only a few of his close friends in on the secret.

And that too is something for which I fault him. True poetry—indeed, true art of all kinds—ought never to lead one deliberately into impenetrable fogs. It ought to say something not only intelligible, but intelligent.

The purpose of art is to clarify, to uplift, to make some statement that the artist considers true, and to make it memorably and inspiringly for others.

In the visual or auditory arts—painting, sculpture, and music—as differentiated from the verbal arts—poetry and prose—the truth doesn't have to be intellectually comprehensible, but it must at least ring true to our feelings, and above all to the dictates of wisdom born of intuition. Indeed, a work of art may express with perfect clarity a negative emotion such as rage, terror, lust, or despair, but in such a case we must draw a distinction between fact and truth. Negative emotions—indeed, in the last analysis all emotions, which (generally speaking) express agitated feeling of some kind—are delusive, because they conceal the truth; they don't reveal it.

Words, on the other hand, overtly communicate ideas. The poet must be a musician in the sound and rhythm of the words he uses; he must be a painter in the color of his images; and he must be a sculptor in the way he molds his sentences. He must also, however, and above all, in some way make sense—unless, indeed, he is deliberately writing nonsense, and inviting his readers to join him in the fun.

Yes, of course he can insert, out of sheer exuberance, a few nonsensical words —like Shakespeare's "Hey nonny nonny no," or Lewis Carroll's "Beware the frumious Bandersnatch." Finally, however, I think he should say something both intelligible and intelligent.

Am I wrong? Shakespeare, now that I think of it, wrote some lyrics that were fairly incomprehensible. I'm thinking of Desdemona's song in Othello:

> *The poor soul sat sighing*
> *By a sycamore tree,*
> *Singing willow, willow, willow.*
> *Her hand on her bosom,*
> *Her head on her knee,*
> *Singing willow, willow, willow.*

Well, I must admit the rest of the poem too, which is meant to be sung, has rather incomprehensible lyrics, and conveys rather a mood, as music does. (I myself have written a melody for those lyrics.) So I guess maybe words that are meant to be sung can legitimately convey feelings without logical insight, the meaning itself being implicit in the feeling expressed. Ordinarily, however, I believe that poetry ought to say at least something, both clearly and well, and ought to say it in such a way as to convey at least a hint of that meaning to the reader or listener.

Auden, after those lines, might have gone on to say something like:

> *Stride on, O mighty hero:*
> *Face the Light.*
> *Gaze fearlessly into those spear-thrusting rays*
> *beyond which lie golden opportunities:*
> *Self-conquest and victory.*

Well, who knows whether he might have considered those lines corny? Writers are notoriously fixed in their own ways of self-expression! Anyway, his two lines describe masculine courage, scornful of feminine hesitancy.

The point is to express oneself strongly, colorfully, and withal to get one's point across clearly (first making sure that one actually has a point to make!): whether it be to express inspiration, faith, cynical doubt, or courage.

The next point, of course, is to express thoughts that are valid and true. The Baudelaires of this world may successfully infect their hearers with their own mental gloom, but the lines of poetry that get quoted during man's hours of need are those which speak the truth memorably.

Love,

"I am only my Guru's instrument. His power is much greater than mine,

SWAMI KRIYANANADA'S ROLE

though I am aware that through me people have come closer to him."

October 12, 1973

Dear _____:

If there is anything in me worthy of praise the praise belongs to God, not to a very unworthy instrument. Seek Him more and more deeply, and you will express Him more and more fully yourself.

In divine friendship,

A devotee asked to become
Swami Kriyananda's disciple | 2

March 22, 1973

Dear _____:

I am only my Guru's instrument. His power is much greater than mine, though I am aware that through me people have come closer to him. But I suggest you keep his photograph on your altar, and concentrate on him in your meditations. You will soon become aware of what a great blessing the world received when he was born into it.

May he bless you always.

In divine friendship,

A devotee asked, "Who is
the Guru, you or Master?" | 3

July 27, 2001

Dear _____:

I remember you well. Thank you for writing, and for sending me your e-mail.

This isn't a superficial question, and it doesn't deserve a superficial answer. It depends on several levels of perception and receptivity.

I would say, however, that inasmuch as I am the spiritual guide of Ananda, and that inasmuch as we have, in my perception, a good rapport, you may consider me your teacher on this plane. Let's put it this way: Master is your Guru, and so also are the whole line of our gurus. I am your spiritual teacher insofar as he inspires me to guide you. It is a role to which I am faithful, but it is not the same commitment as, for example, the bond between me and Master, for the reason that he is God-realized and I am not (though I'm working on it!).

_____ [an Ananda colony leader] is your spiritual teacher, to the extent that you accept her guidance. She's more hands-on than I can be, and is also very conscientious in her role, which she views (as I do) as a service to you, not as teaching you.

None of our roles is fixed in eternity, and can't be until we ourselves are so fixed. Nor is yours, as a disciple, until you are more deeply on the path. You may think of God, finally, as the one and only true guru. (That is how Master himself put it.) Love Him. Obey Him. And be grateful for His guidance in *whatever* form it comes.

I hope this satisfies you. These are subtle things, and can't be declared like mathematical formulae.

In divine friendship,

Devotee questioned Kriyananda's introduction of the Festival of Light into Ananda's Sunday services, urging that these decisions be made "democratically" | 4

February 6, 1987

Dear _____:

I appreciate your sincerity in expressing your thoughts to me so carefully. And after all that effort, I wish I could say in reply, "You've opened up new avenues of thought."

Can you imagine into what confusion my life would sink were my more important decisions made on a basis of dialogue? You put it correctly when you said I felt guided to create this ceremony. I have had to make many decisions similarly, based on inner guidance. Had I not had the courage to take new directions when I felt so guided, Ananda itself could never have come into being. And you yourself would have had no former service format, even, to champion.

You've said you used to go to the services mainly for the inspiration you felt from the people. Fortunately, those people are still there. Why not continue going for their satsang, if for no other reason? In time, I think you may come to appreciate the Festival of Light quite as much as so many others do. (I've had scores of letters so far, thanking me for it.)

In any case, please understand that it is only with considerations involving the outward mind that decisions can be arrived at democratically. Spiritual truths must either be received superconsciously, or not arrived at, at all.

I don't ask you to accept my guidance. But if you have felt inspired so far in your contact with Ananda, might it not mean that, to some extent, you have accepted this guidance already? If this assumption is true, why not give your doubts a vacation for a few months, and see then how you feel? If later you still find that the Festival of Light "grates" on you, that would be the wiser time to decide what alternatives you have left: perhaps to limit your attendance at the Ananda center to group meditations, or to meditate on your own.

I suggest this delayed reaction also as an exercise in surrender. This is something which that fledgling bird in the story from the Festival needed to learn. It might even help you to take that story more to heart. Its concepts, like others in the ceremony, can be understood on many levels, and taken by each member of the congregation according to his own special needs.

If you will examine your own motives carefully, I think you will see that, underlying your rejection of the worship service, is a rejection of certain basic attitudes of discipleship. Your very devotion to Paramhansa Yogananda and other great masters is quite as convenient as it is laudable. For those to whom you pray are no longer with us physically, and are unlikely to embarrass you even in vision, by making you face up to your own weaknesses or, on the other hand, to challenge you to work harder at perfecting your own strengths.

Basic to the spiritual path is a recognition that the truth, while certainly (as you point out) residing within every individual, is also a light of understanding, a touch of grace, that is passed on from generation to generation of disciples. Even societies must pass on their achievements. (Just think how little mankind would have achieved if every generation had had to re-invent the wheel!)

An attitude of receptivity is essential to spiritual progress. By receptivity to the flow of grace that is passed down from the gurus through their disciples, man learns, among other things, to be humble, and not boastful of his own wisdom. You need to learn such receptivity. Were this not the case, you would not have taken such foolish issue with the Festival's statement about self-love—twisting, as you did, a truth that is proclaimed in every scripture.

Evidently you have accepted the Protestant presumption that all men, with or without any spiritual training, are equally competent to understand and interpret divine law. I have long seen this intellectual presumption as a major block in your spiritual life, but have not had your permission to speak to you of your spiritual needs. Now, your letter virtually begs for such a statement from me.

I have often found that those people who waited a bit before judging new developments ended up becoming their ardent supporters. Try it, why don't you, and see if this doesn't happen also to you? The humility entailed in waiting couldn't possibly hurt you, and might prove a major incentive to your own spiritual development.

In divine friendship,

Devotee questioned changes in Ananda's Sunday Service and whether Kriyananda was trying to replace Yogananda as the guru | 5

December 3, 1988

Dear _____:

Thank you for your letter. I'm pleased with your sincerity, though unsure as to how far I can satisfy your desire for an explanation.

First of all, I certainly have no wish to replace Master, or to be installed as the next guru in our line of gurus, or indeed to be considered a guru at all (since I'm not one). As Yogananda's disciple, however, it is right that I express his teachings creatively and not merely parrot them. It is also natural that those who have come to Master through me should turn also to what I have done, and not set that rigidly aside for Master's words alone.

The *Bible* and *Bhagavad Gita* readings are designed for Sunday Services in a way that Master's commentaries were not. Those readings are based on his teachings, and are true to them. There was never any question of substituting my commentaries for his. We never used his, and in fact never had them to use. Amrita [an independent publisher] has put out unauthorized versions, which are, in any case, not designed for Sunday readings.

The *Spiritual Diary* was never a part of SRF's publications while I was in the work. I have made it a point not to draw from their more recent publications, for reasons too personal to go into here, but reasons, I assure you, that have nothing to do with disapproval or disdain for what they have done or are doing. They are doing Master's work, and are doing it (I think) well. Nevertheless, I have been forced to serve him in a different way, and I seek therefore to be consistent to that way.

Still, I see no reason not to have those readings from the *Spiritual Diary* read at our meditations. Moreover, they are altogether different from *Secrets of Happiness*. Why should there be any conflict between the two?

The blessing before eating seems a minor issue. Some people were saying it would be nice to sing the blessing, and someone once asked me if I would write a melody for the purpose. The whole thing really is no deeper than that. Both Master's blessing and the little song I wrote are based on the same passage in the Indian Scriptures.

I have never permitted people to add my name to the prayer to the gurus, and shall look into this matter further now that you've drawn it to my attention. At the same time, it would be idle to say that I am *not* the guide of those who come to Master through me and Ananda. Rather, this fact needs to be affirmed.

Those who want to go straight to Master without a guide are welcome to do so, as indeed you are welcome to do. But if people come wanting my help and guidance in the matter of attunement with him and his ray, what point would be served by not accepting a responsibility which the Guru himself gives to his disciples, and which Master stated specifically he was giving to me? Those people err who imagine their only responsibility to others is to introduce them to Master.

You yourself must decide what you want. I only want to be of help if help from me and Ananda is what you yourself desire. No one ever said the ceremonies are more important than meditation. The very comparison would be foolish. As to whether you feel that the ceremonies, or anything else that we offer, are of value to you personally—that is a matter between you, God, and Master.

I think that perhaps you subconsciously resist the very thought of accepting guidance. At least, please consider the possibility. You might even ask yourself: Would you follow Master himself, if he were living? Much may depend on your answer to this question. Guidance is important to spiritual growth.

In divine friendship,

How should we relate to you, Swami? | 6

[*In a community* satsang, *a devotee asked Swami Kriyananda: "How should we relate to you, Swami? You're certainly a friend, but to many of us you're so much more than that. I'd like to know how I, and all of us, can develop an open channel with you that we'd feel comfortable with. And I'd like to know how to work with that on all levels, not just on the level of personality."*]

Summer 1983

Well, you've asked a difficult one! Part of my answer, surely, must take into consideration not only *your* comfort, but also mine.

You've said you'd like your answer "not just on the level of personality." Yet you've started at that level. Let's then begin there, shall we?

From what I've observed, I'd say it was common for teachers—and not spiritual teachers only—to identify strongly with their teaching role; to tell themselves, "*This* is what I am, and what I like to be." In this respect I guess you might say I'm beyond the pale: I've never really identified myself with the role I'm supposed to fill.

Yes, of course I've dedicated my life to teaching; it isn't that I'm uncomfortable with the role itself. It's only that my desire in teaching is simply to please God and Guru, and to help others. Master told me that this is my path to salvation. It's the goal that draws me. I'm not attached to the path to it. Indeed, whenever I meet others who feel like talking, I'm happy to remain silent—even if I don't always agree with what they say!

I spoke of my own need to feel comfortable in my relationship with you. What is comfortable for me, personally, is the thought that I am your friend in God. When I teach, it is in a spirit of friendship, of sharing with you, and of serving God through you all. You don't *owe* it to me to accept what I say. On the contrary, I feel blessed when anything I say proves helpful to you.

What, then, of *your* comfort? I know it is sometimes awkward for you, used as you are to the thought of a friend and a teacher being two very different animals. You've been through school and college, and perhaps you've been lectured to authoritatively all through your childhood by your parents. And almost always, when anyone has had anything to tell you "for your own good," he's told it to you in a spirit of condescension, as if addressing you from a higher level of wisdom and experience.

What makes it particularly awkward for me in my effort to be first of all your friend is that I do speak with a degree of authority. Thirty-five years on the path could hardly have failed to give me a certain wisdom and experience that most of you, perhaps, still lack. Moreover, I am the spiritual director of this community. Naturally, you see me as an authority figure. I suppose that in some ways I must accept that I *am* one, though I try to step out from under that burden as much as possible by making truth, never my personal wishes, the real authority for all of us. Nor am I one of those teachers or leaders who courts the friendship of those under them by pretending to be merely "one of the boys." In my mind, my sharing with you as teacher and leader *is* my offering of friendship to you.

A tough one to piece together, I grant you! But perhaps this thought will help you: What I seek to do always is let my teaching, and my requests of you, convince you by their own merit, and by the power of truth. I do not hold over you any personal emblems of authority—position, or greater experience, my years with Master. I let the words speak for themselves. I am, meanwhile, simply your friend.

Indeed, it often happens that the words that come through me in this manner come not at all by my will. It sometimes happens, for example, just after I have said, "I don't know" in answer to some question that I suddenly do know. The answer is given to me. Or it may be that I am lecturing, and suddenly I find myself sitting back, as it were, listening with astonishment to what I am saying—almost as if with the reaction, "My, I wish I'd thought of that!"

So what am I saying? If my very service to you isn't really my own, and if that service constitutes my act of friendship for you, where do I even fit in?

The answer is, I don't! What I aspire to be, rather, is a channel for the only true Friend any of us will ever have: God alone. I see each of you, too, as channels above all for my Infinite Friend. And though, naturally, I have particular karmic bonds with some of you (one body cannot relate equally, in an outward sense, to everyone), it is not these bonds that matter most. Indeed, to concentrate too much on them would be bondage indeed. In all cases, it is on an inner, soul level that friendship is sweetest. And on this level, we can be close even when outwardly we seem far apart.

Why then, do I identify more with the role of friend than with that of teacher, if in fact I don't really identify with either role? Well, to begin with, such is simply my nature, my personality. I do identify with the role of friend. But it is an identity that I offer up to higher, impersonal realities.

Secondly, and more important, I think there is more to be gained even from a teacher-student relationship if it can be rooted in deep, spiritual friendship.

Do you remember how once, a couple of years ago, I said to a group of you, "For years I have asked Master to use me as his channel to bless all of you. But this evening I would like to ask each of you to come forward and pray to him, to use *you* as channels to bless me." That was a moving experience for all of us, wasn't it? For it helped us to realize that true, divine friendship means *mutual* giving.

Many of you have mentioned how much more harmony you have felt over these past two years at Ananda, since I began emphasizing the importance of *reciprocal* sharing.

What leader worthy of the name wants to surround himself with "yes men?" The people I enjoy working with are those who think for themselves, who give *me* back energy—and not those who merely sit there, taking it all in like sponges. Passive receptivity makes the flow of energy unidirectional, with the teacher putting out everything, but getting nothing back in return to reinforce his further giving. The student might imagine he receives more from the teacher in that way, but the truth is, he receives *much* less. Magnetism builds up when it moves cyclically. In the relationship of friends, reciprocity comes more naturally and easily.

Here's an example of what I mean. Years ago, while I was writing *The Path*, I invited the members of our community over to my house for *satsang* every Thursday evening. I would read to them whatever chapter I'd been working on last. Well, to my dismay, week after silent week I found them all just sitting there, meditating and (I hoped!) listening to the words, but hardly ever expressing any outward reaction.

Now, please put yourself in my place. Wouldn't you sort of wonder?

Yes, certainly I knew that they were meditating on what they were hearing. But they weren't taking *me* into account. Was I supposed simply to go on pouring out energy to them, without, so to speak, ever pausing for a "refill?"

A one-way flow of energy is an abuse against Nature's very law of abundance.

The farmer who only takes from his land, returning nothing gratefully to it, soon exhausts the soil. God, Himself, showers abundance on those who appreciate it. It is by our appreciation that we attune ourselves to the flow.

As my singing teacher during my college days said, at our first meeting, "Your lessons will be five dollars. It isn't that I need the money; I don't. But *you* need to pay it!" The members at those Thursday evening *satsangs* seemed to be seeing me purely in the light of a sort of spiritual jukebox, set there solely for *their* inspiration!

Well, one evening finally, at the end of a reading, I said to them in exasperation, "Isn't there anyone here capable of saying *something*?"

My point is that you yourselves benefit most when you perceive the teaching process as an *exchange* of energy. This is, as I said earlier, a matter of principle—much more so than of my mere personality. The important thing is to recognize that the giving must be both-sided. Otherwise it becomes poured into a hole that never gets filled. And the easiest way to come to appreciate this reality is, first, on the human level. That, again, is why I stress the importance of friendship.

Toward God Himself there is the beginning of a right relationship when we can offer ourselves back to Him lovingly, and when we don't seek merely to receive Him passively.

~~~~~

Having stressed my friendship for you, and the importance of this role for both teacher and student, it is important for me to make clear the further truth that friendship is only a preliminary attitude. It would be a great mistake to leave this teaching on a merely personal, human level, lest love become emotional, and colored by attachment. The real point I'm reaching for goes much deeper than that.

I've said that I like to see myself as your friend. But by friendship I mean primarily friendship *in God*. Indeed, what I try to be to you is, as I said earlier, a channel for *His* love.

For neither you nor I exist except as shining bubbles in His one ocean of light. Who, indeed, is loving whom? It is all God, loving Himself in His myriad outward disguises! The deep truths for which we, in our *sadhana*, are reaching are all impersonal.

The trick is to realize that, in their impersonality, they are not in any way cold or abstract; that love is the *more* loving for being impersonal—for being freed, that is to say, from the constriction of petty selfhood and selfishness.

Thus, a basic attitude of friendship serves the higher end of helping us to develop attitudes of loving self-giving in our relationship with God. Without such attitudes, high yogic aspirations will ever remain unfulfilled, and the austere impersonality the yogi works on developing remains joyless and dry.

In my relationship with Master I would sometimes find him very distant and impersonal. At first, seeing him thus, I thought he was being cold. In time, however, I discovered that what he was offering to me, and to all of us, was the *perfection* of our human relationship with him, never a denial of it. Far from rejecting our love, he was offering it to God alone, where it truly belonged, and thus giving us the chance to discover, through our relationship with Him, a relationship a million times more beautiful than anything merely human.

Friendship, you see, is right, spiritually speaking, only when it seeks its perfection in God's *impersonal* love. Were I to give you my friendship only as a human being, and to seek your friendship in return only for myself, I would be betraying the charge I have been given to serve you in Master's name. Sometimes indeed, when perhaps I have seemed distant toward you, or even severe, I know that some of you have felt hurt with me, and have wondered if I really did still love you as a friend. I myself, in my human nature, regret it deeply when I must speak strongly to you, but it is my very friendship for you that makes me speak in whatever manner I sense will be most helpful to you. At the same time, I also see friendship as only a doorway to the higher, impersonal love of God. How could it be otherwise, when what we want, as yogis, is the end of our egos?

~~~~~~

Let me underscore what I have said so far. In my relationship with Master, I have found that I'm the most in tune with him when I don't have the thought of what I'm getting from him, but dwell rather in the thought of what I'm *giving* to him. When with my whole energy I give him joy, appreciation, openness, service—in short, my very self—I receive from him the greatest energy and blessings. It has nothing to do with pleasing his ego. Nor—obviously!—does he need my joy. It is rather that that open feeling in myself puts me onto that wavelength on which he himself functions, because his own energy is always directed toward giving, not taking. If I can lift myself at least somewhat up to that giving level, rather than thinking only of gaining for myself, I am able to receive much more. On a lower, taking level I have found that his energy only trickles down slowly, as it were; I haven't exposed myself to its full flow.

In this context I remember when I first met Swami Sivananda, in Rishikesh, India. My impression of him was that I liked him, that he was a nice man. But I couldn't say that I felt very much more. Owing perhaps to the fact that he wasn't my guru, there wasn't that immediate rapport that I would have liked to have with such a well-known saint.

Later on, however, I saw Swami Chidananda, his chief disciple, gazing at him with an attitude of deep, selfless love, devotion, and respect. Implicit in his look was the gratitude offered to one from whom he had received everything. Chidananda himself became ennobled in my eyes by his self-giving attitude. And, seeing him thus, I felt that anyone to whom a man of such noble character could give such devotion must truly be worthy of it. Through Chidananda, I came truly to revere Swami Sivananda.

How different, Swami Chidananda's perfect appreciation, from the passivity of the "yes man" kind of disciple! A "yes man" is somebody who doesn't think for himself, who simply allows himself to live in the shadow of someone else. This is the trap many women fall into in relation to their men. It is the attitude of those disciples who merely turn over to their gurus the entire responsibility for their spiritual development. Don't all the Scriptures emphasize the need also for personal effort on the devotee's part? Why else, indeed, would the Scriptures even have been written?

Perhaps the disciple also helps the guru, by giving him energy for the fulfillment of his mission. At any rate, the disciple certainly gains from what he gives to the guru. Even now, long after Master's earthly life, I find that my highest attunement comes from thinking not in terms of my work, but rather of, "How can I do *your* work?" But whenever I've allowed thoughts like these to come in: "What do I want?" or, "How am I going to grow?" or "What am I going to get out of it, because, after all, you're there already, whereas I'm the one who needs to advance spiritually?"—I've always sunk to a lower level, and there has been no blissful inner flow. In self-giving, especially to Master, I have always gained the most, inwardly.

We must try, you see, but our self-effort must be directed primarily toward deepening our attunement with the guru—not as a person, but as a channel for the Infinite Lord.

~~~~~~~~

So then, what of my position in all this, and where does it concern you? Clearly, I'm not the guru in the same sense that Master is. For one reason, he is a master, and I'm simply not.

But I'm certainly an active link to him—for those of you who live and work here at Ananda, and who try to follow the things I teach you in his name. This is simply the way it is, the way it has always been.

I have seen that those people who thought to attune themselves to Master on their own, without accepting the channel of grace as it flows through those who already have such attunement with him, never receive as much.

Master himself, *while living*, urged the newer disciples to look to his close disciples, and not to him alone, for guidance and inspiration. "Do not imagine," he would say, "that you can please the guru while ignoring his disciples." I recall also how Master told Vance Milligan, a young disciple, "You should mix more with Walter. You don't know what you have in him."

Jesus too said to his disciples, "He that receiveth you receiveth me." (Matthew 10:40)

Consider, by contrast, those who have left Ananda, or who have never joined any SRF group, offering as their rationale that they want to create their own inner attunement directly with Master. They seem to have missed something vital. You can see that lack in their eyes and in their lives— particularly when you compare them with those devotees who live here, or in close contact with other disciples.

The truth is, those who think to go straight to God and Guru, without help from others, have not yet learned the humility necessary to advance much on the path. The wise devotee, rather, knowing how difficult it is at all times to get out of delusion, is eager for any guidance he can get on his journey.

~~~~~~~~

It's so easy to deny the human side in our determination to focus on the Divine, instead of refining the human side into a true understanding of the Divine. I remember one time when I was going through a severe test of doubt, doubting Master—not, indeed, whether he was a master, or whether he was my guru, but rather what it means to be a master. Was he wholly wise? Was it possible for him to make mistakes? Not wholesome doubts, these, to be sure, but real for me at the time, and therefore necessary for me to face honestly.

Master said to me one evening, "Don't doubt God."

"Oh, Sir, I don't doubt *God*!" I replied—feeling the nicety of this distinction.

He looked at me piercingly under lowered brows. "Where," I wondered, "have I gone wrong?" And then, "*Have* I gone wrong?" I was suffering in my perplexity, but, you see, I needed to understand.

The following day I saw Master again. Once more I got the same look. But by this time I was beginning to understand. My error had lain in the attempting to divide those two realities: the Divine, and the humanly Divine. For they were one—particularly so in the case of our fully enlightened Guru.

Wise is the disciple who looks behind the veil of his guru's personality to the indwelling reality of God. As a Sanskrit saying has it, "Though my guru visit the grogshop, still he is the living embodiment of the Infinite Lord."

Wise, indeed, is the disciple who looks behind the veil even of ordinary people, to see only the God within them. But the place to start this practice is by looking for Him in those who are the most in tune with Him, and of course especially in the guru. As Jesus said, "He that receiveth a prophet in the name of a prophet shall receive a prophet's reward."

The light in the stained glass window of a church is different, in a sense, from the sunlight behind it. Its function might be said to proclaim the sunlight to us, whose limited minds need to perceive light more narrowly as separate colors.

Well, then again, how does all this pertain to your relationship with me? You see me, rightly, as Master's representative. And you also see me as your friend. Indeed, I *am* your friend—as true a friend as I know how to be. But what is the highest gift I can share with you as your friend, if not whatever I know and experience of our Guru's living presence? Naught else of what we share together will prove lasting.

I am ever fearful lest I fall from that high purpose. For I am still human; I still can make mistakes. I can still even fall from the spiritual path. To this fact, however, I should add that if our friendship is truly rooted in God, then if ever I should fall, your duty would be to help me, as mine is even now to help you. It would be wrong to say to me then, "Get away! I no longer need you."

Do you need me? That is up to you. But don't imagine that I *want* anything from you, except your own development in God. I am your friend. I am also your servant in God; but one who offers his service, and his relationship with you, daily on the altar where his Guru's image rests. My love for you forms a part of my love for Master and God.

I tell you these things also for my own sake. For I fear delusion. I fear falling into the trap of ego. It is so easy to become proud, when there are others following you. Yet I have to say that so far, with God's grace, I have never felt tempted to want your support or your love for anything but God's sake. I take comfort, too, in something Master once said to me:

He had been talking to a small group of us about some of his minister-disciples who had fallen into the temptation of pride owing to their position as teachers.

"Sir," I cried, "that's why I don't want to be a minister!"

For a moment he looked down at the ground seriously. Then he spoke quietly, but with great firmness: "You will *never* fall due to ego."

Why then do I fear? I fear because it is always wise to hold in awe a power which has held us all in thrall for so many thousands, perhaps millions, of incarnations! But our fear should goad us to love more deeply, and not to live on forever in its shadow. Thus I fear my humanity, but I trust in

God's love, and Master's, and in their omnipotence to save even this frail, struggling devotee, if I continue firm in my love for them, and in my service to all of you.

You are, you see, in a divine way important to me. It is in the human sense only that I need and want nothing from you.

~~~~~~

One thing I'm finding as I stumble along on this path, and that is an inner side of myself surfacing occasionally—a higher reality that isn't me, Kriyananda, but something quite impersonal. Then it's as though Master's inner guidance weren't separate from what my own soul knows.

Indeed, always in my heart there is a feeling, one that I can't really explain, that I don't really exist as a person. This world has never, for that matter, seemed very real to me. But it seems less so now than ever. Increasingly, I simply don't feel personally involved with anything.

And with this thought comes another consciousness that seems to be aware of things not at all known to me, on an ego level.

Do you remember that story of Master's in the *Autobiography*, about his pet deer at Ranchi School? The deer was dying, and Master was praying for its life. Then one night the soul of the deer came to Master and begged him, "You are holding me back. Please let me go; let me go!" The soul even of animals, you see, is omniscient. Each one of us knows everything, on his own deepest level.

Spiritual advancement isn't a question of attaining anything, really. It is only a matter of opening wide the door to a state of conscious being that is ours already, hidden from us only so long as our attention is focused elsewhere. As by regular meditation, the door gradually opens, ego and soul are able to work in closer cooperation together.

It's fascinating, and I can't explain it well, but it's as though there were two "me's" carrying on; and more and more frequently they seem to get through to each other.

The same must be true for everyone on this path.

I read recently about a saint who appeared to his disciples in time of need, sometimes saving them in serious crises, as happened one time in the case of a woman who was on the point of drowning, and to whom the saint appeared physically, and led her across the river by the hand. When next she saw him, she thanked him. But what was her surprise when he replied frankly that he hadn't been conscious of the episode.

A fully realized master must surely know these things on an ego level, too. But perhaps, before one reaches enlightenment, there is a time when the opening between soul and ego is sufficiently wide for the soul to enter into the ego's functions—to do things, for example, for those with whom the ego is involved in ways of which the ego itself is unconscious.

Does all this sound a bit wild? Perhaps it is. Still I've found increasingly that when I've thought of something I wanted to say to someone, that person has had a dream or a vision in which I told him that very thing. I wasn't conscious of coming to him, but sometimes—well, I wonder.

The difficulty of this aspect of our consciousness is that people look for it to the personality, and it doesn't come that way at all. All I can definitely say is that the more I attune myself to that level of being, the better I can help you. And then this friend, whom you know, is not really helping you at all!

So you see, my highest duty, and my constant desire, as your soul friend is to take you beyond mere human friendship to a deeper awareness of the Eternal Friend who resides in our own souls.

You will benefit from our relationship according to the level that you tap. I am your friend, but if you define our friendship in terms already familiar to you, you will remain always at that level of familiarity, and will gain little more from it. See our friendship, therefore, as progressing ever upward, toward the impersonal love of God, which alone is reality.

Remember that whatever I can give to you comes to you through me by Master's grace. Only to the extent to which I can attune myself with him do I receive the grace to help you truly on the path. The more your own faith and attunement goes to our true source, in him, and beyond him in God, the more greatly you will be able to receive.

And remember above all that Master's and God's whole aim is to make *you* perfect—"even as our Father which is in heaven is perfect."

"To me, Ananda is the most wonderful place on the planet.

ANANDA:
PAST, PRESENT & FUTURE

We are proud of what we have, for it is something given to us by God."

January 6, 1974

Dear _____:

Thank you for your letter. It reinforces the general impression I have always had of you, that you are good-natured, sincere, and basically fair-minded. I would like to answer your criticisms carefully. Yet I ask you to accept as kindly as possible the regrettable fact that we have certain basic differences of viewpoint that remain irreconcilable. I think it behooves us as devotees to respect one another's positions, insofar as we are able to understand them.

You express disappointment that Ananda hasn't developed into a community for householders on the spiritual path. Actually, of course, we have quite a few couples who find Ananda compatible to both their spiritual and family needs. What we should say, therefore, is that Ananda hasn't yet developed a milieu for many spiritually minded householders. At this stage of its development it does very definitely need, for its own survival, a certain spirit of renunciation that automatically weeds out numerous good, spiritual, harmonious people—especially, it would seem, householders.

It is too bad in a way that initial sacrifices must be so great, though for those who are temperamentally suited for them the sacrifices themselves are one of the rewards of living here. For a certain measure of renunciation is necessary to everyone who hopes to get anywhere on the spiritual path.

Ananda's present stage of evolution might be compared to the pioneer days of the West, or to the days of the pilgrim fathers. Those settlers had necessarily to be a breed who placed communal needs ahead of their own personal desires. That is not to say that their personal desires and the needs of the community were necessarily always in conflict, nor necessarily very often in conflict. If they truly understood what they were doing, I suspect they rarely saw a conflict between the two ideals; they simply realized that their own personal well-being depended on that of the larger community.

It is much the same in America even today, in the sense, for example, that if America were invaded, many husbands would have to go to war to defend it, and many of them would be killed. If they refused on the ground that they wanted to develop a "healthy" marriage, they might find, if the enemy won, that they had no marriage left to be kept healthy.

But in the early days in America the sacrifices demanded were more frequent, and generally greater. Life was less secure, and people had to cling together as a community far more than was necessary once the land had been settled. Later on, others (families especially) came who wanted the new life without its extraordinary risks. Their consciousness was less community-oriented, but at this time this no longer mattered, for the community no longer needed to make as many demands on their time and interests.

We at Ananda are in the position of being not only a new community, but also part of the vanguard of a whole new social movement. I wonder if you realize how high the incidence of failure is among new cooperative communities? One university researcher a year or two ago found that the average life expectancy of a new commune was only thirty days!

Of the thousands of communities that have been started in America in the past six years, all but a handful have died out. Ananda has the distinction of being one of the three or four most successful communities in the country. It is no small triumph. But we are by no means out of the woods yet. I hope the day comes, and I expect it to come, when families who want a good life in a spiritual community without the sacrifices demanded by the struggle for basic survival will find a place for themselves at Ananda. But it seems increasingly clear that we are not yet the right community for any but people with pioneering temperaments.

To a great extent our problem is financial. Without financial security, families may well experience a strain that single people, and couples without children, never know. But the problem is considerably more than that. Partly, I think, it is our very social upbringing in America, and the expectations that people are led to form regarding what marriage is, or should be.

These expectations are not consonant with a tightly knit cooperative community. Perhaps in this respect this new cooperative movement will be able to evolve new, acceptable, and equally rewarding attitudes towards marriage that will make a more open relationship to a broader "family" both possible and desirable. A comparative study of other societies in the world supports the expectation that this will be possible, perhaps even inevitable.

But you should know that the problem of family vs. community commitment is widespread among cooperative communities. In this respect Ananda is in no way unique.

Rather, our record so far seems to be quite exceptionally good. I've read that the turn-over even in more or less stable communities tends to be high—as high as three to six months. (Recently I noted a boast by a member of one successful community that their turn-over now was "only" six months—this, to emphasize their present stability compared to the earlier days.)

You've referred to the "enthusiastic, hard-working, new thinking, creative people" that have supposedly been alienated from Ananda, and you've suggested that if I had been "great" enough to allow the farm to "do its own thing" I'd have had something to be really "proud of." I hope you are aware that different views are possible in this situation. Let me outline for you my own understanding of it, and ask that you try to see it also from my point of view.

I myself obtained the farm, as I think you know, as a needed outlet for the growth at the retreat. We could not continue to keep families, businesses, and the more communal aspects of Ananda there. I personally raised the $13,500 or so that was needed for the down payment. The people who gave me that money did so out of their faith in what I would do with the land. It was not given so that others might take it over and "do their own thing." I then left Ananda to go out and work to pay the $25,000 or so that was needed for the first year's mortgage and taxes.

Since then I have, in one way or another, been responsible for a large share of the farm's financial burden. So also have the people living at the retreat. So also have those at Ayodhya. To ask that all these sacrifices be made only so that the people at the farm might "do their own thing" would, I think, have been asking quite a lot.

The farm has never been a self-sustaining, separate enclosure from the rest of Ananda, even though some of the farm residents have elected to see it that way. Always it has been part and parcel of the community as a whole. On its own, the farm could never, not even remotely, have made it. (In fact, the largest number of *non*-paying members has always lived at the farm.) Moreover, the rest of Ananda needed the farm. Had the farm seceded from Ananda, as some of its more presumptuous members desired, we'd have simply had to find another piece of land elsewhere to fulfill the same needs for the rest of the community.

If you think the sacrifices even now are too much for families, just visualize what they would have been with the people at the farm standing on their own, paying off a $2,000-a-month mortgage. Ananda farm would not have lasted three months.

I must now give you my own view of those "enthusiastic, hard working, new thinking, creative people" you referred to. You have heard them described by certain survivors of their own group, but there are many people at Ananda who entertain very different opinions of them. I myself find it difficult to recall even one major enthusiastic, hard-working, new-thinking, creative thing that they (as a group or individually) ever did.

They sat for endless hours, week after week, deliberating the pros and cons of relatively superficial issues, and getting nowhere at all. It took them two whole years to decide to get rid of a dog who chased the deer and menaced visitors, and who belonged to no one but had come as a stray. And I verily think this was one of their major accomplishments. It was largely negative energy for the simple reason that it was mainly directed toward preventing various things from being done, rather than toward initiating new, constructive actions. Whatever positive work they got done was accomplished in spurts of enthusiasm, soon followed by discouragement as the job proved more difficult than they'd realized, and then by complaints that the difficulty was not of their making.

It is only now, that their energy has been eliminated, that things are really getting done by the many positive people at the farm who want to work selflessly, not selfishly.

I have never tried to discourage constructive action. Rather, I've always been eager to get people to take hold and do things. What I've always resisted has been the tendency, prevalent in those days, to paralyze constructive action of any kind. The most dynamic efforts of certain persons that I recall were directed towards removing their activities (such as they were!) from under my control—a purely negative action, inasmuch as they need-ed only to step forward with positive ideas and positive energy to have had my support for almost anything they might have wanted to do. Ananda's broader history is full of examples of other people who set out to do something, and then did it. At no time did such people find that the first step to creative action had to be the removal of Kriyananda from having any say in whatever they might do.

But the "creative" people you refer to never belonged in this category of members. Most certainly I resisted them. I knew their attitude would never carry them to success. Their very approach demonstrated their essential incompetence. Such people, invariably, are talkers, not doers. They'd have destroyed Ananda.

Experience is no mean teacher. I've been involved in group living, and in all the problems attendant upon it, for upwards of twenty-five years. I think it is no mere boast, but a simple statement of fact, to say that Ananda would have inevitably joined the vast majority of failures had it not been for whatever wisdom I have been able to gain from my experience over these years.

Had those people truly been leaders and doers, they would have simply gone ahead and done. And in that case, I'd have supported them. But as it happened, I had only to open my mouth to suggest something quite innocuous for many of those "enthusiastic, hard-working" people to ob-ject bitterly that I was dictating to them. Why on earth would I want to dedicate all my labors, and the sacrifices of so many harmonious people, to permitting such "enthusiasts" to do their own non-thing?

You speak of the need for "thinking opposition" to keep an organization "on its toes." In my many years of religious work—I confess I know less about worldly organizations—I have never found constructive work pro-ceeding out of a spirit of opposition. Out of differences, yes. But not out of opposition.

It is interesting in this context to observe that, since I assumed a more defi-nite role of leadership in the community (in response, I should add, to the repeated pleas of most of the people here), I have had to involve myself far less in community decisions. A house divided against itself cannot stand.

It is absolutely essential that we be of one mind on our basic principles and directions. Once that fundamental unity has been achieved, differences become part of a forward-moving energy, seeking new and better ways of doing things, not paralyzing all activity with endless bickering. In fact, Ananda has made its greatest strides only since this kind of "thinking" opposition, as you call it, has been definitely and strongly rejected by the majority.

It will continue to be rejected. We don't need that kind of energy, and the vast majority here are no longer willing to put up with it. Again and again lately I have heard constructive workers in the community express their determination not to have their efforts paralyzed any longer by the small, negative element (which owes its negativity, not to any intrinsic darkness of character—most of them are good people; if they weren't, they wouldn't be here—but only to the fact that it can't accept for itself the direction in which Ananda is moving).

What you and others want is, I'm sure, perfectly fine in itself. You are entitled to feel disappointed in Ananda if it isn't giving you what you want. All I can say is that Ananda has demonstrated an unusual capacity for survival in the direction it has taken; that I don't think it would have survived had it taken any of several alternative directions that have been proposed for it from time to time; and that I hope and expect someday to be able to accommodate people who are less interested in community involvement than they now need to be if Ananda is to remain viable.

Now to some of the other points you have raised:

And so to your statement about _____, "a man you fear or dislike enough to send 'negative energy' to leave the community." Please know, first, that far from "fearing or disliking" _____, I sincerely like him, and probably always will like him. He has many wonderful qualities. I truly hoped, when he came, that he and I would become good friends. By his own discovery, however, he does not belong in Ananda's present situation, for it seems to him to require more sacrifices of his time and energy than he feels he can spare from his family.

Unfortunately, he has so little confidence in his own directions that he feels a need to constantly justify them by soliciting others' agreement and support. He talked to many people here about his own, personal needs in such a way as to leave them feeling, to quote their own words, "depressed, discouraged," and generally, "down." I pleaded with him once or twice not to infect others with his negative thoughts (negative, that is to say, from the standpoint of what he himself is doing), but it was not possible for him to desist. I therefore found myself wishing strongly that he would leave Ananda.

You may call this "negative energy," inasmuch as I do seem to have a strong mind, but in fact my thoughts were directed towards him only insofar as he was putting out energies that were harmful to the general welfare and harmony of Ananda. Had he changed the quality of those energies, my thoughts would have ceased to affect him, for they were not directed towards him, personally. Nor is it being negative to prevent negativity. The most positive thing he could have done is what he is now actually planning to do: leave Ananda, and go his own preferred direction. My wish that he leave, therefore, was also for his own benefit, not for his harm.

You say, "We all know that Master gives us what we need." Yes and no: he does, if we work for it; he doesn't, if we don't. People used to think Master would pay our mortgage without their having to dirty their hands with the crassness of money-making. But he didn't. I myself saved the farm from foreclosure by the very skin of its teeth, a disaster that threatened simply because of many members' impractical and unrealistic, in fact unspiritual, attitude. Master has blessed us because we've done what we could on our own to build Ananda, and to make it secure.

One thing more I should say, out of fairness to those working so dedicatedly here, and also out of kindness to those who sincerely want to live a spiritual life, but who think spiritual living means just "doing one's own thing." The *Bhagavad Gita* stresses the need for sacrifice — *tyaga*. I've observed over the years that those who pitched in selflessly and served the community have grown spiritually.

All too often, however, those who (from whatever reason) withdrew from this attitude have gotten out of tune, have given up meditation, have ceased even from attending any spiritual activity, and have shown in their eyes an inner loss which suggests strongly that it isn't for spiritual reasons that they have withdrawn their energies, regardless of how they might define their own reasons to themselves and their friends. I say this kindly, and with deep concern. And I don't say it personally with *you* in mind, for I haven't seen you enough in recent months to form such an impression about you.

But this, therefore, is the direction we at Ananda shall keep moving in. I am aware that there are other good ways of living, and I earnestly plead with anyone who doesn't like what Ananda is doing that he follow some more desirable (and perhaps even better) alternative. Ananda has had more than its share of "thinking opposition." Always it has found it corrosive, not stimulating. Now Ananda wants to grow harmoniously, constructively, with those differences rather which occur among brothers and sisters, not among antagonists.

Much is happening at Ananda. In many ways it is already the "great" community that you spoke of so wistfully. I would like to think you could be a part of its further growth. If you and your husband should leave, as I understand you are planning to do, our gratitude will go with you for the good that you have done here. You have won friends here, one of whom is myself. I respect and love you both.

I plead with you only, for your own sakes, to support mentally, and not oppose, the good that is happening here. It would not be good karma for you to denigrate Ananda merely because it was not what you wanted. Bless it, and then, if you must, leave. Stay, if you feel that you can; I think you would grow by the association, if you could accept it as it is, not as you might like it to be.

But in any case please remember your own words: "If you are doing Master's will then may my eyes be opened soon." I repeat the same prayer, for myself: if I am not doing his will, may my eyes be opened soon. But I tell you this, I am sincerely and honestly trying to do his will. And I cannot but think that, even if you reject everything I've written in this letter, if you keep it and read it a few months or years from now, you may feel differently about what we've been doing here, and about what we are doing.

At any rate, in the belief that you are, truly, sincere, and though I know your present circumstances may militate against openness to Ananda's prevailing point of view, I have taken the time to write you at such length, and with deep love and affection for you both.

In Master's love,

*[At the age of 90, Mr. Black wrote to Swami Kriyananda, asking
for advice on how to turn the ashram he had founded into a "world
brotherhood colony"]*

January 15, 1988

Dear Yogacharya Oliver:

Thank you for your welcome letter. I am impressed by your courage in
"working diligently," at this late time in your life, to create a colony. More
power to you!

What we have at Ananda now is a real village, with lovely homes, flourishing
businesses, schools that have an excellent reputation, and an experiment in
living that people in many countries admire. We have several branch communities also, including one near Assisi, Italy.

Far more important, we have about five hundred devotees who are living
joyously for God and Master, who meditate several hours daily, and are dedicated to making Master's message of Self-realization known everywhere.

But when I think of the struggle of our beginnings—not so much of our
initial poverty, nor of how simply we had to live; that all had its compensa-
tions: but of the problems I faced in bringing so many people into attunement with Master's ideals—I tell myself, "Once was enough!" Patience and
determination are virtues, but there are other qualities also that one needs
to work on, on the spiritual path.

Most of our real difficulties at the beginning seemed to be related to people.
True, there were money worries. At first I had to go out and earn most of
what we needed myself. True also, there were times when it looked as if
financial disaster not only stared us in the face but was preparing to swal-
low us. But Master always wrought the necessary miracles—in one case
saving our most important (in fact, essential) property with only twenty-
four hours to spare.

I've always believed that one essential reason we won out was that we always
held to the Indian motto, "Where there is *dharma*, there is victory."

Another reason we won was that we held to Master's dictum: "Be practical in your idealism."

And a third reason was our own basic guideline: "People are more important that things."

Even in the matter of practicality, however, my big challenge came from people—from those woolly minded idealists, for example, who insisted they were serving God by going to the river and swimming all day instead of working to earn anything so crass as money. I knew I'd never build a successful community if I simply "laid down the law" to them. I had to learn how to win them, and not drive them, to right action.

People, not things, were the problem. I don't think it would have particularly helped us, in the beginning, to have too much money. Certainly, our present three-million-dollar income would have been our undoing. Had things been easy, people might not have developed the dedication they acquired by responding to outward challenges.

The main principle that I found worked was perhaps to work in cooperation with positive and supportive energy, and not to waste time and energy on those people who were either passive drifters or negative opponents.

In the beginning, our core group of dedicated members was quite small, and the opposition to every constructive idea, dauntingly large. Negative energy, however, has no cohesive power, if one can afford to give it time to disprove itself. What it feeds on, and what gives negativity strength, is the feeling that it has something substantial to oppose.

Usually, therefore, at least where possible, I more or less ignored the negative voices, and just worked around them. When I had to fight them, I made sure in advance that I had the backing, or the power within myself, to win. For even small defeats can loom large in petty minds, and can seriously damage a leader's position in the future. (Best is it, I learned, in the likelihood of defeat, to give in quickly and gracefully, and rescue what one can for the next time around.)

Fortunately, for many years now those people-problems have been overcome. The harmony here now is so great that I rarely have to involve myself in the day-to-day running of things, except, essentially, from behind the scenes.

The most important factor in our success, certainly, has been the fact that every day since our beginnings I have given this whole project to Master, and have asked him to do with it as he would, albeit through our own physical struggles.

I say these things in a spirit of sharing, since you asked me, and not of giving advice. I know you have succeeded greatly in the business world, and that you must know much of what I've had to learn here through years of struggle, and perhaps a great deal more besides.

But let me send you also another book I wrote, one that grew out of the lessons I learned in working with people. It's called *The Art of Supportive Leadership*. I'll also send you a book on Ananda, *Cities of Light*. You may have these books already, in which case you may find use for these extra copies anyway.

We celebrated our twentieth anniversary this year. Please give us your blessings for a continued future of joyful service to Master and God.

In Master's love,

An open letter to Ananda Village members regarding "community" and "ashram" | 3

March 10, 1982

Dear Ones:

I've been puzzled to hear about all the so-called "changes" at Ananda. Do people really understand what is happening? Unless I'm the one out of touch, a mountain is being made out of a molehill. What changes are really taking place? And what are the changes people are talking about?

As far as I'm concerned, the issue is simply this: that we want to emphasize what Ananda is really all about—seeking and serving God. This is a needed clarification, because so much emphasis has been given in recent years to the communitarian aspects of Ananda. Nor has it been wrong to emphasize those aspects: they certainly are a part of what we are doing here. It is just that we need to keep a balance between extremes.

When we go too far in any direction, we need to emphasize the other side again. Were we to get too involved in Ananda as a community, merely, at the expense of the ashram aspect of our way of life we might indeed create a worthwhile thing sociologically, and perhaps many more people "out there" would appreciate what we are doing; but we wouldn't be furthering the real purpose for which Ananda was created: to offer people a place where they can serve God, and find Him.

It's a delicate balance, I know. God has put us in a position of having to support ourselves, as people do everywhere. We can't avoid normal social responsibilities; therefore we must embrace them in a divine way, and hope that we can also set an example of how to live "normally" and still live for God.

The point of Ananda's spiritual focus is important, but it will be utterly betrayed if we insist on treating it as an *issue*. It is too subtle for argument.

A few weeks ago I spoke at the new retreat about attunement with the "ray" of divine energy which flowed through Master, and which continues to flow through his disciples—through you all, that is to say, not only through me. I emphasized that I myself try constantly to attune myself to that ray. Attunement even with Master, I said, (what to speak of attunement with me!) is not a personal thing.

Now I hear that attunement with me is being made an issue. "Must we accept Swami as our channel for Master?" Frankly, I feel cheapened by the question. I am here to serve you all. I try to serve you as a channel of the ray of grace that came to me through Master. Where is the obligation on anybody's part? If you like what I give you, take it. If not, then don't. I've heard from some that you don't like authority figures. But do you realize the extent to which I am in fact your *servant*? What do I want from you? My whole thought is of giving.

The only point that needs to be kept clear is one of self-definition: since Ananda is primarily a spiritual community, those who are accepted here must be those who accept the spiritual basis of what is going on here. Naturally, if they reject Ananda, or me, or the people living here, as living channels of the ray of grace that I have described, then what they must want (if anything) from Ananda is something other than what we have dedicated our lives to doing here. Such people may as well know what

Ananda really is, so that they can understand that the fulfillment of their own dreams lies elsewhere, not at Ananda.

Obviously, those who belong here will be those who are in tune with what is going on. That shouldn't have to be made an *issue*! Obviously, too, if people don't accept me (and others who have been long on the path, and at Ananda), as channels for Master and his ray, they belong elsewhere, not here. But beyond that I certainly feel that every member should seek whatever level of attunement he, personally, feels comfortable with.

And in any case, attunement is something one grows into gradually, over years. Again I insist, it isn't a personal issue, but something very inward— something in fact, between each devotee and God, and much too sacred for controversy.

I don't feel comfortable with the idea of deciding whether or not a person is "in tune." This is something too sensitive, too subjective. Sometimes the devotee who shows the least, outwardly, is the one who feels the most deeply, inwardly.

What we need to see, rather, is whether those who want to live here are supportive to what is going on, or unsupportive. To put it otherwise, it may be difficult to know whether a person is really "in tune," but it becomes quickly evident whether he is basically positive or negative—either in himself or towards whatever is going on around him. We are happy to have people point out the errors here if their intention is to help us correct them. But what is the point of carping criticism? Real gains rarely result from such negativity. (Spiritually, too, such negativity is an obstacle. Krishna says in the *Bhagavad Gita*, "To you *who have overcome the carping spirit* I reveal these truths.")

New and old members should try to be sensitive to each other's position. If an old member speaks, for example, of things he has experienced from individuals at Ananda, he should keep in mind that the best way to share his inspiration is to offer it, merely, not to say, "This is what one ought to be getting from that person." People should be drawn to any good thing because it inspires them, and not because, for some reason they may not understand, they *are supposed to* go that way. The new member, on the other hand, should be sensitively aware that older members may in fact have experienced something in this life that he himself hasn't yet. He should be grateful for any effort to share inspiration, and not hold the common thought of many people in this country: "I already know as much as anyone else."

One thing that does worry me is when people, without at all knowing the facts, simply assume the worst. A decision gets made, for example, and the rumor mill spreads the word, "Look how uncharitably that was handled!" Do you *know* how it was handled? If not, who is really being uncharitable? Part of supporting what is going on is holding the basic assumption that the people who have given their lives to this work are probably people of good will. To hold anger toward them is inappropriate, even when they make mistakes. To *assume* the commitment of mistakes without even knowing the facts is ridiculous. *If* a mistake has been committed, the best way of correcting it would be to come on positively. Negative criticism never tries to be helpful. Its only purpose is to destroy; its only motive is to show others, in the cheapest way possible, how good the critic himself is.

We are here for God above all. Let us keep that thought strongly uppermost in our minds. Everything becomes so simple when we do that!

In divine friendship,

An excerpt from the open letter entitled, | 4
"Ananda's Directions," later placed on the internet

November 16, 1998

Dear Ones:

I think we all feel the need for decentralizing Ananda. The thought has occurred to me that, in the past, when the development of a spiritual work has been determined by one disciple alone, the scope of the guru's teaching has become narrowed. No one disciple can embrace *in its totality* what the guru taught unless he himself is as great as the guru.

When I say, of Ananda, that I think we should concentrate on decentralizing it, I mean, first, that it seems to me our colonies need greater autonomy. Actually, the control exercised from Ananda Village has always been benign. With increasing centralization, however, that control might cease to be perceived as such by other colonies.

My original idea was for our branch-communities to be autonomous. As colonies actually developed, however, it became clear that no one who was qualified to found them would *want* to be separated from our spiritual home at Ananda Village. Thus, I proposed that those early branch-communities, at least, be thought of as a single spiritual family. In this way, people could be shifted about between them according to their own, and the colonies' needs.

There is a danger in centralization, however, of "creeping institutionalism": an imposed uniformity that does not, and cannot, take into account the special circumstances faced by individuals and branch-communities. Our real bond, in any case, is the love and divine friendship we feel for one another, and not our institutional structure. Our soul-bonds don't depend for their strength on centralized control, and might become frayed were centralized control exercised too rigidly.

Should our bonds of friendship ever require strengthening by outward uniformity, Ananda itself would have ceased to serve the spiritual purpose for which it was created.

From our very beginning, I have adhered to the advice Master gave me when I was organizing the monks: "Don't make too many rules," he said. "It destroys the spirit." Thus, I have allowed decision-making to take place, as much as possible, at a "grass roots" level, and have tried rather to nudge things along in the direction—the spirit, primarily—that Master would want them to go in than insist that everything be done in specific ways. This appearance of "*laissez faire*" has been our strength, not our weakness, for it has developed people to the point where they've understood *for themselves* what is the best course to follow.

Naturally, there has had to be a degree of guidance also, or else everything would have ended in chaos. But the guidance itself has had to take into account where people were in their own understanding, and their readiness for whatever step needed to be taken. The contribution of individual insights, moreover, has ensured an all-round development.

It is generally understood, now, that the wisdom in Master's teachings resides primarily in those who have been disciples for many years. Still, it is also wholesome for people to have the freedom to make most of their own decisions, for in this way they develop wisdom themselves to guide Ananda in future in the directions it should take.

November 16, 1998

Sri Ramakrishna's legacy was squeezed into a box of ultra-sectarianism by his disciples, and even more so by their successors. Our Guru commented to me, "Sri Ramakrishna would have turned over in his grave to see what they've done to his teachings!"

Had the disciples been free to develop their own understanding of their guru's teachings, perhaps in their very variety they'd have given a more complete picture of what their guru had taught. Master Mahasaya (known as "M" to readers of *The Gospel of Sri Ramakrishna*) had such freedom. Would that they'd all had it, for then the Ramakrishna Order might have been spared its later developments.

Because that order was formed entirely by Swami Vivekananda, it became defined by his vision, which, lofty though it certainly was, focused on the need in India for social uplift. Thus, the guru's message was stripped of the beautiful spontaneity, informality, and devotion that were so shiningly present in Ramakrishna's own life. Instead, his legacy was pre-empted by the scholarly intellectuals who evolved from the Vedantic emphasis Swami Vivekananda gave those teachings in his efforts to make his guru's vision acceptable to the West.

I'm reminded of something Master once said to Daya Mata: "How you all will change the work after I'm gone! I just wonder, if I were to return here a hundred years from now, whether I'd even recognize it."

Perhaps, though, looking back at Sri Ramakrishna's legacy, it needed the focus Vivekananda gave it in order to survive as a coherent tradition. I don't know. All I can do is add that, if such be the case, what survived was something very different from Ramakrishna's spirit!

His spiritual descendants today claim that, since Sri Ramakrishna was the first master to demonstrate the truth that all paths lead to the same goal, he was the greatest of them all. The Ramakrishna Mission has even campaigned, I understand—with what success I don't know—to be recognized by the Indian Government as a new religion. How ironic, considering that their master's mission was to demonstrate the basic oneness of all religions!

Sri Ramakrishna's place in history is assured, above all, by the example of his own beautiful life. Everything his successors have accomplished, though done in his name, may be considered a footnote.

Paramhansa Yogananda's vision, similarly, is being placed in an institutional straitjacket. Perhaps the narrow interpretation that is being given his teachings by SRF is needed, in the sense that a focus may have been needed also in order to keep Ramakrishna's contribution to the world vital and strong. As in that case, however, the consequence has been a loss for the world.

In SRF's case, "vital and strong" doesn't mean, "inspiring and wise." Though the SRF leaders are dedicated to the organization he founded, the universality of Paramhansa Yogananda's teachings is being ever-increasingly enchained by sectarianism. What an irony! Universality was the very thing that gave Yogananda's teachings their greatest beauty and inspiration!

*In response to objections from
one of Sri Ramakrishna's disciples
to the internet statements*   6

December 25, 1998

Dear _____:

You are right, and I'm appalled that I let those statements get out on the internet. My letter was written for our own devotees, and was, I think, important as a clarification of our own directions. Later, I thought of the internet as perhaps the only way to get through to SRF people who might, eventually, change the direction of their activities. I will check with certain people at Ananda to get their opinions on whether to omit the letter altogether from the internet, or to revise it in certain respects as you've suggested.

Truthfully, I was thinking historically and not diplomatically—nor taking into account the fact that there are indeed, as you say, good monks in the Ramakrishna Order in America today. And, yes, you are right also in saying that Yogananda was careful not to speak out against people publicly.

The other side of the coin is that we have been litigated against for nearly nine years, with no sign yet of a let-up. I myself have been persecuted by SRF for more than thirty-six years. I held my tongue until they sued me, at which point it became necessary for me to defend myself and Ananda.

For four years now, they are the only reasonable suspects as backers in a further legal attempt to destroy me utterly and, if necessary, to destroy Ananda also. (After his deposition of Devi Novak, the main lawyer against us, referring to me, screamed, "You can tell him I'm going to DESTROY him!"). Yes, we've been under attack, and the drama is ongoing. Fortunately, it has made us all stronger and less likely than ever to succumb. But the attempt to destroy us isn't over by any means.

The insights in my paper, regarding decentralization, were important for us. And the examples from history, particularly from Sri Ramakrishna's successors, were virtually essential for making my point, though I'd like at least to make clear that my reference is not to the present generation of monks in America. Moreover, many sincere and wonderful disciples of Ramakrishna have come up in recent years, especially outside the Ramakrishna Mission. And Ramakrishna himself used the analogy of a lamp, which casts a shadow directly underneath it but shines brightly at a distance.

Because SRF has made such an issue of being the *only* true representatives of Yogananda's legacy, the public has come to understand that legacy in institutional and philosophically narrow terms, very different from what he clearly expressed both privately and in public during his lifetime. So—my paper may be important for others besides our own followers. And the lawsuits have forced me to be relentlessly clear as to our true mission.

I am old now, and don't know how much time I'm to be given to finish what I have to do. I speak clearly because I want to leave behind me a legacy of understanding, not of vagueness and confusion.

All this is only to explain what I've done, not necessarily to justify it. If in discussing the paper with others here, the feeling is to change or even withdraw what I've written from further public scrutiny, I'm perfectly willing that that happen. I try my best to be fair, and kind, and certainly don't want to offend anyone unnecessarily. Moreover, what you wrote was definitely the advice my Guru often gave, and the example he, like your own guru, always showed.

So, thank you for writing. Whether I withdraw the letter, or delete certain parts, or explain them further, depends on many factors which will have to be considered carefully. But I deeply appreciate your writing as you did. You were right to do so.

In divine friendship,

> *The manager of an Ananda East West Bookstore facing serious financial challenges wrote: "We are spread too thin. Maybe it would be better to do ten things well, rather than forty things partially well."*

7

October 13, 1998

Dear _____ :

Thank you for writing. And, yes, I very much agree with you. At East West especially, we've suffered from lack of focus. I hope you'll be able to bring people to a focus, and to more of a focus in our teachings. Less eclectic, less scattered, less into everything new as though its very newness and popularity justified our getting wholeheartedly behind it because we think it will sell. I think our people will benefit from more focus, and so also will our customers and their interest in what we are doing.

Did you know that *The Hindu Way of Awakening* is *still* the number one best seller at East-West in _____ ? It's because they work harder at drawing people's attention to it. They display it prominently in the window, etc. The best one to consult on this subject would be _____ , whose impression also has been that your store is too scattered. Too much variety. Just too much.

You mentioned the variety in my own work, and I don't mind your doing so. But two points ought to be kept in mind: 1) Everything I've done has had the "ulterior motive" of furthering Master's ray. 2) Everything I've done has been done with total focus. The President of Warner Books, commented, "It looks like a great deal of variety, but I see that in fact there's a wholeness in everything you've done." And one of our long-time members commented a few years ago, "Though sometimes I've thought you were changing your approach constantly, I realize now that in fact you've always adhered to the central truths of Master's teachings. All you've done is try different ways of bringing those truths out."

I have a kind of mind that can embrace many subjects and hold them together. Not many people can do that, so why ask them even to try? I've offered different avenues for them to take deeper, according to their own inclinations. But nothing I've done has been scattered, either in concept or execution.

I support what you propose for East-West: that is, recognize our need for more focus, less skating over the surface, more *enjoyment* in just doing what we really believe instead of working to promote all sorts of eclectic ideas. The more we do that, the greater will be our success financially, too.

We've thought too "big." There's a need also to think "small," and I think we've reached a point at the store where more of the second is needed.

Love,

Responds to concerns about plans to log certain areas of Ananda Village, making it too "park-like" | 8

May 8, 2000

Dear _____:

I very much appreciated your letter about the tree cutting. I feel that the guidance you received was right. Lower forms of life don't work from ego, and are not deeply concerned about themselves individually. Their karma, as Master said, is a group karma.

Trees do have feeling, as Master indicated, but their feelings—much more than most people's—is for the general rightness of things, and not for themselves particularly, or for personal likes and dislikes. Life and death are, for them, more or less meaningless, and death is not a cause of suffering.

I'd like to add a thought about your lack of interest in parks, and your preference for natural wilderness. Many of our problems in life arise from the way we define things. Thus, atheists reject their idea of God, but believe even passionately in love! Yet God *is* love.

Your definition of modern parks may not please you (I seized on this as the simplest and most easily recognizable example), but I can't imagine someone as sensitive as you preferring chaos to coherence, and coarseness to sensitivity and refinement. Most of us love wilderness, though I think most people like at least to be able to walk through it.

The vibrations of a place can be spectacularly uplifted when the place is developed not with a view to destroying trees, but to making it beautiful and cared-for. The very *devas* are attracted to places where there is pure, devotional energy, as distinct from the unfocused and haphazard energy of a commercial enterprise. For this purpose the ancient Chinese even re-molded the shape of the countryside, and thereby made their world itself a more perfect reflection of heavenly values.

Wildness alone, especially "unkempt" wildness, attracts *rakshasas* and lower entities. Angels are attracted to places that reflect the higher regions where they live.

God put man in charge of the earth that he might bring divine conscious-ness to whatever he touches. If he fails—as he does, unfortunately, all too frequently—he does not bring to fruition his own God-given destiny. Man's sensitivity has been given him by God to refine and develop material real-ity. God needs channels of His blessings on earth. It is not His way to want us to say, "You do it all, Lord. It's your business, not mine!"

Love,

To a teacher whose suggestions
for Ananda schools included less   9
involvement by colony leaders

May 27, 1999

Dear _____:

Thank you for writing as you did. Your letter did not strike me as negative, merely thoughtful and sincere.

I liked a great many of your ideas. I deeply hope we can develop the schools, and agree with the idea of having the schools in a non-parochial setting.

At the recent colony leaders meeting, Ananta said the school in Sacramento is on separate property altogether, owned by the school's founders. Ananta and Maria only have positions on the school board. I told them I thought that was the right direction.

Without the ministerial guidance given to the _____ colony school up to this time, however, and perhaps with less direct involvement by the colony leaders for some time to come, the school there could get off course and become something altogether different from anything that would reflect our ideals. I don't mean the teachers there would take it astray; they are excellent teachers. I only mean that maturity in the overall Ananda work would be an important condition for guiding the school's development rightly.

At the same time, the schools *are* different from the communities, and are, moreover, an added burden for colony leaders for whom they cannot be a principal focus. A compromise must be found. I'm afraid only that, in the name of compromise, we don't sell out something so important to Master's mission.

All of the colony leaders love my suggestions for the schools. They want to see them flourish, not to control them. If they are present at your inter-school meetings—and I think some of them should be, at least to begin with—I think the teachers themselves should lead everything, and the colony leaders only sit by to help with comments.

There is another aspect to this picture, however. The *Education for Life* system itself is larger than the sum total of the schools themselves. I've been blocked in my endeavors to develop it by the fact that the teachers themselves are busy teaching, and by the further problem that their focus is, necessarily, on the students, not on that abstraction, the "system."

I don't know how to manage this needed expansion from individual schools to a system that can create many schools. I'd like the latter, but I wouldn't want schools claiming to teach our system but throwing in anything that comes to their minds, even if it doesn't reflect our system at all.

I'm not narrow in my wish to serve Master's mission. I simply want to give the right focus to what we're doing, because he was an *avatar* specifically sent to fulfill this mission. Whenever people asked him why he did certain things—regarding the schools, as a good example—his answer always was, "That was the wish of Babaji."

We are locked into a universal stream, and need to serve it purely if what we do is to flow most effectively and with the greatest power.

That's why I want ministerial involvement. My hope only is that they'll permit and encourage growth, not hamper it. My understanding, based on the recent colony leaders meeting, is that all of them greatly favor this direction. They feel greatly over-burdened, and expressed relief at my suggestion to separate all the schools as soon as, and as much as, possible from parochial supervision.

In divine friendship,

*On the possibility of opening
an Ananda school in India* | 10

November 26, 1977

Dear _____ :

I had an opportunity in Calcutta to talk with some former students at an American school in Mussoorie. It gave me many ideas for something similar, perhaps in the area of Ranikhet.

For one thing, such a school would be a means of attracting American dollars to India, which would make the development of anything we do there much easier. It would cost no more, and possibly less, to cover a student's round-trip passage and year's tuition in India than it costs to send a child to private school in this country. And private schools are enjoying a boom in America now, because of the growing violence, immorality, and lack of values taught in the public schools.

An English-language school run by Ananda would be a means of providing a rounded education to Indians as well as Americans, and could easily develop into an international school with students from many countries. For Americans it would be a wonderful opportunity, and I think for Indians as well.

It would develop also into our world-brotherhood colony idea. I have been concerned about the difficulty of Indians to receive our ideas with understanding—for example, even so simple a concept as the dignity of manual labor, and doing without servants even if they can afford them. A village of our type could not succeed unless and until all forms of work were considered good, and not demeaning.

I know you will say that the Sikhs have no caste consciousness, but we don't want only a Sikh community, and uprooting that consciousness from the Hindus will not be easy. Those who reject caste tend also to reject religion, and therefore would disqualify themselves from eligibility for a spiritual community. But if we could take children and train them, by the time they completed their education, many of them (judging from our experience at Ananda) would want, after graduation, to join the community.

Once one, even one, such community could be brought to a point of flourishing in India, the difficulty of establishing similar ones elsewhere would be greatly reduced. People would understand what we were doing, and its value, once they saw an actual example. It is while things are in the theoretical stage that understanding is difficult, and rejection easy.

In divine friendship,

*A letter to the Ananda Village
community about water fasting* | 11

November 12, 1990

Dear Ones:

In such a large community as ours, it's difficult to keep everything flowing always in attunement with Yogananda's teachings. Ideas sometimes come up that seem right and good, but that are off on another track. This is where the need for spiritual guidance arises.

Such a thing happened a few years ago, when a certain healer visited Ananda from England. He was a good man, and also, I believe, helped a few of our members. He represented another ray of energy, however. He therefore raised many misgivings in our other members. I myself had been away, but when I returned I saw there was something going on that was in conflict with certain of Master's teachings. I had to step in and correct that situation.

Only recently did I learn of the current "fad" for body purification through water fasting, etc. Now that the matter has been brought to my attention, I'd like to share with you what Master said about such practices.

You'll recall I wrote in *The Path* that when I was new at Mt. Washington I was talked into adopting the "grape cure." The rationale given me was that once I'd purified my body I would find it easier to meditate. The "grape cure" would also, I was told, purify my consciousness. It seemed to me a good idea. After all, I thought: anything to further my spiritual development.

When Master found out about it, however, he scolded me for what I was doing. A pure heart, he remarked scoffingly, is more important than a pure body. Emphasis on purifying the body, I've since found, too often takes people's energy and attention from the real task God has placed before us: that of purifying our hearts.

Looking at the people who are deeply involved in such practices, one must ask: Are they strong devotees? Are they deep meditators? Are they notably pure of heart? The answer to all three questions, as far as I've ever observed, is, "No."

Many of the professionals I've met in this field are sincere, and also good. I'm sure they help many people. Their very emphasis on a physical approach to spirituality, however, almost by definition lacks balance.

Any fast may prove helpful, if people are critically ill. The water fast specifically, however, has been shown also to be harmful. That is, while it has helped in some cases, it has also proved extremely damaging in others. Prolonged fasts of this kind, moreover, are worse than useless for anyone who is not in dire physical circumstances.

Please read Paavo Airola on the subject of the very real perils of water fasting. He was strongly against it. His approach is, I think, sound. It is balanced and based on much objective research.

What Master recommended was that a person fast one day a week on only water, and then, once a month, fast three days on juices.

People will always be fascinated with various kinds of diet and healing. Please understand that I'm not opposed to all such practices, and that much good has come from some of them. Let us remember above all, however, that Master has given us a wealth of material on healing, as on countless other subjects. As his spiritual children, let us depend more on his teachings, and less on the recommendations of others whose final legacy to devotees is often a loss of attunement with our spiritual path.

The person recommending this fast actually commented that Saint Francis himself would have been more saintly if he'd undertaken it. I ask you!

There are other aspects of attunement that I'd like to explore at another time. Please for now, however, keep in mind this basic principle: that we are living at Ananda to attune more deeply to our own teaching, through Master and our line of gurus. This is the ray to which God has called us. It is through this ray, therefore, that He has been so gracious as to offer to help us.

In divine friendship,

Asked for advice on how to respond to a community situation	12

February 9, 2002

Dear _____:

Your question distresses me. As to whether you are being judgmental, that is for you to decide, but it is important to be discriminating, and I don't think it is easy to *act* on the basis of what we see is wrong without a degree of feeling behind our actions.

The solution, I believe, is to meditate and feel God's energy behind our feeling, and not to inject personal emotion into our actions. The best way is to offer one's feelings and actions to God, but certainly it is not to leave them passively in His hands.

You ask if I feel you are being unfair to _____. Well, we *must* be fair. From there, we need to think of being fair also to everyone concerned, and above all being fair to what we are doing in trying to build a community according to Master's ideals. For me, this need is paramount.

Love,

On the potential for an
Ananda work in Australia | 13

2000

Dear _____ :

I'm sorry things didn't work out for you in Western Australia. I know nothing of that area, so can't comment. But several of our Ananda members have tried to establish a beachhead on the continent, and for that reason I returned there three years ago.

My own feeling was that the people, generally speaking, aren't ready for what we have to give, but that if we were to succeed it would have to begin in Sydney instead of on the Sunshine Coast, where our members seemed determined to settle. Nothing is coming of our work there, either. And though a couple did move to Sydney, for now at least, I have no expectation of accomplishing anything there.

It seems best for us to continue spreading our work in America and here in Italy, where the field also is fertile. We ourselves don't have enough people yet to spread any further, though I've always felt that eventually we should have four main centers of activity, including India and Australia. I simply don't think it's time yet.

As for my doing anything further personally, I have my doubts. I'm not involved in organizational activity any more, but am concentrating on writing, and some lecturing. There are others who can handle the rest, and are doing so very competently.

Ananda is thriving on all fronts (except the Australian). More interest being shown all the time; more people coming. Our retreats, both in the village and here in Assisi, are bursting at the seams.

I agree with you when you say, "'Out there' everyone has so much information." What they lack is inspiration. I'm doing my best even through the medium of books to inspire, and not only to inform. That's also why I've written so much music.

Last May a choir of more than fifty came to Italy from our colonies in America to sing my Oratorio in six cities. Wherever they went, they were given standing ovations. One Frenchman came up to me after the concert in Assisi and, deeply moved, said to me (fortunately, I know French), "I don't speak a word of Italian or English, but I was able to understand everything!" It is people's hearts, above all, that need to be touched.

My best wishes to you. I hope you and _____ will be able to visit Italy some day. It's a long distance, unfortunately.

In divine friendship,

| *A "rock 'n' roll, samba, waltz, and cha-cha" dance party at Ananda?* | 14 |

February 13. 1999

Dear _____:

In answer to your question, I certainly agree with you that this kind of dancing is far from the vibration we are working on developing at Ananda. What more can I say? I'm only astonished that the question has arisen.

I will discuss it with _____ and others.

Love,

| *To Ananda colony leaders* | 15 |

April 5, 2003

Dear Ones:

I have just finished re-reading *A Place Called Ananda*. What an important statement it is for the future of our work! I suggest that it be required reading, especially for anyone interested in joining Ananda. What say you all?

In divine friendship,

May 26, 1998

Dear Jyotish and Vidura:

I want to begin this letter by expressing my deep, heartfelt gratitude to you both, as well as to Devi and Durga, for your wonderful spirit of faith and devotion, for your friendship, and for your staunch desire and determination in the face of great trials to serve Master and, to the very best of your ability, to save Ananda. I bless you again and again for what you've done so far and are doing.

At the same time, this letter expresses my concern about certain things, and I want to make it clear at the outset that this concern is for circumstances that may lie outside of anyone's power to control them. My hope is that some of those circumstances will yet offer alternative possibilities for consideration. For it does sometimes happen that circumstances viewed with objectivity—as if mentally from a distance—may actually contain alternatives that would be more to our actual liking.

My concern, of course, is lest the financial pressures of the present cause not only a distortion in our present priorities, but also a permanent shift in Ananda's values.

It was what I saw had happened at Dayalbagh, India. There, since the death of Sahabji Maharaj, the founder, the business faction had assumed control, whereas those whose focus was spiritual had moved out—to the detriment, sadly, of both groups.

It was what happened in a different sense with the work of St. Francis of Assisi. It has also happened at SRF, owing partly, I think, to the fact that Daya Mata continued to hold the position of treasurer after she was made president.

It was what I sought to avoid at Ananda by creating the position of spiritual director, apart from the post of general manager. The idea was for the spiritual director to be removed somewhat from daily administration, and able therefore to keep his or her primary focus on the community's spiritual needs and well being.

I fear to see the spiritual director—you, Jyotish—become as involved as the general manager, Vidura, in the practical administration of Ananda. Certain aspects of our present situation make me uncomfortable for Ananda's future.

Ananda has been a place of spontaneity and joy, of individual self-expression that was not afraid even to verge on eccentricity. Conformity, now, is increasingly becoming the norm.

And this conformity is centered in financial considerations. I spoke to _____ on her birthday the other day. With _____'s expected return in the fall, _____ will have to move out of that house. She sees little chance of finding a residence elsewhere at Ananda because she is either out of the housing pool or too low in it to have that kind of priority. I don't actually know the practical considerations, and I'm sure they are both important and necessary.

At the same time, I can't help reflecting that _____ has been with us nearly the whole of our thirty years existence. I don't want to convey the impression that she was complaining: Far from it, there was no hint of complaint from her. It was I who felt badly, thinking that she might have to move away from Ananda altogether to support herself. I suggested she move to another colony, but she didn't want to be so far away from _____.

I have the impression that this housing pool has produced similar problems for others in the sense of giving priority to people with money over those to whom we owe a larger debt of loyalty. I realize our hands are tied by circumstances over which we have no control, but I think that for that very reason we ought to do everything possible not to bow to those circumstances, except after giving deep consideration to every possible alternative to them—if only to keep firmly in mind that we ourselves, and no outer circumstance, are in charge of our lives.

It is a mistake, I strongly feel, to confuse legalities with *dharma*.

You know that my tendency is to gaze ahead. I'm not concerned only with immediate realities, but with directions for the future. If present needs are going to direct our future development, they could permanently distort some of our fundamental values. As I say, I see developments that make me a little uneasy for the future of Ananda. Perhaps living at a distance, as I am, I see things in a broader perspective than I might, were I there among you.

Some days ago, because of my pending, though still uncertain, filing for bankruptcy, I phoned _____, who had been in touch with the bankruptcy attorney. As he picked up the phone, he announced, "Management Office" in a gruff voice.

Two words—innocent enough, I hope, though in fact there was a suggestion of feeling the importance of that office. Wouldn't it have been more in keeping with our traditions, I thought, simply to say, "_____ speaking," or something of that nature?

The thought that arises is, Are we becoming a corporation, and no longer an ashram? There are some who would reply, "Well, but we *are* a corporation." Admittedly, the law has forced us to become so. Surely, however, there is no need for us to define *ourselves* in those impersonal and worldly terms.

The problem began eight years ago, with SRF's lawsuit against Ananda. Perhaps at that time we could have simply refused to enter the legal arena at all, and insisted instead on our *spiritual right* to express our beliefs as we chose. The law might have been able to prevent us from using "Self-Realization" officially in our name, but it would never have been able to prevent us from using it informally.

Well, that is water under the bridge now. We've made it clear to SRF that we are our own entity. We've won the right to reissue the first edition of the *Autobiography of a Yogi*, and to publish my edition of the *Rubaiyat*. SRF hasn't been able to prevent us from putting out *Essence of Self-Realization*, although they tried to. They haven't been able to choke off, legally or otherwise, our right to express Master's teachings in our own way. They've been prevented from claiming a monopoly on those teachings, as they wanted to do.

These have been important victories not only for us, but for Master's worldwide work. In the process, however, certain values at Ananda have been threatened. I fear that, with this second lawsuit, much may actually have been lost.

People are losing some of the freedom they once had for self-expression. From various things I have heard, there may also be a growing unease over the perceived necessity for bureaucratic control. Is this trend, I ask myself, inevitable to all spiritual organizations? Do they *have* to end up weighting their decisions more and more decisively on the side of financial considerations?

You know that I've been feeling a deep sense of disappointment these past months. I believe it is due more than anything else to this concern of mine.

We spoke yesterday of _____'s and _____'s work, and of your concerns about being able to keep them employed by Crystal Clarity. I understand your difficulty. And I don't want to weigh it against my own central concerns. At the same time, their work is very relevant to my own involvement in Ananda.

For they are part of what might be called my own creative team. _____, _____, _____, _____, and _____ are not so much a business consideration for Ananda as an extension of my own creativity, and the means through which my creative ideas finish their descent, so to speak, onto the material plane. To expect this unit to function according to fixed administrative patterns is unrealistic, in a sense, as it would be unrealistic to expect me to conform to them.

I can well imagine that, were I in a position of still having to prove myself, there would be great objection to letting me work in the unorthodox way I do work. And indeed there has been opposition from certain people for the very reason that what I do doesn't always justify itself financially.

The creativity that my "team" represents happens to be set *within* a business format—Crystal Clarity. But it isn't really a business at all. Nor are our people who are going out singing. Nor are our choirs.

If work of that nature, and our music in general, could be thought of separately from its profitability, and considered rather a long-term investment, important to be kept intact for that reason, at least the issue would be clear-cut. It would then be understood that there are aspects of our work that do require support. Even if, at present, we can bring only a few things to market, it surely is worthwhile to keep the machinery going, especially while I am still alive and able to keep the creativity flowing.

There may even be creative ways of paying some of their salaries. For instance, the colonies all benefit from this creative output. Perhaps they would consent—without letting them feel their arms were being twisted but simply by letting them know the difficulty—to contribute a monthly tithe, perhaps to be deducted from sales at their boutiques, or perhaps by some value added tax on those sales.

I have invested, I estimate, at least $200,000 personally—as a gift to Ananda—in the equipment used in those departments. In addition, I have about 15,000 color slides: another investment (a donation, in fact) of many thousands of dollars more. At present the impression is that that team can't produce the money to justify their employment, except on a project basis. If this is the decision, their focus will simply have to shift elsewhere. And the creative potential of those departments will be vitiated—once again, I might add. The music ministry has suffered continuously over the years in this regard.

Most composers in history have been harried financially, and far more than I have. In this respect I am grateful. Even so, I cannot but feel that in the name of pressing monetary considerations we are denying ourselves something almost as precious as our very survival.

The projects in which this team is involved will not all bear instant financial fruit. Some of them would require outlays of money that we simply don't have, and must therefore await their turn. But there are considerations here that *could* be weighed in the balance, and not dismissed simply because they don't conform to certain existing policies.

Even in normal businesses, there are investments that don't bear immediate fruit, financially. Some of them, of necessity, bear fruit only in time. Some of them, again, bear fruit only indirectly. Research and development is one such category. So also is advertising. So also, at Ananda, is my own creative output. And it has not always been easy to persuade people even of the need for my books and music. (You'll recall that time, years ago, when serious thought was given to suspending the publication of my books "for the present," in favor of two better-selling books, Bharat's and the Ananda cookbook.)

On the other side of this balance, I have to say that, of the many birthday cards I received this year, a significant number of them—quite possibly even a majority—mentioned that what first drew them to Ananda was the music. Many added that it is above all the music that holds them here still.

The books, finally, have won a place for themselves, although, thanks to the disaster we ran into three years ago, their acceptance by certain members remains still precarious. We have much to lose, however, if the music, tapes of lectures and classes, color slides, and similar aspects of our creative work are shelved for more immediate, "practical" considerations.

The fear of what others may say if we maintain these admittedly more long-term investments of time, personnel, and energy in favor of more immediate considerations could set Ananda on a long-term course toward materialism, and toward the loss of its spiritual and creative impulse.

It isn't as if this team couldn't generate short-term income as well. Investment in individual products could be kept small, especially in terms of their long-term, and probable, returns.

1. _____ could devote himself to cleaning up, and preparing for production, the hundreds of old tapes of talks and classes I gave, dating as far back as the sixties. Your energies would not have to be involved in this, but someone could create a tape-of-the-month club of those old talks, and the income from that could be used to help pay his wages.

2. In addition, there are five years of old, weekly radio talks, half an hour each, that could be prepared for sale to members, and even offered as radio shows. I also have the one year's worth of fifteen-minute talks, five days a week, that I did just two years ago. The quality of these is of course superior to the old ones, when I had cheap equipment. But the old ones, also, could be cleaned up electronically.

3. Someone—again, not you, but another person who was freer and able to be personally involved: _____, perhaps—could put energy into getting some of these talks out on radio again. KVMR springs to mind. (That's the local station, isn't it?). This wouldn't be income, but it would be excellent outreach as well as advertising. We need someone to involve himself in getting radio exposure for our teachings.

4. My slides (here, _____ and _____ come to mind) could be turned into small print-runs of beautiful cards with sayings from the Secrets books. The investment here could be quite small; there is no need,

here, to think nationally for now. They could even run the cards off on equipment they already have—real desktop publishing, but in runs sufficient to help them earn at least enough to support themselves. At least it would be preparing a backlog of work that could become a much bigger financial success for Ananda in the future.

I confess I'm becoming worried about policies that set projects like these aside as "impractical." I've tried here to suggest ways that would bring instant returns from them, to justify them from a budgetary point of view. But it's the long term that will show their real value to us.

We may feel we can't handle the output we have already, but that is only for NOW. The potential for future output is not only many times greater, but will be in growing demand if we keep our spirit of devotion and service alive.

Please don't take ill anything that I've said. I want to repeat how grateful I am for all that you are doing. At the same time, the deep disappointment I've felt these past months is, I know, directly related to the seemingly impenetrable wall of material difficulties we've encountered in our joyful efforts to bring *God* to people. I would feel we'd lost everything if we lost that joy in a maze of bureaucratic "necessities." Without joy, what is Ananda?

In Master's Love,

The more good one does | 17

March 1, 1999

Dear _____:

I believe that the best way to meet these carping critics is with silence. The work we are doing will speak more and more for itself. And those critics are already revealing themselves as having nothing to contribute to the world other than their incredible hostility toward us.

"Incredible," I say—yet history provides countless examples of the same behavior. The more good one does, the more one attracts hostility from certain quarters, though also gratitude and appreciation from others.

Love,

April 24, 2000

Dear _____:

I've pretty well lost faith in our legal system. For cases like murder, where only the facts are concerned, it may do well enough to hear first all the facts on one side, then all the facts on the other, and so on.

For cases like ours, however, where facts are not so much the issue as opinions and emotions, the opposing attorney has as long as he wants to prejudice the jury beyond hope of redemption by the defense. Lies can't be challenged on the spot and countered. I myself was not given a chance even to speak in my own defense.

The system is hopeless. A lawyer like _____ can do anything he wants, growing rich while destroying perfectly innocent lives.

I could continue quite a bit in this vein; the important thing is to survive, which I've done by realizing that no one can take away my love for God, and that I have nothing to lose in any case since all belongs to God. Someday I'll recount what a victory that lawsuit was for me and for Ananda. But it was with no help from the system, the judge, or even our own lawyer.

Joy!

September 9, 2001

Dear _____:

There is a great difference, unfortunately, between the way these things are done in Europe and Switzerland. In Europe, one has the government to deal with. In America, where protest is an unfortunate but unpreventable fact of life, one has a truculent public to deal with. If we had allowed neighbors' complaints to be our definition of divine guidance when Ananda was getting started, Ananda would never have happened. Over time, we've been able to show our neighbors that what we are doing is a blessing also for them.

The only course to pursue in the present case is to ask ourselves, "Is there any truth, or justice, in their complaints?" If there were, we should change. But when their complaints sink to the level of protesting in print that we are planning to put up a five-storey building, and other similarly outrageous lies, then it would be cowardly and absurd to bow before their opposition.

There are people in America who fight *everything*, as we know from long and painful experience. Hunter Black's mother, as you told me, had to fight for ten years to get a bicycle path past the city council because certain people protested that bicycles on that path would kill the snails—creatures that people need to control by killing them anyway, if they want lawns and gardens for their homes!

When faced with illogic, the only thing is to look at matters as clearly and fairly as possible. If these dissenters represented a majority, I'd say, "Back down." But they don't. In fact, there are many who recognize what a good thing we'd be doing for their own neighborhood, on land that at present is a wilderness without the slightest ecological value.

It is scenes like this one in Seattle that make me prefer, for now anyway, to live in Italy. So much unfair and unreasonable opposition, based purely on prejudice, emotion, and anger! Frankly, this to me is the worst aspect of America these days.

But as regards our temple, it will be a great asset; many people see it as at least potentially that; the objectors are people of low energy and are not the kind of people who ought to be allowed to control things to the extent that they do. Defeat for them would be a victory of truth over injustice. Victory for them would a victory of mob rule over fairness and common sense. Seen from this perspective, I see no alternative for us except to go ahead and do what we see as right.

Disharmony is a guide to what NOT to do when it becomes too widespread, as opposed to being only the inevitable hot-heads; when it can be justified by reason; when it affects those whom we are trying to help;

when it produces disharmony in our own hearts. Otherwise, the battle of Kurukshetra was righteous, and Arjuna's qualms were born of misunderstanding the realities.

Love,

December 14, 2004

Dear Ones:

The couple who have left are convinced they have their own personal, inner connection with Master, which is a good thing for every disciple to develop. When the inner connection one feels, however, puts him out of harmony with the inner connection others feel, or with their own sense of Master's inner guidance, I think such people owe it to themselves, above all, but also to those others, to go off to where they can develop their connection with Master on their own.

It would be wrong to continue to march together, while out of step with the others. And if those others are trying earnestly to develop their own discipleship—should those departing do so with criticism? I don't think so.

No one way is the *one and only right* way. True disciples, especially, should be tolerant of other ways from their own. I think they, too, should show respect for all.

Too often in my life have I have seen a few dissident voices succeed in getting others to agree with them in their negativity. Anyone drawn into that will find himself taken away from Master's work. There will be no necessity for telling them to leave. They will not be allowed *by Master* and Divine Mother to remain. I have seen this same scenario play itself out all too often on the spiritual path.

There is no harm in reflecting, both inwardly and as a group, on what would be salutary and possible for us to correct. But we can only work together effectively if we work in concert, in harmony, and not in dissonance.

In Master's love,

October 16, 1998

Dear _____:

What this lawsuit has done for me, if nothing else, is greatly deepen my conviction that I want God alone. Nothing, but nothing, else matters. As for going up on appeal: Why ask for reconsideration by a system for which I, and (I imagine) *we* have so little respect? We've won anyway, in the eyes of those who alone matter to us.

Were we to go for an appeal, we'd end up spending even more money, wasting lots more time, and merely risking a repeat of the same treatment we've had already. I don't think it's worth it to any of us.

God is our judge. Why even bother to seek approval from the courts of this world? An appeal would be tantamount to *our* suing. We've never sued anyone. I wouldn't have even submitted that counterclaim had I thought this through adequately then.

In fact, it can only have been by divine will that things turned out as they did. Why not just accept that? This world is not our home, and the lawsuit has helped convince us of that. So—let's just be grateful, and move on.

I do think, however, that I will make a public statement on the subject. For, otherwise, as the saying goes, "Silence gives consent."

In divine friendship,

July 23, 1990

Dear _____:

We've given serious thought to your proposal, and we feel it just isn't "our thing." Thank you for thinking of us. We know you had our interests at heart. Our logical objections to the proposal, however, are several, and these are in addition to our instinctive feelings on the matter.

We've received other invitations to join in what you've called pyramid schemes. No matter how valid the project—and some of the products offered do seem worthwhile—we resist on principle anything that has profit as its prime focus. Our lives are dedicated to the principle of service. This means giving to others, and not thinking of gaining from them.

Naturally, one must gain also, to survive. Everything we do, however, and even more particularly so everything *I* do, is focused on rendering spiritual service. In our stores we sell many things, from health foods to dresses, but even there, our minds are focused on serving God through others. In my case, my work is entirely directed toward consciously sharing our spiritual teachings with others. I don't really believe that any other way would work for me.

Even if we were to reach out to the general public with your product— and I'm sure it's a good product—I would not want to charge them a price that would continue to guarantee me an income purely on the strength of the work a subsequent network of distributors did for me. I'd rather let those distributors have their own contact with the company. If I'm going to profit from a work, I'd like to feel that I'm also *doing* the work.

More is involved, however, almost necessarily so. The people I work with are my friends. The strength of our relationship is one of mutual trust and love. It would be a betrayal of that trust to seek to involve them in a scheme that was intended for mutual gain, when our relationship is based on mutual sharing and love. They might indeed buy from me if I asked them to, but they know I would never ask such a thing of them.

So, _____, thanks for your offer, but the mind-set of this community isn't compatible with this kind of venture. I speak, you see, not only for myself, but for Ananda as a whole.

Again, let me stress that I consider the product itself to be worthwhile. I wish you continued success in your efforts.

In divine friendship,

February 6, 2001

Dear _____:

Thank you for sending me the proposal.

I want to say that I don't want my name, or for that matter, Ananda's name associated with worldly attitudes. Once we feel we must compromise who we are in order to make money, we have already started down the road that certain other spiritual organizations have taken: not necessarily a bad road, but a betrayal of the ideals Master brought to the world.

For myself, I am in the happy position of being able to say that every thing I've ever written is sincere. Never mind what others in the industry are doing. Let's always be *ourselves*.

In divine friendship,

May 4, 2000

Dear _____:

I've certainly no objection to Crystal Clarity Publishers turning a profit! I just don't want us to develop a commercial attitude to the degree: 1) that we lose our devotion, both in ourselves and in our approach to the market; and 2) that we fail to give adequate attention to our members—to increasing their number, and to reaching devotees above all, and others in the hope of turning them in the direction of becoming devotees.

Sales for sales' sake would be a mistake, but successful sales less for the sake of Ananda's income than for reaching people with the truth: Of this I approve heartily. Let many millions come to us that way!

Love,

December 14, 1998

Dear _____:

The whole point of a cover is to sell the book. The problem lies with the thought that marketers, as such, have a special corner on common sense. I've learned over the years to be highly skeptical of so-called "experts." We should keep carefully in mind the fact that this "marketing view" was what nearly ruined Crystal Clarity before.

Often, the "experts" justify that famous saying, which Master loved to quote, "The operation was a success, but the patient died peacefully on the operating table." Their very claim to expertise is the fatal flaw of egotism that eventually proves its own undoing.

We've been down this road before. It didn't work for us. I don't say the direction itself is wrong. What makes it wrong is the competitive emphasis. Merely to BE a "marketing person" doesn't guarantee that you know what you're talking about, or that you'll be right every time. Experience is a liability, often, for it can prevent you from welcoming, or at least being open to, new ideas.

The bottom line, here, is that we do have something, finally, THAT WORKS. Why tinker with it? I'll go with anything that works well, if it also expresses our spirit, and the spirit of the book (which their *Secrets of Life* failed to). But I will strongly resist so-called "expert" opinions that begin with the premise, "You aren't a 'marketer,' so you can't know what you're talking about."

Common sense, not "expertise," should be our guideline. For the present at least, common sense should tell us that we have products, finally, that are doing well. Why not stay with them?

Another even more important issue is, we don't want the marketers telling us, "But we can give you a product that will sell to a wider market." That was where our greatest trouble lay, earlier. _____ and _____ wanted to break into the mainstream market with a product that isn't geared for that kind of market. I write another kind of book. What we needed to do was recognize this simple fact, and not try to compete with Warner or other big publishers. Disaster awaits us if we do.

I am simply not a mass-media author. I've no desire to be. I've no wish at all to misrepresent ourselves for the sake of greater sales. That is why I insisted that Crystal Clarity come under the umbrella of Ananda Church, and not try to be something different. On this point, I do have final say, and shall insist on it. Otherwise—well, I'm simply not interested.

But I'll gladly accept any good cover idea THAT WORKS, and for the right reasons. It's just that they haven't worked nearly so well, until now at least, as the covers we're now using. Give me a better idea, and I'll go for it. But no one should try to sell an idea merely on the ground that "an expert designed it."

Love,

Marketing to "our own" | 26

[Asked about an outreach effort: "We are giving away a free CD. Should we use the reading from The Rubaiyat of Omar Khayyam Explained, *or something more under-standable to the average person?"]*

December 14, 1998

Dear _____:

We're trying to win devotees, not just large numbers of members. The kind of people we want to attract are those who will love the *Rubaiyat* reading. The others—well, we're happy to serve them to the extent that they want it, but they'll never be "our own." I say, let's go with the *Rubaiyat* reading.

In divine friendship,

No good thing can thrive without opposition | 27

May 2, 1996

Dear _____:

Thank you for your letter. I am touched by the thoughts and feelings you expressed. I must say, I endorse them.

To me, Ananda is the most wonderful place on this planet. I suppose it is inevitable that people will try to destroy it. No good thing can thrive without opposition, which serves the purpose of strengthening its own will to grow and expand.

We are proud of what we have, for it is something given to us by God. Our Seattle community, in particular, has a chance now to grow stronger in divine light, in a spirit of service and self-giving, and, above all, in love.

God bless you, ———.

Love,

*"Music doesn't merely <u>reflect</u>
a state of consciousness:
It also <u>generates</u> it.*

CHANTING

---

*A taste for emotional music,
if it is too much encouraged,
will almost certainly
change Ananda's very state
of consciousness, in time—
its underlying vibration."*

[The following letter and statement, "Thoughts on Chanting" were sent to Ananda leaders and musicians. A section of the letter is addressed specifically to the leaders in Australia.]

August 2, 1998

Dear Ones:

I'm attaching a few thoughts I've just written on chanting. I'd appreciate feedback from you, and I suggest you share this attachment with others, especially those who are involved in leading chanting.

Dear ones in Australia: I've been hoping to hear from you. I want to say that none of this is intended to force you into a different direction from what you yourselves feel to go. If my ideas don't inspire you, then please do what does inspire. There have been a few questions about some of your directions, the thought being that they don't seem to be the way we do things elsewhere.

But I realize that Ananda will grow in many directions, and I don't want to discourage a tendency that is inevitable anyway. I do very much hope that our core colonies—those on America's west coast—will maintain their closeness to Master's spirit and way of doing things, as I've tried to teach them.

But I know that many other colonies will spring up, and that while most, perhaps, will be inspired by Ananda, not all of them will do things just as they are done in those core colonies. Some will be different in certain ways—perhaps even in many ways.

If you yourselves want to do things as much as possible the way we do them in America and in Italy, my own energy, certainly, will go out more toward you, but I, and I think I speak for all of us, will support you in whatever way we can in any case. We know you are working sincerely, and with devotion. And I bless you for your courage in trying to establish a work there, which is, I know, a great challenge for you.

If my letter seems critical to you in any way, then please do me the kindness of giving me reassurance—especially on the points I've raised here.

Remember, I haven't heard from you. How can I know anything, if you don't write? But this letter hasn't been written to criticize, because I'd never want to TELL you what to do in anything. How you lead things there is your decision. My love is with you in any case.

To the rest of you, there is another point that I might have raised in the attachment, but felt it better to limit it for now to this letter. It is this: We don't consider appointments to the ministry from a standpoint of people's *desire* to teach, but rather from their humility and worthiness to teach. Shouldn't we do that also, at least to some extent, with the music ministry?

To let people lead chanting only because they desire to, and to turn the job over to them without seeing to it that they get proper training, could in time prove disastrous. It seems wiser to have fewer people leading the group chants. Then, if we want more chant leaders, not to "take them off the street," so to speak—newcomers, in other words—but to give them adequate preparation for such a service.

The music is treated, all too often, as though it were a minor aspect of what we do. It is, however, in fact, central to everything we do.

Love,

~~~~~~

Thoughts on Chanting
by *Swami Kriyananda*

When I first encouraged chanting with guitars—it was over fifteen years ago—I did it because much of our chanting lacked the energy that rhythm gives to a chant. Rhythm is not so important for personal chanting (Master would hold a single note for a long time, sometimes, when chanting with only two or three of us), but it IS important when chanting in a larger group. Lacking this sense of rhythm, I found that the chants were getting slower and slower, until by the end they sometimes sounded positively funereal.

Maybe it was simply the time it takes for sound to travel between the front and the back of a large room, but in fact I think it was more than that.

When leading the chanting, my own playing would get dragged slower and slower. The only alternative would have been to accept a battle of wills between my playing and what was coming back to me from the audience.

We had a few Indian drums that people tended to thump, rather like American Indian tom-toms; the sound lowered the vibration of the chanting, instead of raising it. The inability of Americans to tune in to the subtlety of Indian chanting became especially evident to me at gatherings in Hare Krishna temples, where I found the beat was sometimes of a lower *chakra* variety that affected even the movements people made while dancing. Again, in those temples, I was sometimes reminded of war dances around a tribal fire.

So it occurred to me that guitar playing could help solve our problem. I'd heard this at Peki, [a spiritual group in Italy] and realized that guitar playing was something Westerners were better at. At Peki it gave a more uplifting power to the chanting. The same thing, I thought, could influence our own chanting, and rescue it from becoming a sort of "hymn sing." In fact, the guitars gave a certain power to the rhythm. I think they've added a lot to our chanting, over all.

Then there was also the element of chords. Up to a point, chords were helpful, for they stirred up feeling in the heart. I remember Master, during the chanting at one Christmas meditation, encouraging us, "Whip up the feeling in your hearts!"

But I've worried also about these changes. For one thing, to stir the emotions at the beginning of a chanting session can be helpful, but later on the emotions must be transformed into intuitive feeling, which is always calm and interiorized. How to effect this transformation?

Another point, which I think will not be very well received but needs to be said: Master NEVER played Indian chants for group singing. He could easily have sung *Maha Mantra* ("Hare Krishna, Hare Krishna, Krishna Krishna Hare Hare!", etc.), or one of the other simple chants we all do. I do know that in recounting the life of Sri Chaitanya he once sang "Radhe, Radhe, Radhe Govinda Jai! Spirit and Nature dancing together." But it was usually in the context of that story, and by his translation he gave it a spiritual meaning.

Even in India, the only story I heard of his chanting in a group was of one night when he sang and danced all night. It was in Calcutta. A huge crowd joined him. They filled the house, then the street outside the house, then covered the surrounding roofs. They all danced joyfully the whole night. And the chant he sang on that occasion—in Bengali—was "Door of My Heart."

In fact, he brought to the world a whole new style of singing to God. His chants are NOT like traditional Indian chanting.

So there are several factors I'd like to consider. Let's begin with the last of them. Master's mission was to *spiritualize* America and the West, not to *Indianize* us. He himself loved Indian music, and was exceptionally well versed in the Indian style of playing and singing. Even so, he didn't involve Western audiences in it, and from all I can tell he even sought to inspire the audiences in INDIA with his new style of chanting.

So: Does this mean we should give up the Indian chants altogether?

No, I don't think so. There is much more exposure to Indian culture nowadays than there was in his time. He himself would sometimes sing Indian songs for us, in the Indian manner—Tagore's songs, and others. I have a CD Agni made for me from Indian records that Master loved.

But Master didn't sing those chants that recite all those names of deities. Even when singing to Radha and Krishna, he universalized the concept by his translation: "Spirit and Nature dancing together!" Still, some of the Indian chants ARE beautiful. I'd be sorry to give them all up, and I don't think I'm intruding a merely personal preference in saying so. I simply don't think that, basically, this is what we either want or need.

At the same time, I don't think the mere fact that a chant is Indian is sufficient reason for singing it. Many of those Indian chants are neither beautiful nor inspiring. They haven't a good melody. They produce a lot of noise, but no deep feeling. I think we need to be more selective in the chants we use, and especially to sing those with real beauty rather than select them merely for their Indian-ness.

And I really think we shouldn't sing so many of them. We are disciples of a new ray, and within that ray a new kind of music has been produced. I think we should honor this fact, and emphasize it more.

The next point has to do with emotionalism. Most Ananda members were raised on emotional music, so it comes naturally. I had my own share of this exposure, too, though later in my boyhood, and it never really sank in because I didn't particularly enjoy it. Nevertheless, there is bound to be a tendency to LIKE sounds that remind us of the music we grew up with. And this means liking, and then WANTING, the emotional side of chanting and singing.

I worry about this fact, because music is so much more than entertainment. It doesn't merely REFLECT a state of consciousness: It also GENERATES it. A taste for emotional music, if it is too much encouraged, will almost certainly change Ananda's very state of consciousness, in time—its underlying vibration.

There are three ways of expressing emotions musically: through melody, chords, and rhythm. Even an uplifting melody can be dragged down by chords that are too emotional, and by a heavy rhythm. Chords, if too heavily emphasized, can keep the music on an emotional level. And too heavy a downbeat in the strumming of the guitars will also emphasize the emotions, and feelings that strengthen the ego with their implied affirmation, "I WANT! I LIKE! I DON'T LIKE!"

Another aspect of the chords as many people play them has, I confess, distressed me. For there are right chords, and wrong ones. Too often I've found myself cringing every time a wrong chord is repeated in a chant. If this musical "outrage" doesn't disturb everyone, I still don't think it can really inspire ANYONE. There's a reason why certain chords are right, and why certain others, wrong. Music is a language; it isn't simply a production of sounds.

In our new chant book, I've worked on the chords of my own chants, at least. I didn't feel equal to tackling the chords that have been suggested for all of Master's chants, and I confess I feel slightly guilty about this omission. But I've been trying to do another job, and have had to take time out to do even this much work on the chant book. I hope you'll study these new chords, to the extent that they are new.

How much should we use chords? You'll notice that in my album, *Kriyananda Sings Yogananda*, I hardly use them at all. I chant much more in the style Master used. At the same time, this album is more for individual singing than for large groups, and therefore doesn't even try to be rhythmic.

Back to the question of chords, then: I'd say, don't feel that chords are essential to our chanting. MELODY is what's essential. People who find chords easier to play, and who therefore skimp on playing the melody or omit it altogether, ought to try to learn to play the melodies, and to play them correctly. It isn't enough only to sing them. The practice of playing chords without melody is getting too far away from Master's style of chanting.

Secondly, it would help, as you get deeper into a chant, to get away from playing the chords altogether and concentrate entirely on the melody. Through the melody you'll find it easier to attune yourself to AUM than you will by continuing to emphasize the emotional feelings awakened by chords. Go from outer exuberance to quiet absorption within.

It would be nice to have the Indian drums that are played from the sides (the *mridanga* and *dholak*, for example), rather than from above like the Indian *tablas*. The *tablas* require considerable sophistication to sound good, and even with sophistication they often sound as if they were in competition with the singing.

In my album called (I think) *Songs of the Soul*, Keshavdas's son Murali played the tabla accompaniment, and played it exceedingly well. He played it, however, with personal style and in competition with the singing, not in support of it. In fact, someone asked him later how the chanting session had gone, and he replied, "Very well. I played such-and-such a *tala* (rhythm)."

Lewis plays the *tabla* sensitively and also well, but we can't have him for every chant session, and I think the *tabla* is, in any case, right only for certain chants, not for all even of the rhythmic ones. The *mridanga*, *dholak*, and other similar instruments, played from the side, are easier to play, and are in most cases more natural for chanting than the *tabla*.

But guitars can be great also, if not over-emphasized. Stronger strumming at the beginning of a chant session can yield to gentle finger-picking as the chanting gets deeper. Outer exuberance should be replaced gradually by inward depth.

Sankirtans should include short, then long and then gradually longer periods of meditation. The purpose of all chanting is to take us inside, not to keep us shouting out loud to God.

Most Indian chanting is a recitation of names of God, with an occasional "*namo*" thrown in. Are all those names really meaningful to any of us? We haven't grown up with them. They aren't a part of our culture, nor of the way we think.

I was asked recently in an interview, "To which Hindu symbols do you feel most attracted?" I had to answer, "To none of them, particularly! I'm a yogi. Symbols are for people who feel more drawn to the outward aspects of religion."

Master, too, placed minimal importance on deities, symbols, etc. As his disciples, I think we ought to recognize that many of those Indian chants, most of the names in which aren't even recognizable to us, are more a means of letting off emotional steam than of really deepening our devotion. Forgive me if I offend. I don't at all mean to.

I want also to say, let's be careful that we select chants that uplift us, not those merely that stir us with sweet sentiments. Let us try to use them as a means of internalizing our consciousness—in other words, as a path to God. Let us realize that even in India, much of the chanting is not inspiring, but mostly just makes a lot of noise. I remember a story about a time Sri Ramakrishna and some of his disciples attended a *Vaishnava* festival, and found the music dispirited.

Let's try our best to follow Master's way, and to tune in to the divine ray he has brought into our lives. The more we do so, the faster we'll all grow spiritually.

In divine friendship,

August 17, 1998

Dear Ones:

My recent letter on chanting was intended as a corrective. I've had feedback on the Indian chants, and I must say I love some of them too. What would be wrong would be whole evenings devoted only to Indian chanting when we have our own, Master's especially. But to sing the Indian chants now and then, interspersed between our own, would add to the inspiration rather than deflect it in a different and not necessarily yogic, or not "Yoganandic," direction.

What I'm for, and what I myself have sung, are those that are simple and easy to understand. Too many names only leave people feeling bemused as to what on earth they are singing. It may feel good, but they don't know what it's all about.

I also recommend strongly that we avoid those chants that have complex rhythmic and melodic patterns. They seem to me too mentally involving, at least for Westerners, to awaken real devotion.

I've spoken with Nirmala, who just got out our chant book. We thought to have a separate little book of Indian chants. I suggested we keep their number below ten, and preferably not more than eight, so that people really do think of these as occasional insertions into our own chanting rather than making a whole evening of them. That number, of course, is one I just pulled out of the air; I don't mean it necessarily to be fixed. But limited in number, yes.

I don't feel that Master opposes this decision. It isn't what he himself did, but, as I wrote in my letter on chanting, we are much more exposed to this kind of chanting now than Westerners were in his day. People have learned to love it, and I don't want to deprive them of something that inspires them, so long as it doesn't take them in a *different* direction from what Master gave us.

The role of disciples is not to repeat parrot-like exactly what the guru said and did, but to absorb it and offer it with individual understanding, rooted in inner attunement.

In that same spirit, I recommended to Nirmala a slight change in the way Master himself sang "Spirit and Nature"—you know the one. "Radhe. . . ." Incidentally, it's "Radhe," not "Radha," as I believe it's still written in *Cosmic Chants*. Radha is her name, but Radhe is the vocative form, used when invoking her response.

So: "Radhe, Radhe, Radhe Govinda Jaya! [repeat] Spirit and Nature dancing together!" Then Master had "Vict'ry to Spirit! Vict'ry to Nature!" But he did this spontaneously in the context of the story of Sri Chaitanya's life. It is in fact what the word "*Jaya*" means, in Sanskrit and in other Indian languages.

But "Victory" isn't anything we ourselves say, in English, in this context. For us, "victory" means winning against opposition, not "up with," as it does in Sanskrit. We ourselves say things like "Long Live!" or "Hurray!"— expressions, in other words, that work for us in other circumstances but not really in the present case. So here's my suggestion: "Bliss in the Spirit! Bliss through all Nature!" That's not a literal translation of "*Jaya*," but it conveys the spirit of that word.

Again, I plead with you, let's use these Indian chants more intermittently. They're beautiful, and I, too, love them. But let's think of them as spicing, rather than as the main course.

Love,

Kriyananda emphasizes the "directional"
nature of his statement on chanting | 3

August 7, 1998

Dear _____:

It seems to me I've said enough. Still, let me add—or is it repeat?—just this thought: that to insist on a 180-degree turn usually results in either halted or discouraged energy. We don't want that. Therefore I speak in terms of DIRECTIONS. You might tell _____ that too, and _____, who inclines happily toward the 180-degree corrections without taking into account that few others are happy with drastic measures.

If people find inspiration in what you are now doing, go with it. Your own desire to go Master's way will find the right means of improving the situation gradually, as the possibility arises. It's never good to be drastic, especially about changing what seems to be a good thing anyway.

_____, when things are spelled out too carefully, the whole point of what is trying to happen gets lost. Be guided simply by your inner feelings.

To a certain extent, the problem you voice is similar to _____'s reading of *The Hindu Way of Awakening*. He is offended (though he says he likes the book) that I haven't put in enough qualifying clauses about the good, fine, noble, wise, etc., people who ARE into the mystical side of Christianity, or not into the institutional side, or whatever else he wants to take issue with that would have made that book impossibly long, impossibly dry with so many qualifications, and impossibly dim, one-horsepower energy.

I'd like to write him—though I don't know whether I will—and tell him, "Can't you see, _____, that if all those wonderful people are in our camp, then they are the ones I am writing WITH, not AGAINST! We share the same point of view. Why on earth be offended on their behalf?"

But I'm afraid _____ prefers the kind of writing that qualifies, then re-qualifies, each tiny thought. To write his kind of book, I couldn't have got past the contents of chapter one: I'd have needed 300 pages just to say that much.

I write with a broad brush. Why not take it as a direction, instead of as a directive? Grow into it. I haven't time to work out all the HOWs and WHEREAS's. You all work it out. I'm not running the community now. YOU ALL decide if you like what I say, or not.

I must, however, say what I have to say. I owe that to Master. From there on, it's your community, not mine to run actively any more. I know it takes time to work on directions, but that has always, in fact, been my particular style of leadership, and it is likely to continue to be my style. Let's just say, I'm too old to change.

Many times people have disagreed, even strongly, with what I've said, then have come around to it later in their own time. I'd much rather that than wholehearted agreement, followed by—silence and inaction.

I've no more time to be working things out with you all. YOU work them out. If you like what I say, and find it inconvenient to practice it, I know it will remain in your minds and serve as a constant nudge toward what you know in your hearts must be done. It needn't happen quickly. The important thing is that it be said, heard, and listened to. And then, I would hope, acted upon in some natural timing.

The naturalness of everything is the operative expression.

In divine friendship,

Responds to other comments on
his chanting statement | 4

August 6, 1998

Dear _____:

I'd like to repeat what I said to you yesterday: Don't try for drastic changes. In response to what you heard from people, I don't want to "throw out" anything, but only to make a gradual shift that won't discourage anybody. Nor do I want the dispirited chanting we used to have. You're right, the "dragging" was a general feature at Ananda, and didn't occur only in my dome or the Seclusion Retreat dome. Definitely it occurred also at the Expanding Light.

Let's keep what is good about what we're doing, but not overdo it. Some chords may be helpful. Too much is detrimental. Some guitar is helpful; too much vigorous strumming is detrimental. The important thing is that, if and when we do use chords, they be the right chords. It is beautiful to have chords for the chants, too, when they are being played to listen to instead of to sing to.

As for the ministers, if they feel to lead the chanting, they should do so. If they don't, or want help, fine. But I myself don't want help on the chanting. Before the service we often have chanting, then immediately before the service and during the offertory we have the choir. For help with the chanting during the service, I'd say let the ministers decide.

Love,

August 6, 1998

Dear _____:

Re chanting: It is always best to let new developments insert themselves gradually and naturally into the consciousness of both singers and audience. Otherwise, in this case, there might be a loss of enthusiasm for all forms of chanting, and that would be too bad. It takes time for people to grow into a new idea.

Love,

August 6, 1998

Dear _____:

Some of the simpler Indian chants—"He Bhagavan (O God!)", "Sri Ram jai Ram jai jai Ram", as examples—are lovely. Also those with lovely melodies like "Sri Krishna Chaitanya." I don't want to "throw the baby out with the bath water."

Many of the more newly incorporated chants, however, even I don't understand! My feeling is to cut back by eliminating many of those. The two main motivations for singing them seem to be, 1) they are Indian, 2) they are new and different. The motivation that seems lacking in some of them seems to be that of both beauty and inspiration. And everything else I said on the subject seems to me a cogent argument.

Love,

"I believe that a mere handful of facts, meditated on deeply, will supply one with far greater insights than thousands of facts,

---

INSIGHTS AND COMMENTARY

---

with no time left after gathering them to meditate on their significance. Even one fact, deeply enough understood, will often suffice to explain thousands of other facts."

May 1, 1999

Dear ———:

I appreciate your letter. And of course you're right. When psychology is practiced as you yourself practice it, with devotion and spiritual insight, it can help people greatly. I wasn't addressing the many individuals who, personally, have the wisdom to practice it rightly. I was addressing a movement which, taken as a whole, has become more an industry than a profession.

Forgive me for not making it clearer, but when one sees a need for iconoclasm, one cannot attack the icon with an epee. One must use a mace. At least, that is how I see it. Psychology IS evolving, thank God, but there is much in the field that is damaging to spiritual development, and more and more reports of studies are indicating either that psychology as often practiced is not only relatively unhelpful, but may even be doing harm.

An interesting study, for example, was made a year after a massive lay-off of autoworkers in Detroit. The government was able to afford counseling for only about a third (I believe that was the figure) of the people who'd lost their jobs. The study found that those who had received no counseling ended up better off psychologically than those who had received it. The un-counseled had adjusted better to their new circumstances, had gone out and found new jobs instead of dwelling on their misfortune, and felt much more in control of their own lives.

One critic of the "industry," Noam Chomsky, observed, "One waits in vain for psychologists to state the limit of their knowledge."

Psychologists have touted the benefits of their profession, but by and large have remained silent on its possible weaknesses. Studies have been quoted as proving that the longer a person receives treatment, the more benefits he receives, whereas what those studies actually demonstrated was the very opposite. In other words, the promotional tactics being used by psychologists are too often reminiscent of advertising gimmicks rather than the serious reporting of conscientious scientists.

I don't question that there are many serious therapists. But I have seen the results of a great deal of quackery, and I do not believe that the mind, without the adjunction of intuition, is capable of reasoning its way OUT of its difficulties. What it seems to do is go in circles, from one room of ego-consciousness to another.

You are a good person, with high ideals. That is what you want to see in everyone, and it's laudable of you. Would that as many were like you as you claim. Sadly, I've seen a lot of wounded on the battlefield, as a result of psychoanalytical treatment.

Are they at least better than they were before? What I think is that, perhaps, their psychic limp has become less pronounced. Not much better than that. Meditation, and the spiritual insights you've developed, and a few others are developing, can help people a great deal more.

So, I'm not at all saying, Don't do what you're doing. Keep at it! The world needs more people like you. There's a great deal of confusion and twisted understanding out there that needs to be addressed. But I lived with Master, and I saw how masterfully he helped people: always leaving it to THEM to rise to a higher level of understanding, and giving them suggestions without ever trying to force his wisdom on anyone.

Superconscious guidance is, as you've put it, and as I too have often put it, solution-oriented, and in this sense is very different from the problem-consciousness with which the conscious mind is so easily infected. Classically, psychology tries to get people to face their problems honestly: a worthy effort, but one which too often has led people to dwell too much on their problems.

Solutions can't be found merely by thinking one's way to them. They come from inspiration. And inspiration comes from raising the level of consciousness to a level where it is able to penetrate through the clouds of reason. Self-honesty is essential, but must not become ingrown to the point of becoming obsessive.

Yes, _____, of course I am generalizing. One can't really do otherwise if one wants to address broad issues, unless one is willing to go the statistical route, but then, that route often bogs down in detail to the point where solutions are no longer even sought. My approach is, admittedly, particular. Other approaches are needed also, for final changes to be made. Let's hope my small voice will make a little impact, however.

Please forgive me for offending you. I feel your sincerity and that you are a friend, even though we haven't met. Joy to you!

In divine friendship,

A graduate student asked permission to circulate a questionnaire for his dissertation to Ananda members | 2

Circa 1977

Dear _____:

I wanted to give myself a little time to think over your request before answering your letter. The best I can say is that I don't oppose your asking Ananda members to reply to this questionnaire, if they want to. Anything more than that would constitute in some people's minds a request that they try to set time aside to answer your questions.

And the truth is, I've never felt much in tune with questionnaires of this sort. I find in many, perhaps even in most, cases that a Yes or No answer is simply not satisfactory. Human nature is too fluid to be capable of such categorization.

For instance, "I trust my son/daughter." Trust him/her when? With what? Under what circumstances? Or, "I try to make special time to spend with my daughter/son." I can imagine someone who has to *try* to make special time as being a lot less loving than one who does it naturally, and who therefore might well answer No to this question.

"I respect my son/daughter." I can imagine lots of circumstances in which respect would not be one's conscious sentiment, and yet the seeming lack thereof might involve a much more *practical*, and therefore more truly respectful, attitude than the sort of "buddy buddy" attitude assumed by so many ineffectual parents.

Or take such a statement as, "I do not feel depressed." A Yes or No answer here could easily be determined by how a person feels at the moment of answering the question. Or "I never hold a grudge." I've heard a lot of people make statements of this sort out of a very wish to explain away a grudging mood.

And so on down the line. I'm sure that some good can be got from questionnaires of this kind. It's just that, if asked for an endorsement, I don't see how I can conscientiously give it.

If, however, you feel in my lack of opposition to your asking them sufficient incentive to proceed, then at least I can give you this much.

In divine friendship,

The following two letters discuss the book, Henry I, by Warren Hollister. They were sent to Hollister's assistant, Amanda Frost, who, using Hollister's notes, completed the final two chapters of the book after Hollister's death.

3

[Paramhansa Yogananda stated that in a previous incarnation he was William the Conqueror. Swami Kriyananda has said privately that he believes he was William's youngest son, Henry I.]

January 14, 2002

Dear Dr. Frost:

Thank you for writing. The difficulty I have with too many historians is that they don't, like P. G. Wodehouse's butler, Jeeves (do you enjoy Wodehouse?), "study the psychology of the individual." They study situations and statistics, but show an unsatisfactory knowledge of human beings. Most of them haven't had to work with actual people, nor tried to understand them.

What I like especially about Hollister's and your book is that you made a real effort to enter into Henry's nature, placing yourselves in his shoes. I think the result is masterful.

I could see, of course, from all those footnotes, that both of you had expected a lot of opposition from your colleagues, and had wanted to reply to them as fully as possible when your book came out. I hoped you wouldn't be hit with it, but from my own experience of life—well, one just is!

I knew, of course, that you couldn't argue Henry's lack of selfish motive (assuming the thought arose in your minds, which it may have done). Twice in the book you felt it necessary to make it clear that you weren't depicting him as a saint, though it was clear you thought him basically good. I quite understand, both because there's no reason to say that he was a saint and also because others would certainly have lambasted you if you'd stepped so far out from the traditional line!

The reason I wrote of his devotion to duty was that he confined his ambitions to re-establishing his father's domain. Had he had personal ambition, as Robert Curthose did, he'd have gone on to seek at least some personal conquest for himself. Instead, he didn't try to seize Wales or Scotland, as his successors did: He won them over.

Yes, he was pragmatic, but I think he was also doing what he felt was his duty. Thus, to my mind, there was human feeling involved in his way of ruling. He was loyal, I think, by nature—since he showed such loyalty to his father's legacy. He was loyal when he could be, and expected loyalty of others. Being also pragmatic, however, he worked from his practical understanding of others. He seems, however, to have been hurt by people's betrayals of loyalty. He was a human being, not a machine, and seems to have felt deeply, judging from many accounts in your book.

I find that I empathize with him, having had to encounter many difficulties of a similar nature in my own life. It is from that sense of empathy, of projection, that I believe—perhaps wrongly—that Henry's delays were, yes a tactic, but were also due to natural hesitation, based on a wish to "get it right," and to let what we today would call "the energy flow" work itself out until clarity came of itself.

His abandoning that siege of Falaise in response to Anselm's threat of excommunication suggests to me that he was also anxious to keep himself in the right with God's will. This, too, could have been a reason for some of his delays. I don't think it's unrealistic to suggest that he may also have been influenced by remorse over his impetuous execution of Conan. But, this is what I've done in my own life. I may be only projecting, where Henry is concerned.

The establishment, in every field, is a hard castle to storm! I'm not surprised you're encountering resistance, though I believe your book will end up being accepted as the standard work on Henry I. It is a heroic work.

Perhaps you'd be interested in seeing the first chapter of my new book, *Hope for a Better World!* I'll include it as an attachment. The book is finished, and is even out already in Italian. (In America we are trying to get prepublication comments before the book is actually published, hopefully in March.) Having the "readers only" copy has given me a chance to work on polishing it further.

You ask where I live in Italy, and why. I live in the hills above Assisi, and speak and lecture in Italian at a retreat I founded years ago, to which I finally (in 1996) felt drawn to come and live. It is a branch of a group of communities and retreats that I founded in America. The first of them was established in 1968. All of them bear the name, Ananda.

I also feel at home in Europe, having been born and raised (until the age of 13) in Romania. My parents were "pure-blooded" American—which is to say, the typical American mongrels. So, although I'm American and was raised speaking English, I also spoke Romanian and German (fluently at the time), and then learned French when I was sent to school in French Switzerland. I've always felt at home in Europe.

The second reason I'm here is that people kept asking me to come here. Finally I decided I'd better learn to speak and lecture in Italian. People visit Ananda Ritiro from all over the world—especially, of course, from Italy and nearby countries. The next time you visit Europe, perhaps you can visit here. I'm more or less retired now, so might find myself free enough to take you and your husband around a bit.

It was good of you to write. Best wishes on the reception of your excellent book.

Sincerely,

(*J. Donald Walters*)

December 22, 2002

Dear Amanda:

This is one of those nights I have when I wake up at 3 o'clock and can't get to sleep again. Since you're leaving for France so soon, I'll just jot down a few thoughts for you. You may not get them until your return.

First, I think you must be a very busy person, and am hesitant about intruding. But, I'm happy you answered—"finally," as you put it.

My friend is not a historian, but is the wife of a medical doctor. She does quite a bit of writing, writes well, is literate, and would enjoy a bit of a change in the subjects she writes about. I suggested, after reading Hollister's book, that this might be an interesting challenge for her, and she liked the idea. She does seem to be pursuing it, but I've no idea how far she has come.

It will be a relief to her when I tell her that Judith Green won't be writing her book on Henry. Green, from what I've read of her work, wouldn't have had nearly the human insights Hollister showed. In fact, I must say I didn't really "cotton" to her.

There are many definitions of love. To me, right at the top comes loyalty. Soon after that, friendship, practical support, good will, respect. Sentiment and desire come far down the list.

I can imagine Warren and me liking one another. That's what I feel from his book. I've felt that affinity with you, also—from your letters, and from the last chapters of his book, which I believe you said you wrote for him.

I feel an affinity with Henry, also, and must of course be careful therefore not to project. But in my own life I've learned about loyalty, and friendship. I've been in a position somewhat comparable to that of Henry—not in ruling people, obviously, but in leading many hundreds. And while I haven't land to give them, or money, or power, I've learned that by seeing and appreciating them in terms of *their* interests, rather than of my own, countless numbers feel loyal to me in a way they never would have been if I'd tried to buy them with favors.

That's what I didn't like about Judith's "insights." She seemed to think that a king could only rule with a Machiavellian attitude of buying people's support. So many historians fail to put themselves sufficiently in their subjects' shoes as human beings.

Yes, I'm busy writing. No lecturing just now. My last book, *Hope for a Better World*, will come out in a revised edition in January, and I'll ask my publisher to send you a copy (complimentary). There's a chapter on Machiavelli that I think you'll enjoy. In fact, I rather think you'll like the whole book.

Have a good trip to France, and a wonderful New Year.

Sincerely,

(J. Donald Walters)

A devotee objected to Kriyananda's
condemnation of Russian communism | 5

January 27, 1991

Dear _____:

Please bear in mind that these teachings of the Masters are practical on all levels of human existence. What I said was based on things Master spoke about. He often said that spiritual truths must be made to apply on all three levels, physical, mental, and spiritual, and he was concerned, therefore, about mundane issues as well as with Vedantic truths.

I tried to say to you when you visited here a few months ago that the real issues are not between communism and capitalism, but between total materialism and the higher view, which is increasingly being justified by modern science itself, that behind matter itself there lies a spiritual reality.

If money were truly the God of this nation, as you suggest it is, it might well behoove us, as spiritual aspirants, to leave America and reside elsewhere. But one encounters a mixture of values everywhere, and I have also found much more spiritual hunger in America than in any other country, with the possible exception of India.

I might add, also, that your battle is not with me. It is with old ideas in your own mind. Long ago you bought the idea that the communist system offered freedom and equality for all, and that aberrations of the system were the fault of individuals.

I can't believe that you thought I was condemning the Russian people. Obviously, there are good and bad people everywhere. It would be naïve, however, to claim that there cannot be repressive systems. Repression is the evil.

I believe, and Master often said, that the system in Russia is evil, because repressive. If you disagree, never mind. We are of one mind on the much more important issue, which is that spirituality, not matter worship, is the ultimate solution to human problems.

Love in Master,

A letter to a friend preparing to visit India | 6

April 24, 1972

Dear _____:

I hope you have a wonderful trip to India. You will find the poverty, dirt, and inefficiency hard to take. It may "drive you up the wall" to have to spend a half an hour to an hour in a bank just to cash a traveler's check; to wait hours for a phone call to go through; to find people saying things just to please you, rather than to be truthful.

India has become very politically minded, and has lost much of her spirituality—though, I am convinced, only temporarily. But if you can get down underneath all these distractions, and overlook the noise (bedlam is more like it), the crowds, and the confusion, you will find the age-old blessings still there.

India—the real India—is an ancient culture that has survived the disintegrating influences of time, but has endured many scars in the process. The real India is a land of forest ashrams, simple folk living close to nature, the sound of *bhajans* sweetening the night.

That India has been disrupted by the turmoil and anguish of foreign conquest and domination, by the religious fanaticism of some, and by the even more corroding influence of cynicism from the English. That India is almost hopelessly overcrowded, and unable, with its village attitude, to cope with the crowds. It is aware of its poverty and will have to go through a phase of materialism and of modernization, including urbanization, practical efficiency, and factories.

I think that the real spirit of India may burn more brightly, for a time, in America, where many Hindu souls are being born—drawn to a country that has passed through the worst of its materialism without losing its innate love of nature and of higher values. In an ashram like Ananda, the spirit of India flourishes. And in time, I am sure that India will recover her balance, and return to the kind of simple living which modern progress also makes possible.

India will always be the guru of this planet. For now, however, it may be that her teachings are sometimes better received abroad than at home.

Love,

October 23, 1998

Dear _____:

I think going on the India pilgrimage was a good thing for you, even though you feel drawn more particularly to Master's ray expressed through Ananda in America. It's rather like Michelangelo, who felt he had to study anatomy in order really to get his designs of the human body right.

India is our "background." It helps to ground us in certain aspects of our teachings that we might not "get," fully, were our exposure to them only from the American end.

Love,

April 2, 1975

Dear _____:

One of India's greatest contributions to the world has been its emphasis on non-sectarian, universal spiritual values. By "spiritual values" I refer less to religious teachings than to those universal principles which even atheists manifest—principles of truthfulness, goodwill, and the like, which have always been uplifting forces in human nature.

Many teachers have come from India, teaching (perhaps unfortunately) sectarian religion, but it is not for sectarianism that India is admired and even revered by refined people the world over. Sectarianism is rife in all countries. The particular genius of India has been rather her universal outlook, the all-embracing quality of her culture and her philosophy of life.

In divine friendship,

About an article on yoga and meditation | 9

July 23, 1990

Dear _____:

You've written a really excellent article. Congratulations!

Here are a few changes I suggest, if you're agreeable to them. Mostly they are corrections of fact, or more careful statements of thoughts of mine that you've quoted. In one or two places I've suggested rewordings for you which seem to me more accurate, but of course I don't want to presume to insist.

I have a comment to make on Georg Feuerstein's comments to you (Page 10). Yogananda was a master of yoga, which is a field in which the experts have always insisted on the importance of direct, inner experience over intellectual scholarship. He said that his mission was, in part, "to bring back the original yoga of Krishna." It seems as if his authority in this field vastly exceeds that of Feuerstein. (And I don't in any way mean to denigrate Feuerstein's scholarship.)

Kriya does mean *action*. But Lahiri Mahasaya gave it that name to point out that this is the true, internal *Karma Yoga*, without which outward action alone—and, indeed, any merely outward form of yoga—is rather like a one-legged man. Krishna, in the *Bhagavad Gita*, says, "This *body* is the field of action." Repeatedly he recommends going away for solitary meditation.

Meditation is the internal yoga. *Kriya Yoga* assists one, merely on this inner path.

Krishna speaks of the yogi as being greater than the *gyani*. "Be thou a yogi," he counsels Arjuna, and not merely, "Be thou a *gyana (jnana) yogi*," or, "Be thou a *karma yogi*." Apart from *gyana yoga* and *karma yoga*—"by-paths," as Yogananda called them, to Self-realization because they depend on individual temperament rather than on soul-perception—the *Gita* places great emphasis also on another form of yoga which was not mentioned by Feuerstein: *Bhakti Yoga*. The last chapter of the *Bhagavad Gita*, indeed, urges the devotee to reach such a high level of inner perfection that he can forsake all other spiritual practices and simply love God.

It wasn't only Paramhansa Yogananda, but all of our line of gurus—all of whom were, like Yogananda, great masters of yoga—who said that ours is the path of *Raja Yoga*: not of Kriya Yoga only, but the focusing of all forms of yoga in the inner realization that comes from direct, inner communion with God.

Those yogas which depend on a person's individual temperament have their inner side, too. At this point they, too, become universal, for they lead to the development of intuition, which is "the soul's power," as Yogananda called it, "of knowing God." Thus, they are not different from the path of *Raja Yoga*, but are like contributory streams feeding into the main river of inner, divine perception.

It is the West that, with its heritage of Aristotelian "either/or" logic, tries to separate the different approaches to truth. The Indian vision, on the contrary, of life and therefore of the spiritual path, is unitive. It took me a long time to understand this difference, and to appreciate their unitive vision as more inherently valid than our own analytical, and therefore separatist, view of reality.

You may wish to consider these points in your presentation of Yogananda's teachings, especially.

Thank you for sending us your article. I appreciate the opportunity of being, as I hope, of some help to you in this, your worthwhile contribution to the legend of Yogananda, and, besides, to the story of the impact of India's timeless teachings on the West.

In divine friendship,

About Atlas Shrugged, *by Ayn Rand* | 10

April 15, 1975

Dear _____ :

I've read Ayn Rand's book, *Atlas Shrugged*. Thank you for recommending it. I find corroboration of some of my own ideas in her book, and help from it on certain other ideas.

She's not a great novelist, nor a very profound thinker. Her characters are almost entirely either black or white: the bad, very bad; the good, absolutely good by her standards, which aren't very high.

She hasn't understood her own philosophy clearly enough, for while it is true that self-fulfillment is the underlying motive for all true creativity, and true also that the "looter" consciousness of uncreative people often masquerades as selfless dedication to the welfare of others (while in fact draining them of whatever power they may have), she misses the boat by insisting that what her main characters want is value in return for their investment.

But what *they themselves* show by their actions is that the investment itself—the creative energy they put out—is their highest and only real reward. And this, of course, is forever the mark of the truly creative spirit. The person who thinks, "What's in it for me?" lives on a much lower plane of creativity.

Ayn Rand makes an even greater mistake in equating sincere desire to help others with the "looter" consciousness of uncreative people. She's perfectly correct in the point she makes, that uncreative people have no real desire to help others, in spite of their protestations to the contrary (protestations by which they try to win the good opinion of others, to offset the low opinion they secretly hold of themselves). She's also quite right in saying that no good end is served by helping weak people in their weakness.

But she's wrong in thinking that charity can rise no higher than welfare handouts. And she's even more wrong in not realizing that by generously helping one another, without the thought of "What's in it for me?" we serve ourselves in the highest way of all, for we expand our happiness to include that of others.

This type of fulfillment is the only true motive for serving others. When it is not one's motive, service becomes not a free offering to them, but an insensitive imposition on their free will. But in equating humanitarian love, and worse still, spiritual love, with uncreative "something-for-nothing" attitudes lies Ayn Rand's greatest mistake. And this error makes it possible for her book to do much harm, as well as much good.

For there are many people who, seeing the evil that is communism (and she does a magnificent job of tearing to shreds its tangle of lies), imagine that the cure for communism lies entirely in the free-enterprise system. Unfortunately, not all truly creative industrialists, etc., are so "simon pure" as her black-and-white view of things suggests. Some of the most dynamic and creative of men have been ruthless destroyers as well, driving competitors out of business by unscrupulous means simply because their guiding rule was the thought, "What's in it for me?"

Ayn Rand believes it is the voting power of the weak, uncreative majority that gives politicians their real strength, and that it is by this strength that legislation gets passed against the interest of big business. But in fact, it is money that gives those politicians their power, that buys their influence on crucial legislation, and that topples them again when they rebel. The people like to think they have the final say, and in theory of course they do have it, but in practice it is money that makes possible the propaganda that directs most of their thinking. The weakness of democracy lies not only in the fact that so many people don't really know what's best for them (better that, anyway, than having someone equally ignorant telling them!), but in the fact that they have no sure way of knowing what they're getting when they vote.

The supposed enemies of socialism are the rich. But an enormous body of evidence forces the all-but-unavoidable conclusion that it is the very rich who have financed socialism and communism from their very inception, and who have been the most influential in the enactment of the socialist legislation that has become so epidemic in this country and elsewhere! And it is the free-enterprise system that has made possible this great wealth!

I am very much a supporter of free enterprise, and of the least possible interference by government in the affairs of men. But Ayn Rand's emphasis on the "What's-in-it-for-me?" attitude supports those very aspects of the free-enterprise system which have justified certain people in self-aggrandizement at the expense of others. She has helped to make the conservative cause what it is today—an encampment for another kind of bullies, merely—for people who want to impose their philosophy on others just as much as the so-called "liberals" want to impose theirs. The very effort to impose in any way on the free will of others is the first step toward that kind of monopolistic thinking that has been the breeding-ground for everything evil in modern socialism.

The error, it seems to me, lies in making a virtue of self-aggrandizement, as Ayn Rand does, instead of seeing that the real moral value lies in self-fulfillment. The solution lies not in new (or old) systems, but in helping people to develop the right expectations of life. Such help is possible, for it is only through wrong teachings that people have come to the point of holding such wrong expectations as they do (the thought, for example, that material security is everything). Books such as Ayn Rand's have a tremendous influence on people's minds, and consequently on their actions. The greatest war being fought in our times lies in the realm of ideas. What happens outwardly is only symptomatic of this inner war.

I was, as I said, most impressed with the case Ayn Rand makes against communism and its endless self-deception and insidious corrosion of all that is honest and honorable in human nature.

And of course, I was intrigued with her vision of an ideal, creative community, cut off from a society bent on destroying itself with "looter" consciousness. My practical mind couldn't help doubting that so many dynamic minds could really live happily together in one place. (The failure of Brook Farm community, in the last century, was due mainly to the fact that too many intellectuals and creative thinkers were working together to form the "ideal society.") But that's a quibble. In fact, I had almost exactly the same idea for a novel of my own, when I was fifteen. That was when I actually started planning to establish a community myself, someday.

I hope you won't think I'm merely "putting down" Ayn Rand's book. I found it a rewarding experience, and one that helped to clarify some of my own thinking, and I'm grateful to you for suggesting it. It is because it stimulated me that I've felt inspired to jot down these thoughts, somewhat hastily, while the impression of the book is still fresh in my mind. And whom could I most rightly share them with, but you?

In divine friendship,

October 12, 1999

Dear _____:

Thank you for getting the book to me. And, yes, I completely agree with your assessment of Ayn Rand. I've really no use for her philosophy, which I consider outrageous. So outrageous, in fact, that sometimes it's good to get a glimpse of how the "opposition" thinks. I did like her first book, *We, the Living*. Same philosophy, though muted, and an excellent explanation of the corrupting influence of the false "religion" of communism she grew up with, in Russia.

Otherwise, yes, she's a lightweight philosophically, and I've never been interested in reading this book. But now I've read so many political and financial newsletters praising at least one aspect of it that I'm intrigued. As a person, she must have been high energy, but insufferable.

In divine friendship,

August 30, 2000

Dear _____:

Your letter brought me much pleasure, and also some trepidation. First of all, I want to say that I am most happy to see your interest in the *Education for Life* concept. I wasn't aware that others have used the expression, but I am happy if, as appears from your letter, they have.

I believe that concepts should not carry persons' names, as with the Montessori system. Truth is truth: No one has a right to claim it as his own.

Thus, from the outset let me say that the more people like you can carry this most needed idea to others, the better. If the public schools can accept even a small part of it, that will be better than nothing. If anyone else wants to take the idea and call it his own, I really don't mind at all. Truth alone is what counts. My one concern would be that he not dilute it with ideas that defeat the basic concept.

The education needs I see today are:

1. Modern schooling breeds atheism. Without going into all the reasons for that claim, the results are, I believe, self-evident. Children are raised without moral or spiritual values; as a result, they become cynical, angry, anti-social, and selfish.
The high suicide rate among the young is due to a large extent, I think, to the fact that modern education gives them nothing to believe in. The greatest need of this age is to believe in God again. Modern education *is* essentially atheistic.

2. Children need to be taught values. But if moral values are left on a level of social or personal convenience, they are not "values." They are merely schemes for self-betterment.
The greatest defect in modern education is the modern *dogma*—that's all it is—that spirituality must necessarily be considered sectarian, a matter of beliefs, and therefore not scientific and not a proper subject for education.

The human race has been around a long time, however, and has learned by experience that certain kinds of behavior, and certain attitudes, work and also that certain others don't work. They "work" in the sense that they provide what everyone wants: happiness, fulfillment, an expansion of understanding, inner peace, and success in one's undertakings.

Other kinds of behavior, and other attitudes are negative basically because they produce the opposite results—not always quickly, but definitely so in time.

3. Spirituality needs to be separated from mere beliefs, and founded on people's experience of what actually works. In this sense, spirituality should be taught not dogmatically, but scientifically, which is to say, experientially.

4. Education needs to be geared not only toward helping children to become successful in their work once they grow up, but above all to become successful human beings. And success in this respect means, again, that which gives them what they *really* want in life: happiness, and other acquisitions I've mentioned.

5. The belief that understanding is only of the mind, not of the heart, needs to be balanced by a realization that heart-felt understanding is not a matter of emotion, but of intuition. Intuition strikes much closer to truth than intellectual analysis ever can. And love can understand far more, even in scientific fields, than most people are willing to believe. They think understanding comes by definition. It doesn't. It comes by experience.

6. Music should be, as Plato taught, an important part of every child's education, for only through music can the child "get the point" of any teaching of better ways of living, thinking, and being, by *feeling* their reality instead of being merely able to define them.

Well, I've tossed off the above ideas quickly, though of course I've thought and written about them for many years, so I don't mean to say they've come simply "off the top of my head." But if I were to think longer in the present context, I'd probably come up with several other basic needs in education today. And indeed I think I've covered them also fairly well in my book, which you've read, *Education for Life*.

As I said, I am not familiar with other methods of education similar to what I've presented. The need is there, however, so it would not surprise me if others have tuned in to that need.

I come now to the part in all this that has me feeling some trepidation. Your approach to these things, and mine, seem to me to be poles apart. I am grateful for yours, and believe the *Education for Life* system needs people like you to make it known and accepted.

You ask me about other schools, other writers and educators, other ways of doing things, and of course you have every reason to expect me to be knowledgeable about these things. The plain truth is, I am not. I have never even taught children! My understanding of life comes from experience, and from thought and meditation on that experience.

So, to your questions:

1. Our schools are fairly new. I don't think many people know about them. Those who do, however, have been very well impressed. As for the other traditions you mention, individual teachers in them have loved what we do, but I doubt that we've had much influence on the movements themselves—not because of any lack of interest, but because they are busy "doing their thing," as we are busy doing ours.

2. I don't think other religious traditions know what we're doing in education. I've told our own schools, "Don't limit yourselves by being parochial." Therefore we've named them, "Living Wisdom Schools," rather than "Ananda Schools."

3. I think my (our) philosophy of education could be of universal value. The block to their acceptance is not the usefulness of our system, but people's commitment to other ways, and the government's absurd commitment to banishing spiritual principles from the schools in the mistaken belief that spirituality is the same thing as sectarianism. (Is kindness only a *Christian* belief? or a Muslim? Is kindness excluded from atheism?)

4. We have, not two, but five Living Wisdom schools, and hope to start another here in Assisi, Italy. So far, all of them are connected with our communities, but we are trying, with some success, to give them a separate identity of their own. We'd love to have non-Ananda teachers join our staffs. We'd love to have people of other religions do so. We are not religious. Our focus, to reiterate, is spiritual. Many of the parents of the children in our schools are not Ananda members and, as far as we know,

haven't even thought of becoming members. Many of these people, however, are among our schools' most ardent supporters.

5. I have 175 editions of my various books published in some 23 foreign languages, as well as American editions that sell abroad. I don't know how many translations there are of *Education for Life*. Few, I suspect. People don't think of me as an educator of children; therefore, they'll grow interested only in time. Too bad, because to me the education of children is of crucial importance.

But what I am doing, and my Guru Paramhansa Yogananda did, is work with long rhythms that will have an influence on our culture only in decades, and perhaps in centuries. Someone asked Buckminster Fuller once, "Don't you get a little discouraged, talking everywhere but seeing so few actual results?" He bravely replied, "Not at all! All new ideas take at least one generation, and often two, before they begin to take hold." He was 84 at the time!

6. (You didn't give me a sixth question, but I thought I'd add an answer as though you had.) Yogananda founded a school in Ranchi, India, on which others have been patterned in that country. I don't think many of them are doing much in the direction Yogananda wanted, because they made the mistake of inviting government funding. Nonetheless, there has been good energy in this direction also. I regret to say that I am not current on it.

I very much hope your conference does all the good in which we both believe.

With sincere best wishes,

(J. Donald Walters)

November 20, 2000

Dear _____:

Here are a few hasty answers to your questions.

As for astrology, I believe it is based on true principles, but is greatly over-used and over-depended on. I wrote *Your Sun Sign as a Spiritual Guide,* also, to help inspire people to direct a "craze" more validly. In fact, after nearly thirty years, it is still considered by many people to be a classic in its field.

What I found was that most writers on the subject had gone from assumptions on the sun signs to blanket statements about the people in those signs. However, I simply couldn't relate what they wrote to the people I knew. So I meditated on people I knew in each sign, and tried to intuit qualities that they all had in common. I tried to lift the subject to a more spiritual level.

I do believe there's truth in the subject, because Yogananda's guru was an inspired, and infallibly right, astrologer. But I must say, I haven't seen much come out of the predictions that various astrologers over the years have made for me! Still, as a guide to spiritual progress I think that book has done a lot of good.

I wrote *How To Be a Channel* to try to correct the channeling craze. I'm not at all in favor of mediumship. I wrote the book to get people to try to "channel" God and truth.

In divine friendship,

To a professional astrologer,
discussing Kriyananda's book,
Your Sun Sign as a Spiritual Guide

14

March 18, 1971

Dear _____:

The sun-sign book, which I thought I would toss off quickly in a week, is still not completed. I have only finished Leo, and am evolving ideas as I go along that will necessitate my rewriting Aries and Taurus to some extent.

Specifically, I am universalizing each sign by addressing myself not only to Geminis, Leos, etc., but also to the Gemini, Leo, etc., in all of us—because, of course, we all manifest these various traits to some extent. One of the fascinating things about the signs is how they pin-point basic, universal characteristics in man.

One thing I am realizing is that the reason I have felt subconsciously im-pelled to work on these signs is that it helps me to understand different types of people better, and to see that a piece of advice which might be good for one person would be confusing and unhelpful to another. In line with this thought, I am giving different kinds of spiritual advice under each sign, even with techniques of meditation. It is turning into a book of spiritual counsel!

I am trying to stay away from the idea of "types." People have all these traits; some manifest more of certain traits than of others, but, essentially, we are NONE of these traits, but ever-perfect souls.

I think that what I have found most unsatisfactory in astrology books I have read, especially with regard to the sun signs, is the impression I get that the writers are thinking so much in terms of this "type" and that "type" of person that they forget to think of people as people. The result is that they don't go deeply enough into human nature; all they do is skate about on the surface. One does not get an impression of a human being as seen from within.

And yet, after all, I may realize when I've got it all done that I am only being presumptuous to think that I can contribute anything valid in a field to which so many people have devoted their lives.

Yet I have the strong impression that when I take up any subject, I have only to put my mind on it deeply enough in meditation, and all sorts of new and valid answers come. I find that this is the way, more than by a lot of fact gathering, that I arrive at understanding. I believe that a mere handful of facts, meditated on deeply, will supply one with far greater in-sights than thousands of facts, with no time left after gathering them to meditate on their significance. Even one fact, deeply enough understood, will often suffice to explain thousands of other facts.

With this thought in mind, I wanted to write to you not only to report on my progress with the book, but to ask your thoughts on some ideas that have been coming to me.

I've been puzzling over the meaning of one's rising sign. I know it is sup-posed to govern one's physical appearance—at least to some extent—and to indicate the way we present ourselves to the world, or the way that others see us.

I've always had three objections to these explanations:

1) They are all superficial considerations, yet the rising sign is so important that it alone determines the placement of all houses, and therefore the departments of our lives in relation to the positions of the planets;

2) The way others see us is entirely a matter of what they are looking for, or what they are prepared to see; some will see more our sun characteristics, others more our moon, etc. This is, therefore, entirely too vague an explanation to be of any use at all;

3) The way we present ourselves to the world is not only vague, but also suggests something I don't believe: that we always present ourselves before others with a mask over our faces. Certainly one of the main ways we present ourselves to the world is through our sun signs, which more often than not are very different from our rising signs. And that is why this explanation also is vague. We present ourselves in different ways for different purposes. To say that our rising sign indicates the way in which we present ourselves doesn't give us a strong enough handle to enable us to carry any weight; it is not useful. And of course, it is mildly insulting. We are not all duplicitous!

For these reasons I've never been able to include the rising sign seriously in my thinking. Yet I've known it must be important. So last night I meditated on it, specifically with regard to myself and to two or three other people whose rising signs I know. (You see what I mean about a paucity of facts! I know very few people's rising signs.) And here is what came to me:

My own rising sign is Gemini. (It HAS to be, even though the official time, 7:00 a.m., puts it at 2:19' Cancer.) Very few people see me as a Gemini, yet in my own mind Gemini suggests very aptly my way of handling problems—sort of sending them shooting up into the air, refusing to be tied down to traditional answers and solutions.

Gemini indicates the way I perceive things: analyzing them with a view to finding new angles of approach; interest in many things, but always from a standpoint of the ideas they provide me with, not for the things themselves; a capacity for sustaining numerous unrelated interests at one time, and to enter with enthusiasm into each one of them as soon as I put my mind to it.

Gemini suggests not only the face I show to the world (perhaps it does that), but rather the way I face the world, from inside my own mind. Even that definition won't suffice, because I can face the world with several intentions. If, in seeking to exert my authority over others, I am also facing the world, I am yet acting through my sun sign. So a closer word would be the way I perceive the world. Yet even this is not enough; I perceive it also through my inner attitudes, which are suggested by my moon sign.

What is the rising sign? It determines the placement of my houses, or life departments. This means that it's in my ninth house, my "house of religion," that I receive Jupiter's rays. In my tenth house I receive the combined rays of Mars and Uranus (in my solar horoscope; Venus in my sidereal chart). *Receiving*, surely, is the key word: How we receive our impressions of the world, including the challenges and problems with which it presents us. This definition includes the way we face or perceive the world from a standpoint purely of receptive consciousness.

This definition doesn't contradict the more common ones, for the way we receive our impressions determines also our immediate, superficial reactions to them. Yet it doesn't limit the influence of the rising sign to these superficial reactions.

If an impression (or a situation, or anything external) is important enough for us to want to react to it by impressing our authority outwardly in return, we take it deep inside first, gather our forces, and then come out with a reaction that is very different, usually, from the quick, superficial reaction that was only a sign of the way we had received the impression (news, remark, challenge, or whatever). This deeper reaction will, of course, follow the influence of our sun sign.

As I think of it, I see that there HAS to be this receptivity provided for in the chart, to counterbalance the externalizing flow of the sun sign. The moon, though receptive, doesn't quite tell the whole story, since it indicates our subjective reactions.

In fact, the moon seems to play a dual role. It indicates not only the attitude with which we view the subject of authority (or let me say, rather, the personal attitude with which we view it), but also the personal attitude that we bring to bear on the impressions we receive. In other words, I not only receive my impressions of the world through a filter of ideas and creative questions; my personal attitude toward these ideas is distinctly Leonine (my moon being, as you know, in Leo). What they mean to me, the special interest they hold for me, is how I can use them to spread enlightenment to other people.

The way in which I externalize myself (impress my authority) is Taurean in its persistence, etc., but my personal attitude, again, indicates the special interest this work holds for me, which is Leonine: the wish to share, to enlighten.

So we see that the moon is the pivotal point between the rising sign and the sun sign. Our personal attitude lends the color of special meaning that we give to the impressions we receive, to our perceptions of the world around us; our personal attitude, again, determines the way we, in turn, seek to impress ourselves on the world.

Sidereally, my own case is not a good example, because only my moon changes signs; rising and sun signs remain the same. Yet it is true that, though I am still a Gemini in the way I receive my impressions of reality, my personal attitude toward those impressions is definitely Cancerian, not Leonine. And I think as I view other people whom I know, that this definition holds up, that the sidereal placements are more in keeping with our relationship to reality and the universe.

For a real consideration of the houses, therefore, I think one should work with the sidereal chart, as these concern our relationship to the totality of life, and not only to the solar question of how we shall impose our authority on others. (In this last sense, Mars and Uranus belong in my tenth house, which is where they are tropically; but in the previous, more universal sense, Mars belongs with Jupiter in my ninth house, which is where it is sidereally.)

I'd really appreciate your views on this, so that if I'm really off base I can know it before I commit any horrible blunders in the book I'm writing. But I must say, it feels completely right to me, and clarifies things that were never clear before without contradicting anything that has been claimed for the rising signs by long tradition.

By the way, on the subject of Solar Returns, isn't the position of everything on one's birthday of that year supposed to indicate the trend of the whole subsequent year? Am I to take it from this that those influences haven't yet begun, and won't begin until May 19 (my birthdate)? And that Saturn's placement right over my sun at that time is an influence that will hang over me for one whole year thereafter, even after Saturn has drifted off into Gemini the following month?

In divine friendship,

P.S. People who don't so much externalize themselves (exert their authority), and who are by nature more receptive than aggressive, may manifest in their lives more their rising signs than their sun signs. Right?

"In all situations relating to interpersonal matters, human feelings are an essential consideration—

LEADERSHIP

so much so that reason is never the whole, or even the primary issue."

Dear _____:

The most important thing to keep in mind is that no position and no talent is more important than any other in God's eyes. We are all of us simply serving God. It is our honor to be able to do well whatever He gives us to do, but it is not our glory. It is good, in fact, for leaders deliberately to take on serviceful jobs occasionally—cooking, sweeping, washing dishes—simply to keep that perspective clear.

I remember once in Encinitas a group of us monks were leaving for Mt. Washington in a van that had only two seats, in the front. Those sitting in the back had to make do with cushions. Dr. Lewis, seeing me sitting in the back, said, "You ought to be up front." "Why?" I asked. "Because," he replied, "you're in charge of the other monks." "For that very reason," I replied, "my place is here in back." I was surprised that he couldn't see the obviousness of my reasoning. But then, he'd been a dentist all his life, and not in a position of leadership over others.

Try drawing the others out. Ask for their advice, for instance, whenever possible, even if you don't really feel you need it. This is a way of making others feel included.

If possible also, let them have the last word. That is to say, let them feel that you accept their suggestions, even if you've already had the same ideas before even asking them. After all, what does it matter where the idea comes from, or who had it?

It's important not to give the impression that you've thought the whole thing through already and they were simply agreeing with your own conclusions. This kind of response leaves the other person thinking, "Why bother to make suggestions, if they are neither needed nor wanted?" This is not a good way of developing team spirit, nor of encouraging leadership qualities in others. It is much better, as I said, to leave others thinking that an idea is theirs, even if in fact you've already had it yourself.

The important thing, in this context, is not to be swayed from your own inner center, and not to accept ideas that are likely to put your overall plans at risk. Within the larger framework, however, it is often possible to go along with second or even third-rate ideas without risking anything serious, if in the process there's a chance of helping to develop in others a greater sense of responsibility.

It is also important to have the patience to draw others into *your* creative flow. Otherwise you'll find them grumbling that *their* energy and creativity seem to be held cheap. And of course you don't mean to do that at all. So give them a chance to shine.

As for yourself, don't ever think of shining. Just think of doing as well as possible whatever needs to be done, and of getting others to help you do it.

I find this helps even when something so dependent on my own creativity is involved as writing music, or a book. Suggestions from others may always prove helpful. Often, I admit, the feedback I get strains my patience, and I have to remind myself that it is God's work, not mine, and that He may indeed, sometimes, say something useful through others.

As a matter of fact, He often does. Mine, then, is the job of sifting, and of not allowing myself to be drawn out of the inspiration I feel in the project. This takes effort, sometimes, and a strong hold on patience and will power, but I've found it proves worthwhile on many levels—to the project itself, and to the overall dynamic of group spirit.

May Master bless you always.

Love,

June 27, 1998

Dear _____:

Here is a thought you might find helpful, one that you could share also with others. In delegating authority, don't just turn a job over to others, as if "washing your hands" of it. Expand your consciousness, rather, to include them and what they are doing in that job. Make them and what they do a part of your own reality.

This doesn't mean overseeing everything they do too meticulously. It doesn't mean breathing down their necks, as it were. Simply offer them your spirit, as if to sustain them. Those who tune in to you will, in this way, do things better, will accomplish more, and will unite to create a harmonious whole in the overall work instead of becoming separate entities, each going his own direction.

Love and Joy!

Advice to project leaders on winning others | 3

Dear _____:

They're all of them doing their best, as also are we. Correcting them will work best if it comes FROM them, rather than TO them. As I hinted to you on the phone, let's forget about weeding the garden. It's big, and could make us weed-conscious rather than flower-conscious. Let's work rather on developing our own little patch, and on making it beautiful.

The more successful we are in those efforts, the more the others will tune into that direction and follow it as well as they are able. But if we try to tell them how to proceed, especially if our advice isn't earnestly sought, they'll only become tense, thinking, "Are they trying to tell me I'm wrong?"

I think the three of you will make a great team—especially if you work together with love and joy, lightheartedly, even good-humoredly, about any differences between you and others. These differences, as we know by now from a long life of trying, are simply bound to arise, and in fact needn't always be a bad thing.

I suggest that you let others have their own space to come around in their own way, and in their own time. The change, to the extent that it happens, may take a few of them several months. What of it? If we ourselves do a good thing and don't give anyone the slightest impression of self-righteousness, I think we'll build up a magnetism that will draw everyone into a new vortex.

This music scene is so important, I'm very anxious that it be approached harmoniously. Moreover, this is the only way to make it work. And I think it can work gloriously—to everyone's lasting joy.

Humor is often the best nectar for making things work. It often does so much more effectively than strong medicine.

Love,

On letting change take place gradually | 4

August 6, 1998

Dear _____ :

I'd like to make a further point: Don't feel that you have to change things drastically. It is always best to let change take place gradually and naturally. People need above all to grow into new ideas. So don't feel pressured. It's enough to know that this is a desirable DIRECTION to go in.

Love,

Cautions an Ananda colony leader not to fear offending wealthy parishioners | 5

November 7, 2002

Dear _____ :

I hope you like the version of chapter three [of *God Is for Everyone*], sent this morning, better than the one I sent you yesterday. I confess, however, to a slight uneasiness in your reaction. I would not like to see you develop the tendency, so common to priests and ministers everywhere, of fearing to offend your more wealthy parishioners on the matter of material possessions.

I don't agree with you on the subject of making this story taboo because it deals with creativity. Creativity too, after all, is part of delusion, as long as it springs from egoic desire.

Love,

June 13, 2000

Dear _____ :

By now I have heard several views on these funds. I think the best thing you can do at this point is give it to _____, or to _____, to be put into a fund specifically marked for _____, and step out of any position that could, or might, be regarded as controlling. The bad blood that might result from not doing so could damage many other things in future relations. The good blood from this concession, on the other hand, could help those same things in future relations.

Money has many times throughout history been a cause of conflict and strife. The human element—the friendship, trust, and harmony—is more important than money. And though you yourself feel that this is precisely what you may not feel certain of having in them, if you don't "bite this bullet" you'll damage things irreparably for the future. It isn't worth it.

They, too, want what you want, and I'm very sure at this point that they'll never spend that money for any other purpose. They will, however, remember that you didn't trust them to, and the more conscientious they are about fulfilling their side of the bargain the greater the bitterness that will remain in their hearts.

At present, I should add, there is no bitterness. But I see clouds on the horizon. In all situations relating to inter-personal matters, human feelings are an essential consideration—so much so that reason is never the whole, or even the primary issue.

You have your own feelings; they have theirs. Were you to back off, I think it would go a long way toward smoothing other things, in future.

Love,

January 15, 2001

Dear _____ :

I am distressed that _____ has not told me the whole story. He gives me whatever he thinks will please me. But what can please me, really? Only this: to see things done in a godly way. Otherwise, what is the point of the music itself?

At any rate, don't hesitate to do what is right, *dharmically.* I know you both believe in the music, and don't discount its importance. But we believe in God and Guru, first. If the music scene doesn't serve the cause of *dharma,* it cannot be pleasing to God and Guru, and has no more value than a speck of dust.

Leaving my personal feelings out of the picture, then, but understanding rather that my feelings support whatever is right, don't fear to do whatever you have to do.

Love,

"I would say
we are <u>true</u> Christians,
and <u>true</u> Hindus,

YOGA &
CHRISTIANITY

---

and <u>true</u> anything
that holds that
divine truth is inward,
not institutional."

November 3, 2000

Dear _____ :

Your question is very easy to answer, but more difficult to understand. However, I think you'll understand without difficulty.

What we teach is not at all a mixture. Yogananda taught that truth is one and eternal. Christ taught it. Krishna taught it. We have Christ on our altar, and have deep devotion to him. In fact, Yogananda told us Jesus had appeared to Babaji, our first guru (after Jesus himself) in the Himalayas and asked him to send someone to the West to bring people his inner teachings.

I don't know whether you've read *Autobiography of a Yogi*, or my book, *The Path*, which is about my life with Yogananda. I would say we are *true* Christians, and *true* Hindus, and *true* anything that holds that divine truth is inward, not institutional.

In the same way, speaking personally, I don't really belong to any nationality, though my passport is American. I was born in Romania, of American parents; lived there thirteen years; have lived in many countries including India. Above all, however, I feel myself to be a citizen of the world, and manage pretty well to get along in eight or so languages. Here [Assisi, Italy] I lecture in Italian, but I've also lectured in French, Spanish, and some German. English is, of course, my mother tongue. I speak Bengali and Hindi, though not well because educated Indians mostly speak English and wouldn't let me converse with them in their own languages! Romanian I've pretty well forgotten, though I could pick it up again in a month or so if I had a reason to.

As for religion, it isn't that I'm against institutions. They certainly have their place. But for myself, my interest and devotional direction is Self-realization, viewing God, not the ego, as our true Self. Finding God, and helping others to find Him, is my only interest in life. Other interests are all subordinate to that aim.

I hoped, here in Italy, to develop some sort of dialogue with the Church. But I was severely rebuffed by the local bishop; since then I have stopped attending their church services and bow to them in my heart, only, from afar.

I lived for six months at New Camaldoli, near Big Sur, California. They were hoping I'd convert to Catholicism and join their order, but I could not have done so sincerely. I respect the Catholic monastic orders, however, and particularly that one, and I feel at least in spirit that we are working toward the same ends.

I think, however, that by the local church authorities I am viewed, if not with hostility, at least with considerable suspicion and reservation. Thousands come yearly to the retreat I have founded; they bring money to the area, and visit the pilgrimage spots (the Porziuncola, etc.) with deep devotion, but they are considered—well, different.

I think the day will come when the Church considers me and what I stand for to be a major threat. That day hasn't come yet, and I'd love to think it never will, for we don't in fact threaten anyone. We represent, however, a dynamic teaching, and the bishop thinks in terms of holding his flock together under the outspread wing of the Church. That is not my faith or my interest.

In divine friendship,

A follow-up to the previous letter | 2

November 3, 2000

Dear _____:

Again I want to emphasize that what we teach is not a mixture of anything. I say this because I know this is the concern of modern Catholic theologians. It is a teaching *essential* to all religions. That is, it addresses their essence. Much could be said on the subject, if you're interested in pursuing it.

As for your earlier letter, on the subject of openness to other religions: Yes, I told the local bishop [Assisi, Italy] that I myself loved to go to mass, and encouraged our people to do so; said (and always say) that these (Ananda's) teachings make people better Christians, etc., and that I have never tried to convert people. His response to me was, shall we say, unsettling. I've never gone to church again, except to meditate in the Porziuncola, nor have I urged anyone else to do so.

That doesn't mean I'm hostile. After the earthquake here in 1997, a little village nearby was virtually demolished, and their historic little church was destroyed. I offered to raise the money to build them a temporary chapel, with the suggestion that if and when the little church (really, just a chapel) was rebuilt the one we'd built could be used as a meeting hall or a schoolroom.

Months later I got a letter from the bishop saying, in effect, "On the 18th of this month [March, 1998] I am scheduled to consecrate a newly-constructed, temporary chapel in the village of Isola (the village here referred to), which will later be used as a meeting hall once the old church has been rebuilt." Great idea! thought I. One can't get much of a sound out of only one hand clapping!

I suspect, and have heard, that the Catholic Church in America is more open in its attitudes. The Church here tries, but there are many factions. The local bishop is one of the rigid conservatives.

In divine friendship,

On responding to dogmatic attitudes | 3

January 26, 1988

Dear _____:

I am deeply concerned about the remarks of the bishop of Assisi [Italy]. I don't think it will suffice to gloss over his reaction to us by telling him once more that people who come to us become better Catholics. In many cases they do. Nor do we convert people away from the Church. No harm in saying these things, because they are true.

However, we've said them before, and the bishop is reacting as though we hadn't spoken. I think he is getting heavy energy from the priest in San

Presto. It's a pity I never went to see that man. I think also that we must take this as something God has sent us—a test, certainly, but one that can strengthen us if we meet it with faith and good cheer.

It is important, I think, not to lose our own inner center when dealing with this matter. We can lose it if we assume too much of an attitude of wanting to reassure the bishop, and that local priest. I think we are going to have to be strong in ourselves, and in our inner convictions. It is possible this thing will build up into determined persecution of us, but the more we stand our own ground instead of trying to meet them on theirs, the less they will be able to touch us.

After all, the Communists, the Masons, and any number of groups are actively hostile to the Catholic Church, and have been able to hold their ground. We are in no way hostile; in fact, we deeply appreciate all that the Church has done. Virtually, we are in *their* camp!

The difficulty is that through our very similarity to them, and openness to them, they may be able to strike at us. It is important not to try to speak their language—that is to say, not to enter into the sort of dialogue where we hope to persuade them of the deep ties we feel with them.

It's too bad, but they have developed their arguments over centuries to the point where, if we try to speak their language, we will find the doors of logic utterly closed to us. They will try to force us to use their definitions, their theological language, and to reason according to their premises. In their own field they reign supreme. Their weak point is that they are talking to themselves.

We have no choice but to leave them there, while following our own lines of reasoning. Silence, not reasoned argument, is I think our strongest force at present, until such time as a few of them show a willingness to speak with us a *shared* language. The bishop is, obviously, incapable of doing so, has no desire to do so, and almost certainly is unaware that any language but his own even exists.

Love,

Late 1980s

Dear _____ :

I was happy to get your letter, and the article you wrote for your congregation.

Your article was interesting, but may I suggest another emphasis? The Vedantic view of reality is really only for those very few who are deeply versed in the furthest subtleties of Hindu thought. Few spokesmen, even for Hinduism, would be able to relate to this division between communion and union as you have described it. Most would be more comfortable with communion than with union, and even if they recognize Vedanta as expressing the highest truth, their concern is with more immediate realities, which can be conceived primarily in dualistic terms.

The real difference between West and East lies in the more *active, outward* emphasis in Western teaching, as opposed to the more *passive-seeming*, because *inward*, emphasis in Eastern teaching. The Westerner is not so much inclined to *commune* with his neighbor as actively to reach out and share with him, or serve him. The Easterner is more inclined to commune with him inwardly. The Western emphasis is on doing; the Eastern, on deepening one's sense of being.

The time has come in the evolution of civilization for these twin ideals to be united.

Incidentally, when I was studying the New Testament in Greek, at college, our professor pointed out that the true meaning of "Love thy neighbor as thyself" is, "Love thy neighbor; he is like you." A Vedantic rendition would be, "Love thy neighbor: He is a manifestation of thy greater Self."

Thanks for writing, _____ and blessings to you.

In divine friendship,

Dear _____:

You speak of the "tension" between "elements" in Christian spirituality and elements in Eastern spirituality. I read something the other day that struck me as a particularly good point for people experiencing stress in their lives. In paraphrase, what the writer said was, "Stress is a perception of reality." I would say the same thing of your use of the word "tension." There is no tension between the teachings of Jesus and of Krishna, or of any of the great masters. The tension arises in our efforts to *understand* their teachings.

Always, when I contemplate the deeper teachings, my first question is, "What did my own Guru say?" Second, "What did our other Masters, including Jesus, say?" Third, "What do the scriptures say?" My basic and unshakable conviction is that contradictions cannot exist in the teachings of the truly wise. The difficulties come in our interpretations.

My second question is, "What example did my Guru set?" For it often happened that he clarified by his example points that were not readily understandable in his writings. Master is, if you will, my "bottom line," but if a point is not yet clear then I will refer also to the examples of other teachers, as a means of understanding Master's message more clearly.

There are many ways of presenting the truth. We'd only get confused if we tried to follow, or even to justify, them all. Master's is the way God wanted the truth presented for this age, and for us, his disciples. I never challenge him with the objection that other masters *seem* to have presented it differently.

The Hindu teachings have a reputation for being world-rejecting. And, in fact, there are teachers in India who have emphasized a world-rejecting attitude. The *Bhagavad Gita*, however, which is the scripture we follow, states at a certain point, "*By works alone*, Janaka and others of the ancients attained Me." The teaching that all is a dream must be paired with the understanding that it is *God's dream*, and therefore inherently right and just. It is we who, by confusing the plot, make the dream ugly.

We read Master's emphasis on matter as being a dream, but we don't see him refusing to take responsibility for his role in the dream. He did more work than ten, or a hundred, other men. Many of those, on the other hand, who work out exquisite definitions of God's involvement in the world, etc., don't show nearly the power to transform the people whose lives they touch.

God in the world—God beyond the world—God involved or not involved: What does it all matter in the long run? One breath of divine love, and theology ceases to be relevant.

I think I work better for being non-attached to the fruits of my labor than I would if I let my ego get involved. I wouldn't work nearly so hard if I didn't feel an intense desire to help people to find what they themselves are looking for: joy in their lives, peace, understanding, and love.

In Master's love,

About Jesus and the Bible | 6

April 6, 1998

Dear _____:

Everything I read about the life and teachings of Jesus shows him to have been a complete *sannyasi* [renunciate], and to have taught the way of *sannyas*. The kingdom of God, he said, should not be sought "here" or "there," for the kingdom of God is within. Take no heed for tomorrow, he said, for God knows your every need.

Even his teaching to love one's neighbor as oneself is linked to the first commandment: to love God with all one's heart, soul, mind, and strength. "Seek ye first the kingdom of God," he said, "and all things else shall be added unto you."

Jesus shows infinite love and compassion, but shows no approval for worldliness, even of the type you describe. Rather, he said, "Be ye therefore perfect even as your Father in heaven is perfect." Even his descriptions of heaven are not of the astral heaven of popular fancy, but they fit perfectly the ideal of cosmic consciousness. (An example he used was the parable of the mustard seed.)

As I read the Bible, Jesus was looking for souls that were pure and wanted God rather than going out among the masses as, himself, a man of the masses.

Last evening I saw a beautiful and inspiring movie called, *A Man Called Peter*, about the life of the minister, Peter Marshall. It is well worth seeing. Still, that doesn't mean I went along with everything Marshall said. For example, he described Jesus in one sermon as very much a man of the people, with his big carpenter's hands and his "fellowshipping"—a man, in short, rather like Peter Marshall himself, the subject of the movie.

I see nothing in the Bible to support such a view of Jesus. Nor do I believe that such a man would have had the magnetism to launch a new religion. Jesus was a man of God, trying to draw as many as had "ears to hear" to the divine quest. He converted Mary Magdalene because she was ready in her soul. He forgave the woman taken in adultery, but he didn't condone the adultery. What Jesus was teaching in that story is that we should not judge one another.

You say that creation is "good, good, good." What do you mean by "good"? Is it good, for instance, that the moose in the Alaskan tundra suffer agonies from the stings of insects and from internal parasites, through no karmic fault, evidently, of their own? Is it "good" that there is suffering everywhere, along with—I grant you—joy? Was it wrong of Krishna to say to Arjuna, "Get away from My ocean of suffering and misery"?

By "good" you can't mean "good" as we human beings understand the word. And if not, the word loses meaning for us. This, to me, is a generalization that doesn't hold up under inspection.

Creation is good in that it carries out God's design, but that design, as I see it, is that it affords Life the opportunity to evolve to the point where Life, through man, discovers the long-hidden secret of existence.

Man is sinful, but man is also the crowning achievement of creation, and a wonderful achievement for all his stumbling, sinning, and struggling. It is his final end in God that is wonderful, not his ignorant fumbling while he voyages. Yes, of course truth is life affirming, but Life with a capital L.

Does God really reveal himself through our fears, etc., as you say? To this extent only: that through our fogs of delusion there is still the light of Truth. But I do not accept that human suffering is itself a revelation of God's presence; it is only a revelation of our need, and perhaps of our conscious longing, for Him.

Another thing I cannot and do not accept is that any truth can be a uniquely "Biblical view." Truth is truth. Great masters in all religions have realized it, regardless of any inherited, or perhaps I should say, imbued religious tradition. It is to them we should look for guidance in these matters, not to scholars, thinkers, and theologians.

God does work through history, but I don't really know why Christian writers have made such a big thing of this; it suggests their focus is outward, and not on the kingdom of God within ourselves—superficial, in other words, although for all that valid. The masters themselves take an interest in world events, and guide them as they can within the karmic limitations people themselves impose.

Thank you for writing.

In Master,

| *Did Jesus speak of "embracing the world"?* | 7 |

April 5, 1998

Dear _____:

It would help me to be able to point to some specific teaching of Jesus' where he himself (not St. Paul) speaks of embracing the world in any sense. Yes, I know he said, "Render unto Caesar the things that are Caesar's, and unto God the things that are of God." But in that statement he didn't say what we give to Caesar we give to God.

I know he mixed with publicans and the like, but I read that to mean he went wherever he saw love for God, regardless of religious or social position. I do not read it to mean he was a man of the people in the sense one would normally understand the term. Master said he even went to Samaria ("he must needs pass through Samaria") because he knew there was a fallen disciple of his, who in fact was the "woman of Samaria"). He went to the dunghill, so to speak, of this world to find the few rare gems.

Now, it would help me to find some passage where he said something like "Accept the world, and your life in it, for God's sake." After what you wrote you must have such quotes, and I can't think of a one.

Love,

April 8, 1998

Dear _____:

In the context of your last letter, you've convinced me. In fact, what you describe of Jesus is very like Master himself—not when I knew him, but when a young man. He "played the game," not with human personality, for there was no ego there, but with divine joy, embracing God in everyone.

Yes, I'm glad to read everything you've said. My own view was too austere, based on Master as I knew him and on the many saints I have personally known.

In fact, in my chapters on the *avatara* [in *Hindu Way of Awakening*] I state how an *avatara* has no need to be so austere. And Master wasn't. Nor, I now realize, was Jesus. Thank you.

In Master's love,

August 4, 2002

Dear _____:

The reason I've not tried to answer your questions is that they demand long answers, and one feels challenged to answer such questions when they are closer to the surface in one's own experience and memory. For instance, questions on reincarnation would have been more fun to answer fifty years ago, shortly after I'd done my own wrestling with the issue.

Questions on the Eucharist would have been more interesting for me when I was studying Catholic history and theology—again, 40-50 years ago.

That's why I've encouraged our churches to give our newer members the job of answering newcomers' questions. After a time, these matters become so settled in one's own mind that one just doesn't feel like entering the waters yet again. They become no longer meaningful. Yet I've had all those questions myself. It isn't that I wonder at your having them.

I wrote you some months ago that I felt sad over your difficulties. The sadness was based on the fact that for so many years I've tried to build bridges between the teachings of India and those propounded in Christianity, and I've been forced to admit that my efforts were unsuccessful. I'd hoped to bring meditation to the churches. I even started a movement, which I called "the movement of inner communion." I used to go to the churches. With devotion I attended mass.

I was forced in the end, alas, to accept that it just wouldn't work. The people I was able to reach were not those devoted to the churches, however sincere they were in their own Christianity. They were those who had, like myself, left the churches in disillusionment. Too bad, for the teachings are the same—yogis teach the same practices that were taught long ago in Christianity itself.

There's a lot in the Bible on reincarnation. I've mentioned some of this material in *The Path*, in the chapter on "Reincarnation." These truths don't exist merely on a theoretical level: Lots of reputable people have *remembered* having lived before, and have demonstrated the accuracy of their memory.

A fascinating book on the subject is *I Have Lived Before: The True Story of the Reincarnation of Shanti Devi* by Sture Lonnerstrand. Reason also supports the "theory" hands down. But I no longer feel enthused enough on the subject to go into all the arguments. To me, reincarnation is simply too obviously a truth to bear further discussion.

As for the Eucharist, there's nothing wrong with it as a dogma. I'm perfectly aware of Therese Neumann's experiences, and don't in any way challenge them. The same sort of points could be made regarding many other religious experiences, in other religions.

I, too, have been greatly inspired by church services. And there's a church in Siena, Italy, where the wafer itself is held to be particularly sacred. I've had wonderful meditations there. It's the *exclusivity* of Christian dogma that I reject.

Well, _____, I thought to go further into these matters, but honestly my heart simply isn't in it. I no longer try to convince those who have been conditioned to believe otherwise. That's why I was sad: I didn't see what I could do to bridge these matters *for you*. I was writing *The Promise of Immortality* for another audience, and would have liked so much for you to feel a rapport with what I was saying, but I'm simply forced by the facts to accept that Master's teachings won't reach everyone.

I *am* convinced, however, that they will reach increasing numbers of people who have grown up with new ideas and a new outlook. In saying this I don't at all mean to be slighting. But I don't see how to build the bridge you want. Or at least, I have to say the job isn't mine to address. No doubt someone will do it, someday. Every attempt so far to do so, however, that I've heard or read has been, in my opinion, merely a one-horsepower kind of energy. If it finally convinced anyone, it left hearts dry, not inspired.

I'd like so much to be of greater help.

In Master's love,

*"Yogananda's work isn't personal at all.
Yogananda wasn't personal. As he
put it repeatedly, 'God is the Guru.'
His teachings weren't personal.*

SELF-REALIZATION
FELLOWSHIP

*God was using him as the avatar of a
new age, to change an entire civilization.
Don't let anyone tell you that
one organization, one person,
one statement can ever, even remotely,
define what he brought to the world."*

Self-Realization Fellowship (SRF) is the organization Paramhansa Yogananda founded in 1925. It is larger and much wealthier than Ananda. Swami Kriyananda was part of SRF from 1948 until 1962, when he was dismissed. The letters in the following section give the reasons for Kriyananda's separation from SRF and an overview of the relations between the two organizations over the years.

~~~~~~~~~

Letter to an SRF monk │ 1

1973

Dear _____:

How very good it was to see you again—after nearly thirteen years! And how wonderful to be in one of Master's places again! The vibrations at the Lake Shrine are so uplifting, I cannot but feel that everyone who comes there must go away in some way changed.

Let us continue to pray to God and Master that the seeming distance between us become demolished. We are all serving him. It behooves devotees to feel an underlying oneness even with criminals, what to speak of their own *gurubhais*.

But the way of *maya* is to emphasize differences, just because they are superficial and slight, from a wish to safeguard one's own integrity. (After all, there is no danger of devotees becoming confused with the Mafia.) We need therefore to keep in mind that the surest way of safeguarding our own integrity as Master's disciples is to live by his words.

I think the walls are crumbling, and I am very happy to contemplate that possibility.

Brother, would you please see that _____ gets the enclosed letter? I think Ananda may be the best place for him, now that he has left the order. Here he can continue to serve Master. All of us here consider ourselves Master's disciples, and all must be SRF members to join. I even have a job for _____, if he comes. Anyway, I have suggested to him that he at least come and see what we have.

God bless you, brother. I hope we meet again soon.

In Master's love,

In a series of letters, an SRF member urged
Kriyananda to reconcile with SRF—or else refrain
from any activities outside that organization

2

September 14, 1978

Dear _____:

Why don't we leave it at this: that I truly feel that the work I am doing is one that Master wants me to do? I feel his guidance and his blessing on it. As I wrote you earlier, I have not taken on this work without much meditation, and sincere prayer for guidance.

I think Master wanted me on my own because his work, this work, could not have been done within the larger framework of SRF. Even my books, which he told me to write, would never have been published had I been in his organization.

I see now that this is what he meant when he told me repeatedly, "You have a great work to do." A "great work" implies a work of this type, rather than activity within a work that has already been established.

I should perhaps add that it was not my choice to leave SRF. I offered to wash dishes for the rest of my life, rather than be separated from my Guru's organization.

After I was put out of the work, I sent donations to it, but my checks were either returned or were never cashed. I offered to distribute Master's books in bookstores, and my offer was rejected. I was told in a telegram that I could do nothing to serve my Master.

It was only then, and because the one service I could not render him was to do nothing, that I had to turn within to seek his guidance directly.

I might conclude by saying that I hope very much that someday Ananda and SRF will be able to work together, but the next steps in that direction will have to be taken by them. I have made all the offers I can, including several times, in years past, offering to give Ananda to SRF. (Their reaction was to suspect me either of trying to foist my debts onto them, or to get rid of Ananda because it was too much trouble for me.)

I hope that this explanation helps you to understand the situation better.

In divine friendship,

[Editor's Note: SRF filed a lawsuit against Ananda in 1990. After 12 years of litigation and three SRF appeals, including one to the U.S. Supreme Court, Ananda won more than 95% of the lawsuit.]

1999

Dear Kriyananda,

I just finished reading your booklets, *An Open Letter to the Board of Directors of SRF* and *My Separation from SRF.* Thank you so much for sharing your feelings and beliefs and for exposing what is going on in SRF.

I joined SRF two years ago and became a Kriyaban over a year ago. Since that time, I have heard a few rumors about SRF and was not sure what to believe. I tried very hard to just dismiss the rumors because I wanted to believe that whatever SRF did, it had Yogananda's blessings.

Three weeks ago, I met a woman from Ananda. My reaction to her was very negative in that, as soon as I heard where she was from, I felt cold towards her. When I walked away, I felt a great sense of guilt. I knew that the way I responded to her was not right. I knew where those feelings were really coming from. I thought of how God and Yogananda love us all, and how we are to love all. I had been questioning SRF all along, but as I said, I tried to dismiss it.

Then I found a book put out by Amrita Foundation, titled *The Second Coming of Christ.* It says it is the "original unchanged writings of Paramhansa Yogananda." When I began to read it, I realized that Yogananda's writing was very different from what SRF puts out. I called Amrita and after listening to Priscilla, the lady in charge, I was in shock.

At first, I believed that SRF had only changed the way it was written and not the message itself, which upset me deeply enough. But after reading your booklet, I find that SRF even changed the message. I am not sure of the extent that this is being done, but my feeling is that it is important to read what Yogananda wrote in its unchanged form.

SRF had sent me a booklet in an attempt to refute what you have said. They quote you as saying that Yogananda admonished you, "Edit, but don't change a word." They did not deny that he said this. They just tried to prove that *they* did not change a word. They fell short on that.

Plus, in the SRF booklet or leaflet, they brought up that there is a sexual harassment lawsuit against you. To me, that was stooping low. It was an attempt to make you look bad so we would not believe what you had to say.

It told me that they had no other recourse because they don't have proof that what they are doing is not wrong.

It saddened me greatly that they have done this to Yogananda's writings. It saddens me also that now I cannot trust them. I now feel that perhaps all the gossip I have heard about the SRF Board of Directors is true. If they can do this to Yogananda's writings, where is their loyalty, and what more can they be capable of?

I recall one woman in SRF telling me that she took the nun's training. She said they were horrible to her. One monk told her, "You would not believe what goes on here." I tried to dismiss that, too, but I have noticed over the last year that I have suffered on a spiritual level due to hearing all these things. But I have also wanted to know the truth.

I do not feel that I can be in a religion that is like this. Now I find that I can't even talk about my feelings to other members of SRF. If I try, I am met with resistance.

I talked to someone who is on another spiritual path. He told me that someone else from SRF had also talked to him about how upset he was about the editing. That man also said that SRF told him he was not allowed to read *The Path*.

This reminds me so much of the Jehovah's Witnesses. They, too, try to keep people quiet and won't allow them to read other materials. They, too, talk about loyalty and try to make you feel guilty.

When I was finding all this out about SRF, I thought of walking away. But I felt a lot of guilt, as if Yogananda would leave me if I left SRF.

At this moment, I still have one foot in SRF, because I have not made a certain decision about what to do.

I did call Mother Center to ask about the editing. What the nun said did not ring true. She told me that Yogananda edited all his works again before his passing. She denied that SRF had changed any words. So she is saying that the new *Whispers from Eternity*, the later editions of the *Autobiography of a Yogi*, the commentary on the *Bhagavad Gita* all have his blessings.

You were there in his last years. Was he doing that or did he consider his work on the *Autobiography* and *Whispers* finished? Why is the 1929 edition of *Whispers* different from the 1949 edition? (At least I think it is.) It hurts me to know that they have many more writings by him and that they alone will edit them.

The way they have treated you, according to the booklet you published, rings true after hearing what that woman said about the nun's training.

This may be a very naïve question, but I read in a book on meditation that when you reach cosmic consciousness, you know right from wrong and always do the right thing. Yet Daya Mata, who I am told has reached cosmic consciousness, is allowing these things to happen. And what about the other members of the Board of Directors? Are their own meditations just not that powerful? Or are they too busy running the business of SRF? Perhaps I just thought too highly of them all and expected too much.

I was shown an article on SRF that was printed in the *Los Angeles New Times*. It made SRF look really bad. When I questioned Mother Center about it, I was told that I should consider the source.

The newspaper said that Daya Mata lives in a mansion. Mother Center told me that Daya Mata's home is small, just a retreat, and that wealthy homes have been built up around it. The newspaper said SRF paid $333,000 in hush money to a woman who had an affair with a monk. SRF says it is not true, and so on and so on.

Also, I was told that the Kriya that SRF teaches is not the same as what Yogananda taught. Is that true? Is it also true that Yogananda told us not to read other books by other religious teachers? SRF quotes him as saying that, both in the lessons they send out and in the leaflet they sent to me. It is his handwriting, but is it being interpreted incorrectly?

I quote: "100% Self-realization and the living link of the gurus, and not divert your mind to any other teachings or work. Passing out literature of other teachings confuses and unsettles the minds of new and even old students. So I shall be happy if you concentrate minds of students only in SRF."

It helps me to know that even Yogananda thought of leaving SRF. Can you enlarge upon that?

I feel that you have done a great work. I have always secretly admired your brotherhood colonies. I feel that you have had to go through so much with SRF, but it has brought so much light on what SRF is doing. We all need to know and not be such blind followers of yet another religion.

God's love to you,

———————

~~~~~~~

Swami Kriyananda's response
December 13, 1999

Dear ———— :

Your letter has put me in a bit of a quandary. I want to be helpful to you, for you seem to me a sincere devotee, and I usually try to support such people. On the other hand, I am also loyal to Master, and it pains me to write anything against the organization he founded. I would remain silent on the issues you've raised were I not convinced that SRF is harming in important ways the cause for which he created it. I am unable, moreover, to write or speak with the questionable sincerity of "political correctness."

The purpose of that "Open Letter" was not to hurt anyone, but to shock the directors of SRF into realizing how many people they themselves were hurting by their lack of charity and even of interest in others, all in the name of institutional exigencies. When I reflect that my (our, rather) letter doesn't seem to have had any effect at all, I wonder if perhaps I was wrong in writing it.

There are issues at stake here, however, so important to the future of Master's mission that I feel that in good conscience I have a duty to speak out.

Moreover, I did feel Master's guidance in writing it, and his indignation at the issues that letter confronted.

He made a statement again and again—it is one I take very seriously—that he'd been sent to the West to bring back "original Christianity." What was it that caused Christianity to drift away from its origins? I am convinced it was exactly what SRF is trying to bring about in Master's work at the present time. For the old problem was institutionalism versus individual Self-realization.

Institutionalism is SRF's idol, too, and is the way they define their service to our Guru. Institutionalism takes precedence in their minds over people's needs and the devotee's individual quest for Self-realization. In the minds of SRF's leaders, Master wanted the name "Self-Realization" applied uniquely to *his own* organization. Whereas his concern was for a principle, theirs is for the medium he established to promulgate that principle.

It was because Ananda chose to include that principle in its name, as an affirmation of our discipleship to Master, that SRF first threatened to sue us in February of 1990. In fact, they began trying to silence me with threats as long ago as 1962—nearly forty years ago.

I think you know that they actually did file a lawsuit against us later, in 1990. This was only their first lawsuit against us, though they've claimed that it has been their only one and deny involvement in the suit that was filed in 1994, which you know about. (Their disclaimer means only that they are anxious not to be *perceived* as being involved. Their *indirect* involvement, however, is unmistakable.)

The SRF directors have often said to me, "You weren't with Master a long time, as the rest of us were." The truth is, only two of them—Daya Mata and Ananda Mata—were with him many years longer. Master himself often reminded us of Christ's words, "The last shall be first." The other still-living direct disciples who are also directors came only a year or two before me, or, in Brother Anandamoy's case, one year after me. The newer directors came years later, and never knew Master.

All the directors, however, seem to consider it presumptuous of me to offer any suggestion for their own or for the work's growth. Personally, at least as far as the work is concerned, I don't agree with this attitude. I am sincerely serving Master's mission to the best of my ability, and am doing so in the way he himself told me to do.

I was personally with Master as a disciple for the last three and a half years of his life, and got to spend quite a bit of time with him alone. When he accepted me as his disciple, he said to me, "I give you my unconditional love." (How those words have strengthened me through the dark nights I have lived!)

Some of the SRF directors have told people I hardly knew him at all; or that I was never with him privately, only in group situations; or—the latest "news," from the SRF center in Palermo, Italy—that I never met him at all.

There are other disciples who, like me, regret what seems to them also the excessive institutionalization of Master's work, but they have chosen to remain silent. Should I follow their example? I have tried to do so. My conscience, however, will not let me say nothing on a subject that, I feel, concerns an important principle.

Moreover, they attack the work I myself have founded in his name, though I was forced *by them* to serve him separately. How can I permit them silently to destroy this, my own service to my Guru?

Moreover, I do not agree with a statement Tara Mata (Miss Pratt) made to me shortly after I myself was elected to the Board of Directors. "In a corporation," she said, "no one has a right *even to think* except the members of the Board of Directors." To my mind, disciples have a sacred duty to serve their guru to the best of their ability, which means using their brains and not only their bodies or their bank accounts.

This need is especially great in my own case, for Master told me repeatedly, "You have a great work to do, Walter." [Master called him "Walter".] The SRF directors scoff at the idea that he could have said such a thing to anyone, but I can only reply that I *know* what he said. I am, moreover, his disciple, not theirs. They insist that, if he did say anything remotely similar, he meant to apply it to everybody serving the work. In fact, he made it very clear that he was addressing his words to me, personally.

If I am right in my feeling that he wanted me to speak out in that "Open Letter," maybe good will come of it after all, in time.

Meanwhile, I may add that I feel closer to him than ever; that Ananda is thriving; that its members are growing spiritually and are widely loved for their humility, kindness, and devotion; that our several branch communities are flourishing; and that in our unfortunate confrontations with SRF (which to us have been heart-rending) we have at least won steadily. Even the second lawsuit, which went against us, was no defeat for us, for we have emerged from it stronger spiritually, and with greater public respect than ever.

What has pained me more than anything else, as I've stated repeatedly over the years in letters to Daya Mata, is that people are being hurt by SRF's indifference to its members' spiritual needs. In my view, those needs are of paramount importance, and are the whole reason for which Master founded SRF.

I recognize that many people have a need to belong to an organization, and I don't want in any way to damage their loyalty to SRF. On the other hand, the very principle of Self-realization cries out for strong, independent seekers. Many of these will not be interested in outward affiliation of any kind, since their search is for God, and is therefore inward.

SRF, like the traditional Christian Church, seeks to persuade people that discipleship means outward affiliation with Master's organization, including the acceptance of guidance from officially appointed representatives of that organization (even if the guidance comes, as it often does, in the form of letters from the head office, written by disciples whose experience in the teachings may be far less than the correspondents').

There are many people, moreover, whose contact with SRF has not given them the inspiration they sought, even though they have been deeply devoted to God and Guru. Those who have been drawn to Master through me have told me many times that they found no help from SRF, and could never have come to him if it hadn't been for Ananda.

I have never urged them to choose Ananda over SRF. Rather, what I've told them is, "Go and see for yourself. Compare, and then make your own decision. But remember, both paths are serving the same Guru, and both of them are doing good work."

Over the years, to my deep regret, I've found myself obliged increasingly to refrain from giving this advice, for Ananda people who have gone there have too often been treated unkindly, or have been greeted with a kind of proselytizing zeal that had the obvious motive of winning them away from me. The sad thing is, I don't think anyone at Ananda is *anti*-SRF— unless it be to the extent that his experiences with SRF representatives have wounded his love.

I think perhaps you've never read my book, *A Place Called Ananda—Part One*; otherwise, you'd have mentioned it. That book tells more of the story of my separation from SRF than you've read. I would not have written it had I not been forced to do so by their continuous efforts to respond to people's questions about me with damaging innuendoes, such as, "Oh, if you *only knew* the real story!" (In no case has the speaker himself known the story!)

Now, as I learn from you, they've decided to confront the issue more openly by putting out their version of what I call their "second" lawsuit, obviously with the purpose of inflicting as much damage on me as possible. At the same time, as your letter indicates, they haven't admitted, and indeed never would admit, even the possibility of any fault on their own side.

One of the reasons I wrote that "Open Letter" was to get the SRF directors to see the extent to which they were being untrue to Master by suing us. Apart from my hope that they'd change the way they treated individuals, I also hoped the letter would persuade them to drop their lawsuit against us. This second hope too, however, has been disappointed.

Indeed, my concern was far greater than their treatment of individuals. What I wanted above all, and what I have sought repeatedly to do, is encourage a right direction for the future of Master's mission.

Since 1990, I estimate that SRF has spent as much as fifty million dollars in a three-pronged legal attempt: to destroy me; to separate Ananda from me; and, if necessary, to destroy Ananda itself. These are things that to me and to others are obvious, but that they simply do not seem to understand. SRF's persecution has made me, and the Ananda members, stronger in our service to Master, and has in this sense been a blessing.

The kind of money SRF has at its disposal, however, and its willingness to use it toward our destruction, have pushed us to what has repeatedly seemed our limits, for it is our very survival that has been threatened. So far, thank God and Guru, we've done remarkably well. However, we haven't their vast financial resources. Thus, it hasn't been easy to keep going in the face of such determined, often underhanded, and always unrelenting opposition.

Life's tests are, as I said, a blessing if we meet them with faith. The energy we've had to put out to survive has resulted in enormous growth for us. In fact, since SRF initiated its lawsuit in 1990, we've established flourishing communities in Palo Alto, Sacramento, Portland, and Seattle, as well as in Assisi, Italy. We are starting a community on the east coast, in Rhode Island. In all these communities some 800 resident members reside.

We've built churches (*mandirs*, we call them) as outreach for all our communities, including a justifiably famous mandir-dome near Assisi. We've bought bookstores, all of which are doing well in a time of all-but universal depression for book stores. In fact, we've done so much more than all this that to describe all of it might seem like boasting.

How much more beautiful it would have been, had we been able to grow in a spirit of harmony and cooperation with SRF! Their estimate of our motives has been wrong from the very beginning. They've thought we were competing with them, but in fact all we've ever wanted was to walk by their side in a spirit of friendship. They've thought we *needed* them, but this has never been our reason for wanting to cooperate with them.

Twice in fact over the years, during my discussions with Daya Mata, I offered to give Ananda to SRF. My intentions were generous, and were rooted in my devotion to Master. They were without ulterior motive; indeed, I actually said to her, "After accepting this gift of Ananda, you may send me away if you like. I'll go willingly, reassured that Ananda is wholly Master's."

The second time I offered Ananda to her, all she answered was, "We wouldn't want to inherit your debts." Evidently my offer meant nothing to her except that Ananda must be in danger of imminent collapse—"a consummation," as Hamlet might have put it for her, "devoutly to be wished"! To this hint that I had to be in dire straits to be making such an offer, I was forced to say, "And I wouldn't want to give you Ananda, if your only purpose in accepting it was to destroy it."

Years ago, the minister of the First Methodist Church in Pasadena outspokenly opposed the new Christian Science Church in that city. Later he had the good grace, and also the sense of humor, to claim credit for building that congregation! "I talked so much against them," he admitted, "that people went over to see for themselves. Many of them remained!"

For me, the hardest part in serving Master separately from SRF has been that the very people who have been so dedicatedly opposed to me are my *gurubhais*. Worse still, they are people I love dearly, and to whom I feel very close.

I know that those who knew me years ago love me, too. They have made it clear to me, however, that their priority is not the friendship we feel for one another, but their service to "Master's work." Fair enough—up to a point. After all, we are devotees of God first of all; anything outside our relationship with Him is illusory. Friendship too, then, ought to be viewed by us as having its existence in Him.

My fellow disciples, however, are guided by a policy that was initiated, and insisted upon, by Tara Mata: "In every situation, always ask yourselves, 'What is best for the work?'" Her advice might sound good, were it not understood by all concerned that what she meant by "the work" was not the spiritual well being of the SRF members, but only the power, the fame, the worldly importance, and the financial strength of the organization.

In June of 1990, some of Ananda's leaders met with the SRF Board of Directors in Fresno, California, to discuss the lawsuit SRF was threatening against us. Our meeting took place at my suggestion; I had hoped to avert an expensive and mutually harmful struggle. At that meeting I reminded Daya Mata, "Master told us, 'Someday, Self-realization will be the religion of the world.' He *can't possibly* have meant Self-Realization Fellowship, Inc."

Daya Mata, to my utter astonishment, replied, "That's" (a pause) "your opinion." *How could there possibly be* two *opinions on such an issue?!* Could Master really have envisioned a sort of super-Catholic Church taking over the world? Evidently, they are convinced that he did. It was just this "ideal" that took the churches far from the true teachings of Jesus Christ. In light of their conviction, the obsession the SRF directors show with eliminating me from the scene becomes understandable.

Nothing short of a direct declaration by Master himself, or by Babaji or one of our other masters, could persuade me that God wants a super-institution in this new age of energy, this *Dwapara Yuga*, as Sri Yukteswar called it.

How often Master said, both privately and in public, "SRF is not a sect." Unbelievably, Tara Mata, after quoting those very words to me, said (with what I could only think was amazing presumption), "Well, we *are* a sect!"

No, I think what is being reenacted between SRF and Ananda is the early history of Christianity. If I am right, then SRF represents the very energy that caused the early Church to depart from its original teachings.

On this point, incidentally, you might be interested to read a new book of mine—actually, it is only Part One of a much longer book I am work-ing on, which will be called *The Promise of Immortality in the Bible and the Bhagavad Gita*. I've had this slim first volume printed as a Christmas pres-ent to Ananda members this year. It is called, *The Eternal Christ*. In it I've gone into this subject as deeply as I was able. This little volume is not avail-able in the bookstores, but I believe it can be ordered from Ananda.

To me, the question, "What is best for the work?" has always meant, *"What is the best way to spread Master's teachings? How can people's hearts best be opened to them? How can their spiritual needs best be served?"* The SRF directors see me, for this reason, as the enemy of "the work," as they define it, even though they consider me at the same time, personally, their friend (or so I believe—perhaps wishfully).

I've never considered them my enemies, nor even the enemies of Master's work. I think of them as not only my dear friends in God and Guru (for when I give someone my friendship, it is forever), but also as my co-serv-ers in Master's work.

I disagree with certain of their directions, and I believe it would be in their own interest to act more like disciples and less like the directors of a busi-ness corporation, for they don't even fit into the business mold. At heart, they are devotees. Truthfully, I think it goes against their very grain to feel obliged to maintain businesslike priorities.

They themselves would certainly say that it is none of my business to con-cern myself with their spiritual progress. And of course they'd be perfectly right. At the same time, I don't believe concern for others is the same thing as meddling in their affairs. Moreover, the future of our Guru's work *is*, certainly, my business. Master himself made it so, by discussing it with me at some length, and by telling me I had a great work to do.

I have failed to get the SRF directors to see things differently, so I must accept that I can do no more in this direction. They, for their part, cannot believe that I have any right to think about their directions at all. So I guess we have simply to agree to disagree.

Daya Mata once, when I'd expressed an opinion that was at variance with her own, said to me, "The Board thinks differently. Don't you think you ought to go along with the Board?" I was a Board member myself at the time, and was, in addition, the first vice-president of SRF.

In Fresno, in 1990, she led us in a prayer that Master's will be done on these legal issues. We joined her wholeheartedly.

During the lawsuit they then filed, however, and after they'd lost on every count, Daya Mata couldn't accept their numerous, considerable defeats as Master's will. SRF therefore appealed, then re-appealed, then appealed yet again. As she told me during her opening words at that Fresno meeting, "I can't face Master as long as this problem remains unresolved." The "problem," of course, was Kriyananda. Years ago, she'd defined it to me as such.

What was that first lawsuit all about? SRF wanted us to stop using "Self-Realization" in our name. We, for the sake of harmony, proposed other alternatives—though "Self-Realization" is, for us, the name of Master's very mission. One of our alternatives was "God-Realization"; there were several others. SRF rejected them all. Soon it became obvious to us that their complaint about our name was only an opening gambit.

In the papers they filed, they added other demands, the following ones particularly: that we stop quoting any of Master's words without their permission; that we only display our Gurus' photographs on our private altars; and that we not use Master's "name, image, or likeness" in any advertising or publicity. It was on all these issues that their formal complaint was written.

Eventually they were defeated on every count—losing even the copyrights on Master's books. Later, out of what can only be called a desire for revenge, they attempted to seize the copyrights on all my own books—not with a view, obviously, to publishing those books themselves, but simply to bury them.

I allowed Ananda, albeit at first reluctantly, to publish the first edition of *Autobiography of a Yogi*. I had wanted SRF to be the sole publisher of that book, but our legal team pointed out that not only had SRF lost the copyright on that first edition, but that anyone else, consequently, was free to publish it. Wasn't it far better, they argued, that it be published by devotees of Master's? I agreed, partly also because I was as shocked as they were at some of the changes SRF had made in Master's autobiography since his passing.

———, I didn't want to go into these matters at length. For one thing, there are simply too many of them. For another, I feared that to air them wouldn't be helpful to you or to anyone else. Yet I feel I must respond meaningfully to you in *some* way, rather than not responding at all. To leave your letter unanswered would, I feel, be unfair to you, and also to anyone else with a sincere desire for answers on these issues.

My silence would indicate, besides, that to me nothing more was involved than the relatively insignificant question of the treatment I, personally, have received.

The SRF directors are—I believe, or want to believe—no less desirous of serving Master's work than I am. Their concern also, however, is for how the work is perceived by the public, whereas mine is primarily for how it can inspire people. Otherwise, I am not much concerned for the public's perception of either SRF or Ananda. Truth is my God, not people's opinions.

Daya Mata, at a meeting I had with her in Pasadena in 1970, asked me to stop telling people that I'd been dismissed from SRF. "Recently," she said, "I called a meeting of all the monks and nuns and said to them, 'I know some of you have heard it said that Kriyananda was dismissed. I want you to know, he was *not* dismissed. He *resigned*!'" Shocked as I was by what she was asking of me, I could see no alternative but to reply, "That isn't true, and you *know* it isn't true!"

"Well," she answered, "you *should have* resigned!"

Isn't there a suggestion, here, of the communists' definition of truth? To them, truth is whatever helps communism, and falsehood is anything that hinders communism's expansive ambitions.

Disciples need to ask the questions you have. And since you have appealed to me, I need to answer you in good conscience—supportively, if possible, to you as an individual, and above all supportively to Master's mission as I understand it. I would not be so arrogant as to say that I know absolutely what he wants, but I do try sincerely to understand his will, and in most things I do feel his guidance.

You showed integrity in your regret for having behaved coldly toward that Ananda member. I agree with you: Master would not want a disciple of his to behave that way toward *anyone*. He himself never did so. Didn't he tell Daya Mata, "When I am gone, only love can take my place"? Love is driven from our hearts if we deny our good will to others merely because they disagree with us, or because we disagree with them.

Master also once commented sadly to Daya Mata, "How you all will change the work when I am gone! I just wonder, if I were to return in a hundred years, whether I would even recognize it." I've reflected, since then, that his words to her were, "you all."

One thing that has caused me deep pain has been the fact that I have not, in all these nearly forty years since my separation from SRF, heard *one single* inspiring story come out of SRF. I don't mean "inspiring" in the sense that someone has been reputed to have attained cosmic consciousness: Who, indeed, can really know these things? People show their inner consciousness by their outward actions. It's the actions I'm talking about: deeds of simple charity, kindness, humility, concern for others, self-sacrifice for the needs of others; determination to place *truth* ahead of any convenience. I have *not heard even one* such account. I've longed to hear them.

Surely in the normal course of events there would have been many such stories. Surely also, therefore, I'd have heard at least a few of them. Instead, every story that has reached me has indicated a lack of charity and, alas, a spirit of meanness and intolerance. How greatly our Ananda members would love to hear inspiring stories about Master's disciples! They would certainly repeat them to me. Moreover, I've begged them for such stories.

The only story I've heard is one that was meant to show Daya Mata's compassionate spirit, but that to me seems like scraping the bottom of an empty barrel. It concerned an SRF member who was dying of cancer. She received a personal phone call from Daya Mata. This was gracious of Daya, but was by no means, for a busy executive, heroic or extraordinary.

What pains me is to hear this given as proof of Daya Mata's saintliness. There is an overtone in this story, moreover, of condescension on Daya Mata's part—not because she was busy, but because she is so spiritually important. She herself has declared, "I didn't ask for this position" (the presidency), as if the position itself mattered all that much. (*Someone*, after all, has to fill it.)

The head of a religious institution ought, surely, to define his position in terms of the opportunity it gives him to serve others, and not in terms of the preeminence it bestows on him. Ananda members want, as much as I do, to think well of Daya Mata and of all who are senior disciples to themselves. They *want* to be inspired.

Until SRF initiated its lawsuit in 1990, I only hinted at the pain I'd been suffering for years. Even since they filed their lawsuit, I've done my best to soften our members' hurt and anger. My closest friends, people who have been with me since the founding of Ananda, asked me, "Why did you never tell us?"

On the subject of editing, you should know that Master himself *wanted* his words to be edited. He knew he hadn't mastered the English language. More than that, he didn't want to go painstakingly through a manuscript sentence by sentence, to make sure its meaning was pellucidly clear. Most writers accept the help of editors, if only because this phase in the writing process can be very tedious besides being, to a great extent, mechanical.

I do in fact do all my own editing, but I can easily appreciate why Master wouldn't do so. The way he worked was entirely intuitive; the laborious process of reasoning wasn't for him. I myself often compare editing to plumbing: a process of putting words together in such a way as to make the meaning flow smoothly. Master, however, wrote from pure inspiration. Really, even had he been a master of English composition I can't imagine him working arduously to smooth a field he'd already leveled.

Evidently you, like most people, don't realize the extent to which a written idea needs polishing in order to delight, instruct, and inspire the reader. The last chapter of my own most recent book was one I'd worked on until I considered it finished. On reviewing it, however, I found it needed more work. In the end I went over it *twenty-two* more times!

Conscientious editing is hard work; sometimes it seems like trudging through heavy snow. Not to do this work, however, is to be unfair to the reader. He might get the idea anyway, with a little effort, but he might also miss important nuances of meaning. Important concepts might slip by him unnoticed. He might even get wrong ideas.

Readers tend to be somewhat superficial, especially on their first reading. In attempting to grasp Master's deep wisdom, they might, if the text was not polished, get only a general impression of the meaning, or else feel that, whereas the material itself had to be wonderful, they weren't awake enough to absorb it fully.

I can't tell you how many people used to tell me, with regret for the fact and blaming only themselves, that when the SRF magazine came to their homes they would quickly turn to Master's commentary on the *Rubaiyat of Omar Khayyam*, but then find their attention wandering as the commentary simply failed to register with them. It was, in fact, the quality of the editing that put them to sleep, not Master's actual writing.

To write on spiritual matters requires not only literary ability, but the practical experience of teaching people, and of listening to their questions and to their problems with the teachings. One must be aware of ways in which a reader might misunderstand the message. It isn't such a simple matter as letter-writing.

There are countless ways that a thought can be misinterpreted. One must avoid writing condescendingly, which would be insulting to the reader's intelligence. On the other hand, one must respect the fact that he may not be familiar with the concepts. To explain, yet not over-explain; to write simply while at the same time not over-simplifying; to search for the right word without taxing the reader's linguistic knowledge: these are some of what might be called the *fulcrums* of good writing, without which a work may waver between the heavily cumbersome and the childishly simplistic. Clear, insightful, and joyful editing is a taxing job.

Master once said that in the astral world one simply puts his vibrations into a book. "When I was working on the *Autobiography*," he said, "Divine Mother really disciplined me!" Even so, Laurie Pratt (Tara Mata) did the heavier editing work. She would make a suggestion; Master then would check her work to make sure it reflected his intentions. When necessary, he explained those intentions carefully to make sure she'd grasped them fully.

Very few writers, I might add (from their own description of their way of working), pay much attention to these matters. But then, very few writers write well, conscientiously, and with proper respect for their readers.

Master was obliged to work with editors who had no real appreciation for his spiritual greatness. Some of them were so presumptuous in their ignorance that they intruded their own thoughts into the editing process, without even trying to tune in to *his* inspiration. Some, again, had done a lot of metaphysical reading, and considered themselves knowledgeable in such matters. They let others' ideas intrude into the work they were supposed to be doing for Master, simply not realizing the deep nuances of meaning in his writing. When you read his supposedly "original" words from the old SRF magazines, what you sometimes get is such careless editing, and not Master's full inspiration at all.

There was a small book of his on the Cosmic Mother that one of those editors had taken from transcriptions of his talks, then edited for publication. This woman's work was literarily adequate, but it departed from Master's meaning, and failed to reflect his vibrations. He had the whole thing thrown out.

Nowadays, were someone to discover that book and see the publication date on it, he might well pass it around as "Master's original work." But Master complained to me, personally, of his experiences with that woman, both as a disciple and as an editor.

It would be good for you also to understand that what made its way into the magazines was often little more than a first draft. The ideas are there, but the way they appear is like furniture that has yet to be planed, sandpapered, and polished.

The first editor with whom Master was really satisfied was Laurie Pratt (Tara Mata). One is not likely to hear Miss Pratt's praises liberally sung by

Kriyananda, for it was she who got me thrown out of SRF. Nevertheless, she was both fully competent as an editor and, far more important, she was also a devoted disciple.

Her desire was to express *Master's* teachings, not her own ideas. Inevitably, no doubt—being a writer myself—I do have a bit of a quibble with her editing style, which I consider a little high-handed and peremptory, as was she, herself. This is only a question of style, however. Writers seldom agree completely on such matters. The important thing in Miss Pratt's case is that she was more than competent: She was excellent.

More and more, as I myself slave over editing—particularly when I work on Master's words, though also in working on my own—I find myself appreciating the skill, insight, and energy she put into editing Master's *Autobiography*.

SRF, careful as ever to disparage me when it can, misquotes something Master said to me. What he told me in 1950 was, "Work like lightning, but don't change a word!" Pretty impossible, wouldn't you say? How can a person edit without changing a word? What he meant, as I now realize, was, "Don't change a single idea."

Obviously, he was coming from his experience with so many editors who had taken that very liberty. In other words, he wasn't implying criticism of my own editing, since I'd done no editing so far. Indeed, the work he was giving me to do at the time didn't involve editing at all! His instruction to edit was a guideline for my work in the future, one that I've taken very much to heart. SRF makes it sound as though he was criticizing something I'd edited already, of which he disapproved.

Here is the "inside story" of that episode. I was twenty-three at the time: too young and inexperienced in the teachings, as well as in writing itself, to touch his writings with an editorial pen. There were, however, many things Master needed to do while still in his body, to indicate future directions for individuals, or for the work. Many of those directions would become relevant only in time—perhaps after the individual had developed spiritually, or when the work itself was ready for them.

A good example of what I mean here was the insistence with which he urged people to create spiritual communities—"world brotherhood colonies," as he called them. He actually tried to create a model for such communities in Encinitas during the forties.

The attempt might be called a failure, since it was abandoned, but all that the abandonment meant was that people weren't yet ready for the concept. Seen in the light of future directions for the work, however, the project was not a failure at all. He remained deeply interested in it, and never missed an opportunity, especially in public lectures, to interest people in starting communities. I couldn't count the number of times I heard him speak on this subject. Always it was with great fervor and enthusiasm.

If you should happen to read my own autobiography, *The Path* (this work is really far more about Master than about myself), you will find a fair amount of information on this topic. SRF today claims that he changed his mind about communities. I was with him personally, however, and I know that he absolutely did not.

Daya Mata's comment to me on the subject, when I raised it to her in about 1958, was, "Frankly, I'm not interested." I don't criticize her for not being interested. One must be true to oneself. No individual, moreover, could embrace Master's entire vision for the future; it was simply too vast.

He never changed his mind on this issue, however. Only four months before his *mahasamadhi*, he was still speaking enthusiastically of the time when his concept of "world brotherhood colonies" would be embraced throughout the world.

So then: back to things he said or did, for which the time was not right, and for which he himself could offer only guidelines, therefore, for the future. Before taking me out to Twenty-Nine Palms in January of 1950, he said to me, "I asked Divine Mother whom I should take with me, and your face appeared. I asked Her twice more just to make sure, and each time your face appeared. That's why I am taking you."

The thought of editing his words frightened me; it was so obviously beyond my youthful, inexperienced powers. Actually, all he ended up asking me to do was cut out and paste old magazine articles onto typing paper, so as to make it easier to re-set the type. Mindful of his instruction not to change a word, however, I thought, "And he wants me to *edit*?" What did he mean? All I dared to change were obvious typographical errors, of which there were a great number. What confused me was his definition of this work as "editing."

For three months I remained alone, struggling with what turned out to be one of the major tests of my life. Looking back now, after many years, I realize that he'd never really expected me to produce anything worthwhile. He was looking ahead to my future. Perhaps he wanted to see if I'd be steadfast in trying to do *his* will.

He did ask me, however, when his work was finished, to offer actual editorial suggestions for the manuscript.

People have stated—unworthily, and also untruthfully—that when Master saw what I had done he hurled my work angrily into a wastepaper basket. As if he could ever be angry! and as if he could ever be ungracious! But that wasn't what happened at all.

What actually happened was that Miss Pratt—quite rightly, I might add—ordered that my work of editing and pasting be discarded, and the material typed out afresh. It's what should have been done in the first place. Perhaps Master hadn't realized what bad shape those magazine articles were in.

I was working in the garden outside his hermitage a few days later, when I heard him scolding Dorothy Taylor, his secretary, for throwing out the work I'd done. His words reached me clearly, for he shouted them: "I wouldn't go through what he went through to do that work, not if you gave me a million dollars!" Then again, for emphasis: "Not if you gave me a million dollars!" I couldn't help smiling at the thought of his doing *anything* for a million dollars!

Later he tried to comfort me, but I replied, "Master, Miss Pratt did the only thing possible. No one could have worked from the copy I submitted." Master, at least pretending amazement, exclaimed, "You are *defending* her!" Then, to reassure me, he said, "But that was *good* work! All those capitals!"

I'd known it was useless, in fact, even while I slaved over it. It wasn't Master's way to explain himself in these matters. He left it to us to work things out by tuning in to his consciousness if we were able to, and grasping his wishes intuitively.

Soon after that discussion, he said, "Walter, I predict you will make a good editor someday." A few days later he told me, "Your work in this life is writing, editing, and lecturing." I replied, "Sir, haven't you yourself written everything that needs to be said?" With a slightly shocked look he answered, "Don't say that! *Much* more is needed!"

Now, _____, please read at least a little bit of the book I edited called, *The Rubaiyat of Omar Khayyam Explained*, by Paramhansa Yogananda. I'm sure you will notice that I changed the wording, for it is different from *Wine of the Mystic*, which again is different from the original version that appeared years ago in the SRF magazine. I think my version sounds more like him than theirs does, and more than do the old magazine articles, from which I was forced to work.

I was extremely careful, however, not to change a single idea in his writing: not to add an idea, and not to omit an idea. If I thought some other idea might help to explain something in the text, I added it under the heading, "Editorial Comment." I was as conscientious as I possibly could be in the editing.

I also did my best to preserve the poetic vibrations of Master's writing, for he obviously wanted this book, like Omar's *Rubaiyat* itself, to read like poetry. He himself once said he'd been a poet in a former incarnation. Later on, I was recording this opus for an "audio book," and on reaching the last chapter, I broke down and wept at the sheer beauty of it. Several minutes passed before I could continue reading.

Please then, after you've read a little of that book, read *Wine of the Mystic*. Judge the differences for yourself. SRF's version is not identical with his original, either, but I think my version captures better his intentions, his spirit, and his vibrations.

You spoke of the supposedly "original" *Second Coming of Christ* that appeared in the old magazines. Please read carefully again at least a portion of what Priscilla published. Presumably you aren't yourself a writer, otherwise you wouldn't have raised this issue, but I think you will agree that the message could have been expressed more clearly, simply, and inspiringly—in fact, closer to the style in which Master actually spoke. (While editing his words, I've had the blessing of being able to hear him speaking them in my mind. This seems to be an ability with which I was born, but also one he augmented: to tune into the rhythms of a person's speech.)

Master in those days was obliged to write hastily, for there were monthly interpretations to be got to the magazine on a wide variety of subjects: the *Bhagavad Gita*, the *Holy Bible*, the *Rubaiyat of Omar Khayyam*, and other articles besides. He was also giving weekly talks in the churches, and directing a growing organization. Yes, of course, he *might* have simply materialized his written works, but that isn't the way most masters do things, and it certainly wasn't the way he did them. As he himself expressed it to me, "By editing my writings, you yourself will evolve spiritually."

Have I specific complaints about the way SRF edits his writings? Well, for one thing, I'm uncomfortable with their heavy promotion of SRF as an institution: It seems to me they should stick more to Master's emphasis on universal truths. For another, SRF often waters down his statements, doubtless to make them palatable to what they consider the general norm of understanding, so that his writings will offend no one. The reader gets the impression that the editors are used to declaring truths as if pontifically, but not to teaching or actively sharing them with others.

Another defect is that, in several cases, they've actually *deleted* his humor. (Evidently, they considered it not properly dignified.) They seem not to be interested in communicating an idea, or in helping others to grasp its importance. They are their own audience, and seem satisfied if they themselves are persuaded. As a result, they often "write down" to people.

They use pedantic words that I never heard Master use himself, and that I can't even imagine him using; some of those words aren't even in the dictionary. The idea behind this aspect of their editing seems to be to impress the reader with Master's erudition. Yet he himself was unabashedly unscholarly; his own autobiography makes this fact very clear.

Frankly, much of what I have read of SRF's editing seems adolescent. It mixes metaphors. It includes more than one thought in a single sentence (something a qualified editor would separate into two or more sentences). Their editing shows a lack of awareness of the rhythmic quality of Master's writing, and in fact of the importance to writing of rhythm itself. And they seem to feel that once a thought has been expressed correctly, they need strive for nothing more.

There is nothing in their editing of the very real charm in Master's style of speaking. As a result, his writing as presented by them seems often more mental than heartfelt. Yet his own writing came very much from the heart. I've described their editing as adolescent mainly because it represents an attempt to sound intellectual on the part of persons whose own nature is, like Master's, genuinely devotional.

As for the editing they do of his spoken words, I was myself present on a number of the occasions when he uttered the sayings that SRF has published. It was I, in fact, who submitted quite a few of those sayings. About twenty-five percent of those which appeared in early editions of *The Master Said* were contributed by me, so I know exactly what he said. I know how greatly some of those sayings were altered, and how much some of them were "laundered."

I've been blessed—perhaps by Master?—with an unusually clear memory, especially for the spoken word. Even words and phrases that he spoke in Bengali and Hindi—languages I didn't know at the time—I remembered accurately, even to the tone of his voice, and was able to verify years later, in 1958, when I went to India.

In one of the sayings for *The Master Said*, what he actually said was, "The dreamer is not conscious of his dream." That's a sentence that needs editing, because, obviously, the dreamer is conscious of his dream or he wouldn't be dreaming. In *The Master Said* the sentence was edited to read, "The dreamer is not cognizant of the hallucinatory fabric of his dream." (It would take a master to be able to speak like that!) When I used the same quote in another book, I said, "The dreamer is not conscious of the fact that he is dreaming." The simplification is, surely, too obvious to explain further.

Another sentence involved a vision Master had had of a saint. Boone had asked him who the saint was, and explained where the vision had occurred. Master said, "I see so many, how can I remember which one you mean?"

We both exclaimed with surprise at this fact of many saints appearing to him.

Master then said, "Why be surprised? Wherever God is, there His saints come."

They edited it to read, "Wherever a devotee of God is, there His saints come." Their wish was to make him seem humble. Well, I too am a devotee of

God, and can't claim to have been so "pestered." What he said very definitely was, "Wherever God is." The editor couldn't accept that sometimes he spoke in that impersonal sense of divine identity.

Did Master do the final editing of his works, as SRF claims, before he left his body? Emphatically not!

The two editions of *Whispers from Eternity* to which you referred—the 1929 and the 1949 ones—are not good examples, for in fact both of them were published during his lifetime. He himself told me this was the one book he had taken the time to edit personally. I myself have always considered it a literary as well as a spiritual masterpiece. There is little difference between these two editions, though I did hear him complain about a word that Miss Pratt had altered for the 1949 edition. It was in his poem, "God! God! God!" He lamented, "Why does she keep insisting on the word, 'clamor'? Every time I change it back to 'noises,' she makes it 'clamor' again!"

The really drastic changes in *Whispers* appeared quite a few years later: in the 1958 edition, I believe it was. There was no poetry in this edition, for Tara herself was not a poet. The edition was prefaced also by a letter, purporting to be by Master but in fact, *as I and other insiders knew*, written by Tara herself. This letter thanked "the editor" for her labors on the book.

What happened later was that a number of people, among them Priscilla and myself, complained about the excessive (and unpoetic) changes in this edition. SRF finally backed off—a rare thing for them to do—and agreed to reprint the earlier version as an alternative edition (in response, as they put it, to the sentiments of people who still liked the old edition). Actually, Daya Mata herself was not happy with the liberties Tara had taken with the new edition, and expressed to me her dissatisfaction with it.

You've been told that Daya Mata has "reached cosmic consciousness." This seems to be an important issue in SRF. How do I stand on it?

Once, while still new at Mt. Washington, I asked her, "What is Christ consciousness?" She replied, "Christ consciousness is when you see everyone as your brother or sister." I couldn't help thinking that this explanation didn't really address the issue—at any rate, not philosophically, and not as Master was wont to explain this and similar matters.

Let us in this case, however, accept her definition and ask ourselves: Has Daya Mata herself shown this kind of sisterly attitude toward everyone? Would someone who sees humanity as composed of brothers and sisters try to destroy a brother disciple? Would she spend fifty million dollars (my estimate) to attempt his downfall, and the obliteration of his service to Master, when no other opportunity to serve had been granted him?

Would she, even while spending such vast sums of money with intent to harm him, be willing to contribute no more than $200 a month toward the support of an aging SRF minister (Kamala Silva) who was in desperate need of care? This particular minister didn't live at Mt. Washington, but she was much loved by Master, whose disciple she had been since a girl in 1924, and to whom she'd remained faithful and devoted all her life. (I myself was paying $800 a month out of my own pocket at this time to help her, from a monthly salary at that time of about $1,000. It was I who wrote the SRF directors for assistance in this matter, so I know the whole story personally.)

Other members of Ananda were assisting Kamala also, by donating money and rendering her personal service. SRF assumed at the time that our motivation for helping Kamala was political, but this assumption lacked any supportive evidence, and showed how easily people project their own attitudes onto others.

What benefit could we have derived from helping Kamala? There was no friendship to cement there, nor any hope of future collaboration. Years earlier, in fact, she had hurt me deeply by refusing even to see me.

It was soon after my dismissal from SRF, when I was feeling spiritually abandoned, and was desperately lonely for contact with members of Master's spiritual family. Ananda and I (the Ananda members knew nothing of how hurt I had been by her) wanted only to care for someone whom Master had loved, and who loved Master, and who had now become old and helpless.

Would a person who viewed herself as a "sister to everyone" refuse to increase the stipend of another person, an aging relative of Master's, which was sent to her monthly because of a promise Master had made her?

India had passed through years of inflation since that promise had been made; the sum Master had promised, which at the time had been generous, was now the equivalent of about two U.S. dollars a month. The woman had pleaded with Daya Mata by letter that the amount be increased, explaining that she was faced with rising medical costs. Daya Mata replied that she was honoring Master's promise, and would continue to send the same amount as before.

Master had also given permission to this relative to live out the rest of her life in the home of Ananta, her father-in-law and Master's deceased brother. Again, would anyone who saw that woman as a sister in God—leaving aside the fact that she was a loved member of Master's family—have told her to leave her home so that it might be converted into an ashram (though eventually it became an apartment house)? Would this person (Daya Mata) protest that she had been generous to that woman, and plead, "Why, we gave her another home to live in!"—when in fact this new "home" was the so-called "carriage house," or garage, belonging to the first house: a little structure with only one window, and an open drain in the floor?

Ananda, during the time when we were struggling to raise the money SRF forced us to spend (by vicious and perfectly needless legal papers, submitted again and again by SRF's lawyers with, obviously, no other purpose than to bankrupt us), paid $15,000 for the purchase of a home for that aging relative of Master's. (The exchange rates made it possible to buy her a very comfortable house, and just what she wanted.)

What must SRF's reaction have been to Ananda's generosity? We don't know, but experience has taught us that they probably assumed we were acting from political motives. I can't imagine any benefit we might have gained thereby, politically or in any other way.

The truth is, we simply couldn't find it in our hearts to leave this relative, to whom Master had pledged his word, abandoned, without a home deserving of the name, and without medical attention. What was our benefit from this "deal"? Simply the satisfaction of having maintained Master's promise to her, and treating her with kindness.

I've done my best to make excuses for SRF's actions over the years, and also for their lack of action. And when the *Los Angeles New Times* printed that scurrilous article—the first of two as far as I know—about the uproar among the Mt. Washington neighbors over the projected transfer of Master's body to a crypt at the Mother Center, I wrote the newspaper and told them that in my opinion it was eminently fitting for Master's body to be there, regardless whether Ananda members would have access to it. (The newspaper had been trying, by letters and phone calls, to fan a feud on this issue between Ananda and SRF.) I also gave them an argument that no one seems to have thought of before: Having Yogananda's crypt at Mt. Washington wouldn't significantly impact the flow of traffic up the hill, since visitors to the crypt at Forest Lawn generally visit Mt. Washington also.

The Board of Directors phoned Ananda to express their thanks for my letter (which the *New Times* never published, unfortunately). We hoped this phone call signified an easing of tension in SRF's attitude toward us. As usual, however, we were naive.

I learn from you now that SRF has published what you've described as a "booklet" or "leaflet" citing that second, scurrilous lawsuit against us as "evidence" against me. Obviously, they are as determined as ever to "resolve the problem of Kriyananda."

Shortly before the second court case, Daya Mata said to me, "None of this is personal." Of course, it does manage to seem fairly personal to me. Their subsequent reference to that court case in an attempt to turn people against me does seem to be, as you put it, "stooping low." Even in the name of a supposedly "greater good," I cannot consider it honorable to impugn a person's character.

My "Open Letter" didn't do that. Though it drew attention to mistakes that I felt (and still do feel) need correction, it didn't say, "That is the kind of people they are: liars, business people, and callously indifferent to the needs of others." What it did was only try to correct, not to condemn.

The truth is, during the trial which you say they've described in their "booklet or leaflet," I was given *not one* chance to speak in my own defense. In its refusal to give me a hearing, this lawsuit paralleled with startling exactness SRF's dismissal of me in 1962. Every criticism the lawyers in this last case made of what they imagined to be my character—except only that of sexual harassment—was identical with Tara's accusations in 1962, and was self-evidently fed to the lawyers (who didn't know me at all) by SRF's leaders.

As for the charges of harassment, harassment of *anybody* is completely foreign to my character—as everyone is aware who has ever really known me.

The case was a lie from beginning to end. I am sorry to find SRF announcing it now as the truth.

Several lawyers have said to me, "Truth isn't what the courts are all about: All that matters is winning." In our own dealings with the law, however, we have always made it a point to select lawyers on the basis of their integrity and honor above all; only secondarily for their legal skills.

On to another of your questions: Yes, of course Master wanted disciples to read his own works, and not dilute their spiritual focus with other, lesser teachings. But to extend that advice as far as SRF has taken it? Well, you decide that matter for yourself.

As for your question on Kriya, I won't answer it here—not because I can't, but because this letter is already long enough.

I am very sorry for the pain you've experienced. I won't try to suggest what you should do, but I think that, if a person wants to keep his sanity in this world, his greatest need is for a sense of humor!

In divine friendship,

P.S. You may wonder why I have written you at such length. I've done so partly, as I said, out of concern for the distress you feel. I am also aware that anything I write on these matters cannot be stated casually; better than tossing it off lightly would it be to say nothing at all. Our ministers also will find what I've written helpful in answering people who question them on similar issues, as does happen. Whatever is made of this letter, please rest assured that any personal reference to yourself will be changed so as to make it unrecognizable.

Discusses an SRF monk who was once a friend | 4

2003

Dear _____:

Achalananda (Stanley Guy) came to Mount Washington in the early fifties, while I was in charge of the monks. He was one of two possible choices for someone to send to India with me; I often wished he'd been chosen, for he was a friend and was supportive to me. Instead, however, Tara said Allen's [another monk's] horoscope was better matched with mine, and he was the one sent.

In fact, Allen proved to be a disaster for me, as you've read in *A Place Called Ananda*. He has since left the work, and I've heard nothing further about him.

I met Achalananda, briefly, in Bombay years later, at a *satsang* given by Daya Mata. He'd obviously assumed—safely, and understandably—that I must be a fallen soul and shouldn't be spoken to. He knew nothing of what had really happened, but assumed that since I was out, I must be in the wrong. I understood where he was coming from, and have never had anything against him for it.

I saw him recently in an interesting video on the *yugas*. He has aged, of course, as have we all. He also seemed more in his intellect than in his heart, though of course the subject itself was of intellectual, rather than devotional, interest. Still, I'm interested in getting a feeling for who, why, what, and where he is in relation to Master, the path, and anything else, should you get a chance to speak with him.

I'm not asking you to probe too deeply. And I don't ask you to mention that you've been in contact with me. I'm certain he's completely loyal to Daya. I wonder: is he *intelligently* so? Is there anything about Daya in that organization that I've missed? I have many reasons for thinking she isn't following Master's will, but I'm always willing to be shown that I'm wrong; how else does one grow?

I guess what I'm saying is, I wonder how someone who was a friend, whom I always liked and respected, and who I believe to be deeply sincere, could have so opposite a *take* on things from mine. He is *much* senior to Vishwananda, who also seems sincere. Yet Vishwananda seems to be too much the organization man to be willing to question any official directive. Are both of them like that?

I've been so completely out of touch for so very many years, that I feel almost a stranger. Yet Mount Washington, to me, is still home.

What a strange road I've traveled!

It looks very much as though SRF, in reaction to Ananda, is hemming itself in ever further, becoming "monastic" (proudly so, in other words), and shutting out the world even more rigidly. You'll be able to tell me, when you come.

I know that the monks a few years ago were saying to people (certainly getting this concept from Daya), "Master came to the West to found a monastery." That's Daya, completely. But that attitude won't get the word out! It won't help all those who "humbly ask for help." And it isn't the way to found a religion.

When Master was William the Conqueror, Daya was his daughter Agatha. He sent her to Spain to marry the heir to the throne. She, however, wanted to be a nun. She prayed to be spared this terrible fate (marriage). When the ship arrived in port, she was found dead on her knees. It sounds inspiring and beautiful. Daya still takes it as evidence of her dedication to the only true ideal: God.

However, Master was her Guru, and the fact is, she disobeyed him. In this life, too, she is disobeying him in the sense that she wants his work to be a cloister, not a world mission. She has her own ideas of what's right, just as she had then. As Agatha died without completing her task, so Master's work is dying under Daya. Both "deaths" are, supposedly, in God's name! How ironic!

Blessings,

On the pronunciation and spelling of the name of Yogananda's foremost disciple, Rajarsi Janakananda | 5

March 17, 1999

Dear _____ :

A point I'd like to take issue with is Durga Mata's [an SRF nun's] insistence that Master named St. Lynn "Rajasi," not "Rajarsi." Durga was not an educated person, and had no knowledge of Sanskrit terms. Nor, for that matter, did Rajarsi, who pronounced his own paramguru's name [Sri Yukteswar] "Seeruktetraji." Nor do names really matter; it's the spirit that counts. When one is actually dealing with names, however, they DO count.

I myself was present when Master presented St. Lynn to the community with his new name and title. I have a trained ear for languages, and knew something of the Sanskrit terms even then. I distinctly heard Master say, "Rajarshi."

This title is, moreover, a scripturally recognized appellation dating from ancient times. It is short for "*raja rishi*," and was attributed to kings who were also great saints. King (Maharaja) Janaka, was one such royal *rishi*; he was a great master of ancient times and was, in fact (as Master told me himself), a former incarnation of Lahiri Mahasaya. This fact, and his giving St. Lynn the name "Janakananda," reinforce the rightness of Master choosing the title "royal *rishi*," since St. Lynn was indeed a "royal *rishi*" according to modern American understanding, as was King Janaka in his own times.

Because the second "r" in "Rajarsi" is very lightly pronounced in Bengali— a very slight roll of the tongue—anyone who was not accustomed to this sound in other languages (for example in Spanish) and who knew only the American exaggerated, but not rolled, "r" would be unlikely even to hear it. I myself, knowing other languages as I did (including Spanish), caught it easily and unmistakably. Daya didn't catch it, and insisted for years that Master had said "Rajasi."

I later tried to convince her that "Rajasi" doesn't make sense. It isn't really even a word. SRF, seeking justification for their error, combed what texts they could find, and finally came up triumphantly with the discovery that one scripture gives "Rajasi" as a name for the Divine Mother.

This was quite beside the point: Why would Master give St. Lynn a title referring to the Divine Mother, then follow it with the name, "Janakananda"? Moreover, Rajasi is, simply, a feminine form of the second of the three *gunas*, which is known as *Rajas*. Divine Mother as Rajasi is the Divine Mother manifested through *rajo guna*. This is no title to give anyone!

In India everyone insisted the title HAD to be *Rajarshi*. I myself renewed my efforts to convince Daya Mata, as I'd been doing for years. She finally admitted, "There may have been a slight 'r' when Master said it." There was. Of course there was.

Her own attunement to Indian languages was a subject of good-natured chaff among us—so much so that one day, after we'd kidded her for repeatedly mispronouncing the name of one of the ashram servants (his name was "Rambochan," but she kept calling him "Rashabom," "Rajasthan," and other variations I can't recall), as she was going up good-humoredly to her room, she turned around on the landing to face us, and, with mock gravity, announced, "Well, besa me mucho!" It was a line from a song, and one of the few foreign expressions she could remember. I'm sure she didn't realize what it meant: "Well, kiss me again and again!"—though I think she'd only have chuckled had we brought this meaning to her attention—which we didn't do.

Durga Mata has further muddied the waters with her insistence that Daya changed Rajasi to its present form. The fact that Rajarsi signed his name "Rajasi" doesn't mean a thing, except that he simply didn't know any better, and went along with what people assured him was the right form. "Rajasi" does NOT mean "king among saints." "Rajarshi" *could* be taken to mean that, though it usually is not interpreted that way. But in fact St. Lynn was, and Master considered him to be, a king among saints.

Love,

P.S. Here is one more point: The "s" in Rajarsi is pronounced "sh." This is how Master said it, and how Bengali is written and, usually, transliterated. In other words, an "s" followed by a vowel is always pronounced "sh." Scholars (but not Master) sometimes put a dot under the "s" instead, but to me (and also to Master, as he himself told me) it seems useless to have such diacritical marks, which no one understands except those who know the original script anyway.

My own vote is that we spell it Rajarshi.

In his 1994 Christmas letter to the Ananda community, Kriyananda describes a deep spiritual experience he had while recovering from open-heart surgery. This is an excerpt from that letter.

6

December 23, 1994

Dear Ones:

Last Sunday night in the hospital I became aware of an actual force trying to bring Yogananda's work downward: to confine it in the pettiness of definitions and formal organization. And I felt a mighty force combat this pettiness, to open up his teachings and mission that it become a doorway to the New Age of Dwapara, which is to say, of energy.

I prayed deeply until well after 1:00 a.m., trying to attune myself more deeply to this expansive power. And I felt that that expansiveness *will* win, *must* win. I also felt that it is quite impersonal, caring not a whit for forms, persons, positions, dogmas; that *whoever* tunes in to it, no matter what that person's spiritual path, will serve as an instrument for this great wave of divine light and energy that is sweeping over the planet.

It occurred to me to write an article for a magazine: "Yogananda's Mission, and Yours." His work, you see, isn't personal at all. Yogananda wasn't personal. As he put it repeatedly, "God is the Guru." His teachings weren't personal. God was using him as the *avatar* of a new age, to change an entire civilization.

Don't let anyone tell you that one organization, one person, one statement can ever, even remotely, define what he brought to the world. The present legal tiffs are not between two organizations, but between two different "takes" on his cosmic mission.

The dark forces (I definitely felt them as that) want to keep him small: a loving saintlet, the "beloved" founder of an organization, etc. The forces of light want to use his life mission to change, inspire, and guide all humanity.

It is a glorious work, one so important, and so great, that we, as individuals, count for nothing at all except as we offer our lives to the service of Divine Love.

January 5, 1995

Dear _____:

I wrote of universal principles. You've personalized my statement by making it seem boastful. I would never say, "I represent the truth." I have a right and a duty, however, to say, "I believe I perceive the truth of a matter, and am doing my best to attune myself to that truth."

Master wrote in the *Autobiography* that even masters can make minor errors of judgment concerning principles, errors for which their gurus may reprimand them. It is wise always to look at the principles involved, and not only at the persons who are trying to exemplify those principles. The argument, "Don't you think So-and-So *ought* to know best" is a weak argument if only because it demands the suspension of normal reason and common sense.

Oh, true, if Master, who was always compassionate, were to appear unfeeling in a certain circumstance, the proper reaction of a disciple *would* be to say, "I must not have understood him in this instance." If even a saint, however, shows himself too often to be unfeeling, and too seldom compassionate, the disciple would be justified in asking himself whether the actions are not truer to the person than his own devout expectations of that person.

In the present instance, what is involved are grand and impersonal principles. To boast that one *represents* such a principle would be, as you said, delusion. To believe in the principle, however, and to do everything one can to support and serve it, is the duty of every devotee.

If one believes, on the contrary, that because a good person is acting against that principle therefore the principle itself must be wrong, this belief must be considered a delusion. For surely you will not say that it is right *on principle* to oppose the universalizing of Master's message.

The two principles of contraction and expansion can be kept in a state of harmony and rest as long as both are accepted as necessary to the total picture of reality. When these two concepts are set at odds with one another, however, it is that conflict, and not the concepts themselves, that raises the question of good and evil.

I feel that there *is* a cosmic force which is wholesomely determined to universalize Master's work. To combat that force, rather than letting it work itself out to its natural conclusion, is what I call evil. That is to say, the friction resulting from this conflict produces disharmony.

I do not say that Daya Mata *represents* this evil, any more than I say that I represent this good. That she is—I hope with good intentions—acting in support of this obstructive force is, however, I do believe, true. And I see no point in saying, "She *couldn't* be supporting it." We can all make mistakes.

A matter of this sort must be approached in light of the principles and concepts, not of the persons involved. Universality simply *has* to be what God wants for Master's mission.

One also serves the cause of evil, or disharmony, when one tries deliberately to harm others. This is especially so when the harm is committed in the name, not of truth, but of untruth. To welcome _____ with open arms, for example, and support her in what could only have been, and are now revealed to have been, lies about Ananda, is not godly behavior no matter who the perpetrator is. To encourage treachery to Ananda in the name of loyalty to SRF is, again, not godly behavior.

I repeat what I wrote in my Christmas letter: There is something very big trying to happen in Master's mission. If I can be shown that my perception is wrong, and can be convinced that it is wrong, I myself will willingly admit my error and change my actions accordingly.

In the meantime, however, I cannot accept it as error merely because a fellow disciple tells me I am wrong.

I too lived with Master. I know what he told me and others. I have every right to my own understanding of his words and teachings, and must insist on that right as preferable in every case over blind acceptance of someone else's understanding, especially when that understanding goes completely counter to everything I myself deeply believe to be true.

In divine friendship,

*To Ananda's "legal team," commenting on
a letter from Daya Mata discussing the
possibility of settling the SRF lawsuit*

8

Dear Ones:

Here is a letter I've just received from Daya Mata. My own letter made it fairly clear that if we couldn't reach any mutual understanding, there was no need for further correspondence. So on this point, at least, we seem to be agreed.

She speaks of having tried to settle [SRF's lawsuit against Ananda]. The first step toward settlement, especially when one is losing, is to see what points one can concede. They, on the contrary, have done nothing but continue to make demands. What kind of "greater understanding" has she ever sought in our relationship? Nothing but my own acceptance of how wrong I've always been, and how infallibly right she's always been. She has never conceded a single point.

She says Master never told her to settle. Her own words to me in Pasadena (and I have a good memory) were her statement that he said to her, "*Settle!*" What am I to make—what am I *ever* to make—of her unwillingness to stand behind anything she says? She denies our (my, that is) "vicious charges" of complicity on their part in the Bertolucci case [sexual harassment lawsuit]. It has always seemed to them beneath their dignity to answer our charges. Simple denial, they seem to think, is sufficient. We've been lied to too often, however, to believe anything they say. What we need is some sort of proof.

Their main objection from the start has been not so much to anything I've done as to the mere fact of my continued existence. According to them, I should have died. (Ananda Mata actually dreamed, in 1959, that I'd left the work and that soon after that I died.) Or I should have become a shoe salesman, or *anything* except try to continue serving my Guru.

They did their best to destroy us, and then they claim I've been *adharmic* in "wresting away" Master's copyrights. The inspiration for doing so was, in fact, Jon Parsons', but it was the logical consequence of their own attempt to muzzle me. They tried to stop me from even quoting my Guru's words. Now they are getting their own karma back at them.

But they cannot see that anyone but them can be right on anything. With this attitude, it is impossible to reason. They have never seen that their treatment of me had to have negative consequences for them. I imagine they are convinced even now that they have only acted with pure and loving intentions!

I myself have struggled with that question of Master's copyrights. I want to do the *dharmic* thing, and, to be honest, I have worried lest my actions displease him. Reason, however—Jon's, Sheila's, all of yours, my own— has persuaded me that we have behaved rightly. I don't feel a need to struggle with this question any longer.

They have denied my right, as his disciple, even to quote him without first applying to them for permission. Moreover, they have repeatedly changed his words to suit policies that I consider flagrantly in conflict with his oft-stated wishes. Their argument that I "came years later" is absurd. Master himself frequently quoted Christ's words, "The last shall be first."

Their argument of my Johnny-come-lately status may be balanced also against SRF's absolute refusal to accept that he said anything to me directly, including of course his repeated statement, "You have a great work to do, Walter," and his prediction that my work would be writing and lecturing. (Yes, he included editing in that prediction, too.)

Their argument of my lack of any right even to *think* about the directions of his work may be balanced, finally, against my perception, which one would think at least worthy of some respect, that their basic premise of his work as being the organization rather than the teaching is a false one.

No matter what I have said, they've refused to discuss it, much as one might refuse to discuss an intelligent matter with an idiot. In fact, given their perception of me as a liar (a projection of their own tendency to tell flagrant lies), no intelligent discussion is possible anyway.

Daya writes, "Many words have been spoken or written to you in an attempt to reach an understanding." What words? The only "understanding" she's ever shown an interest in has been my total acceptance of her every dictate.

She writes that I have tried repeatedly to "divide and conquer." When have you ever known me to do that? You all know me as a man who does his best always to "unite and let truth conquer." In fact, they've never had the slightest idea who I am. Daya's recent letter merely reaffirms that fact.

The clinching argument for my editing his works is not that, owing to the court's decision, those works are now "up for grabs." It is that their editing is so bad it is embarrassing.

If they'd had the humility even to consider suggestions from me, I would have offered them humbly and would have done my best to be of service— to Master, of course, not to them. But they've rejected even obviously valid suggestions simply because I was the one who made them.

The important point, of course, is that his works be given the best treatment possible. Daya's statement that I came "years later" is irrelevant. If someone came even today who could serve Master better than I or than any of us has done, I would applaud, not condemn. The issue is *what*, not *who*.

There is nothing more to be said. I didn't think there was. My main reason for writing was to say that I simply don't care any more. Master is my Guru, not Daya Mata. Sure, I love her, but my policy must be directed by truth as I understand it.

Love,

To Ananda's lawyers about settling the lawsuit | 9

November 11, 2000

Dear Rob and Jon:

I have the impression that both of you would like to do your best to bring about a settlement between SRF and Ananda. It is important that the two of you understand certain things that Jon knows to some extent, but that Rob, being newer to the case, couldn't possibly know: namely, fundamental attitudes on the part of SRF that no reasonable person, accustomed as one is to the normal give and take between human beings, could possibly believe to be true.

I'm concerned, because as long as you think there's a chance of meeting them part way we'll be forced to spend a great deal of money quite uselessly.

SRF has a fundamental mind-set. It is absolute, because they are convinced they are doing God's will. We ourselves consider their attitude dogmatic and arrogant to the point of obsession, but whether they are right or not, they are not open to bargaining. This means they will never cede a single point in the simple and perfectly normal hope of gaining a concession on some other.

SRF believes utterly that it is on God's side, and however irrational their position appears to us, there is no doubt at all that they will never budge from it. They claim to want to talk "in good faith." All they mean is, their own "good faith"!

I ought to know. I've been associated with them for 52 years. I was for some time their vice president, and was on their inside councils for many years as well as being a monk there for 14 years. Don't, please, dismiss these statements as either uninformed or prejudiced. *I know what I'm talking about.*

Ananda has tried repeatedly, since their first threatening letter in February 1990, to find points it can concede. That we have failed is not due to any intransigence on our part.

In 1997 I invited them—by no means for the first time—to meet and discuss with a view to settlement. What I wrote them went in effect as follows: "Judge Garcia has refrained from finalizing his judgment purposely to give us a chance to, as he put it, 'practice [our] own teachings.' We have reached a point in this case where Ananda has won virtually everything. I don't want to be in a position of being able to declare to the world, 'Ananda won. SRF lost.' I want to be able to say, instead, 'SRF *and* Ananda both agreed to....' In that way you will save face, which is what I want for you, for our Guru's sake. For it will hurt his public name if we can't come to some agreement."

SRF met us in Pasadena. It was a very harmonious meeting. But somehow they formed the impression, no doubt from my conciliatory tone, that we were malleable. They did nothing but ask for concessions, meanwhile offering none in return.

In the name of harmony we agreed to most, if not all, of what they wanted. Thereupon they requested more concessions. At that point we began backing off. Gradually it became clear to us that they were going to demand *everything* they'd claimed since the beginning of their lawsuit.

SRF cannot think in terms of winning some, losing some. They are not even capable of seeing this as a case of "all or nothing," though I think they must see that nothing is what they may be left with in the end. Instead, they see it as a case of "all . . . all"; they are certain even now that some miracle will save the day for them.

The principals on their side are quite elderly; Daya Mata will be 87 next January. She has made it clear to me, however, both in writing and in talks with me, that she will fight on to total victory as long as breath remains in her body.

Please don't imagine that they will back down on any point. If they promise to do so on something not even significant, experience has convinced me, as well as the rest of our legal team, that they won't keep their promise until the final legal nail is hammered into their coffin. *They won't give up*.

I have had a great deal of experience with them. Much of it has been at close quarters for (as I said) fifty-two years. Don't, please, come in with the thought that you will bring about harmony, when I and countless others have tried and failed.

I myself have done far more than most people would dream of trying under such circumstances. My own people consider me almost obsessive in my efforts to bring about harmony at virtually any price. (At least twice over the years I actually offered to *give* Ananda to them, in the thought that it would at least be part of the same basic mission. So deeply did I believe in unity. Yet Daya Mata's reply to my second offer was, "We wouldn't want to inherit your debts": as though the only possible reason for my exceptionally generous offer was that Ananda had to be on the verge of bankruptcy!). I have failed in my efforts. I will never succeed.

The simple facts are these: They think themselves to be fighting in the cause of God and Guru. They consider me an instrument of Satan, and have said so. They have also charged me repeatedly, in public, of being a Judas. They have never shown themselves capable of logical reason. For one thing, they have never shown respect for any point of view but their own, even in little matters. To them, other points of view *simply do not exist*. I am not referring only to the present case.

In every matter, they always reason from an entrenched position. They never give reasons for their position, but only declare themselves in such a way as to silence all opposition. To understand this attitude, it must be kept in mind that, living as they do in a quasi-cloistered state, they are unaccustomed to being contradicted in anything, and especially in their views of what is right or wrong.

The only possible alternatives are that they cede defeat out of a fear of going to trial, or that this case actually does go to trial. No concession on our part can possibly result in anything but the conviction, on their part, that we are weakening.

I don't think they want to go to trial; they have too much to lose in the resulting exposure. This is the only hope we have of avoiding what we, too, would of course prefer not to go through. The difference between us, however, is that we aren't afraid of going to trial.

Maybe they'll decide to give up. They'll never compromise, and they'll never stop until there is no alternative left to them. Despite Judge Garcia's ironic statement about their appeal to the U.S. Supreme Court ("Don't hold your breath!"), we must count on their "going for broke." And when they lose, they'll make the usual noises about Satan and all the rest. Even now, word has come back from them (but this is pure rumor) that, living in Italy as I do, I must have Mafia backing.

Please believe me. Otherwise, we'll only lose a lot of money. Even if they talk compromise, all they can possibly mean in that posture is that they want *us* to compromise. After that, they will only insist that we concede everything, including all that we've won so far in this lawsuit.

Sincerely,

To an LA Times reporter after an interview with Kriyananda | 10

June 20, 2001

Dear _____:

You asked me during our interview how I could still be a friend to someone who had betrayed me deeply, and for so many years. Since then I've pondered how to answer you, because I assume you had a sincere desire to know.

There are two kinds of love. The first is given *in response* to love received. It is conditioned by what it receives. The other is a *commitment*. As Shakespeare wrote in the sonnet that begins, "Let me not to the marriage of true minds...." He continues, "Love is not love which alters when it alteration finds."

Love that comes with commitment is one's own to give; it doesn't depend on anyone else's attitudes or behavior. The way Daya Mata chooses to treat me is her affair, not mine. My feelings are my own responsibility. Were I to retract them, I, myself, would suffer more than it would be worth to me. Were I to allow myself to be angry, or to hate, I would cheapen my own self. By loving instead, I feel calmness, inner joy, and a wish to help her if I can.

Though I feel I must fight back now in defense of the work Master has given me to do, my hope is that even at this late stage of her life she may recognize her mistake, and change. More than that, I feel it my duty to defend this work. For it isn't mine, and my determination to defend it is not for myself: It is to persevere in my duty.

In divine friendship,

2002

Dear _____:

If we want to make any reply to SRF, I suggest it be individually to those who ask. Here's what we might write:

> A Reply to SRF's Paper "Protecting a Spiritual Legacy"
> *[in which SRF implied that they had achieved victory in their lawsuit against Ananda, when in fact 95% of the issues were decided in Ananda's favor]*
>
> Well, SRF hasn't been wholly candid in their announcement. We are tired, however, of the confrontation circumstances have imposed on us. Naturally SRF wants to show its best face. We can't really fault them for that.

Certain people have expressed their displeasure over their public statement, which tries to blame Ananda and make it seem the loser in their lawsuit against us.

I say, Let people simply compare SRF's statement with ours, and make up their own minds. We've been as truthful as we could, but in the end what does it really matter? The important thing is that we can now carry on without further fighting.

At Ananda, and I suspect equally at SRF, there has been a huge sigh of relief now that the lawsuit's over. We can now both serve God and our line of gurus according to our own concepts of devotion and belief.

Ananda hopes that we can all gradually become friends. I know that we at Ananda feel that way, and I believe many in SRF feel that way too. Communication needs to be developed between us. This has been the greatest lack.

May there be increasing harmony between us in the years to come. Meanwhile, we extend our sincere love and friendship to all our *gurubhais* (fellow disciples) in SRF, and everywhere.

Love,

"Morally and spiritually, the whole world is in a state of great confusion.

WORLD CONDITIONS

I can't help thinking that much, much more suffering lies ahead before humanity will learn its needed lessons."

January 9, 2000

Dear _____:

Master spoke of three things: a depression, which he said would make the one in the thirties look like "a picnic"; world war; and a "cataclysm." He spoke of the causes of the first two: money mania, greed, and materialism, for the depression; communism and a clash of old and new values (*Kali* vs. *Dwapara Yugas*), for the war. He didn't define or describe what he meant by "cataclysm," but obviously ascribed, whatever it will be, to world karma.

Therese Neumann also said something interesting that may touch on more than one of these points. She told an American soldier that America would suffer economic destruction as a result of the break-up of its landmass.

Everyone in this century whom we'd consider a saint, or to have had heavenly visions (such as the many visionaries who have seen the Madonna, including Padre Pio who also endorsed what some of the visionaries had seen) has spoken of *great* trials.

As for the first of Master's predictions, there was no specific timing on it. However, no one seems to disagree that we are in an incredible financial credit bubble. No bubble in history has failed to burst, in time, leaving countless people bankrupt. The people during every bubble have considered their times "the exception." There never has been such an exception. Moreover, it looks increasingly as if the stock and bonds market is getting too hot to last.

As for war, I think people are waking up to the fact that communism is about as dead as a hibernating grizzly bear. Putin, Russia's new "boss," has eyes like a crocodile; I don't think the deaths of hundreds of millions of people would be anything more to him than an interesting statistic.

What I've suspected, moreover, is that the break-up of "Mother Russia" has been a wound that many a Russian will simply not tolerate forever.

The Russian mind doesn't react swiftly, as the American does. The Russian broods, nurses its wounds, and awaits its opportunity—preferably until the enemy gets the idea that maybe the bear is dead after all and walks over and bends down to take a closer look.

Master spoke of communism as a very real and global threat, and not one that would simply blow away with a sea change in the economic scene. The Madonna at Fatima said the same thing in 1917 (or was it 1918?), when communism wasn't even perceived as the great threat it has since become. The same thing has been said by many others.

Meanwhile, the old communist guard hasn't faded from power. The KGB, the politburo, the satellite "republiks": All of them are the same people, merely dressed up in new clothing. The KGB is very active in, and perhaps even *as*, the present Russian Mafia. Russia as a nation has known ruthless dictatorships for centuries. They've had no actual experience in democracy. "Democratic sounds" have been made, and have been applauded by wishful thinkers in the West and elsewhere, but such has been the inexplicable pattern of thinking among "liberals" since the Russian revolution.

I don't believe Master would have believed a word of the praise that has been heaped on modern Russia. It isn't "modern." It's the same bear, disguised as a rug. When people write of "the former communist system," my thought has been, "I'll believe it when I see something else actually at work." So far, the "new Russia" thing seems a shill.

No, I think war is definitely a likelihood.

Master spoke of the timing of the economic crash and world war in vague terms—something like, "toward the end of this century." We're past that end, but we're in the same "time zone." I'd say we need to be very careful.

We here in Italy have gone to the American consulate in Rome and given them our e-mail numbers. A wise precaution, I think. If an emergency arises, they'll do something to get Americans out, if possible and if things don't simply move too fast for them.

What about "cataclysm"? Master shouted this word in church one Sunday morning: "You don't *know* what a TERRIBLE *cataclysm* is coming!" I've always thought cataclysms were natural, not man-made. Therese Neumann suggested this one would be natural. Master, during that lecture, was talking of the coming economic disaster. That was the context, but did he mean more? Could Master have meant cataclysm in terms of its overall effect on humanity? Possibly. Or could he have meant—as I always used to think he did—something geologic and global?

A book Byasa recommended to me, *When the Earth Nearly Died*, a long, exhaustively researched, and fairly persuasive inquiry into something that seems to have nearly occurred around 9500 B.C., describes what must certainly be called cataclysmic, because it is attributed to the near approach of a heavenly body from outside our solar system.

We've seen something of that nature with the Schumacher-Levi comet, which hit Jupiter fairly recently. Considering the Earth's far smaller size, such an event would certainly be far more traumatic for Earth than it seems to have been for Jupiter. Such things are possible, and seem to have happened more than once during the Earth's history. When we say, however, "Okay, what about *this* year?" the answer, obviously, is that the likelihood is minimal.

Still, here we are at the beginning of a new *Yuga* (another question: What was a cataclysm like that last one doing hitting the earth in the middle of *Satya Yuga*, the spiritual age?). It does seem at least possible that when Master said "cataclysm," and when Therese Neumann spoke of land changes, they meant something much larger than a man-made disaster.

The Y2K predictions didn't materialize, but they forced us to prepare in case of any need in the future. Then of course the question: "Aren't you afraid, living in Europe?" No, not at all. I don't think anyone at our center is. Our lives belong to God and that means also our deaths.

Love,

The timing of Yogananda's predictions | 2

Late 1980s

Dear _____ :

I've found that, in the matter of timing, the prophecies even of masters seem to be qualified in their accuracy. On the other hand, we've no way of knowing from what depth of intuitive perception they were speaking. From an absolute level, one assumes they are infallible. There are other levels, however.

I would think that, normally speaking, the masters address *directions* of karmic flow, more than the timing involved in the working out of the karmic law. Certainly there are also predictions that involve karma which can be corrected by ameliorating karmic acts. The probability of war can be nullified, for example, if sufficiently nullifying activity is directed towards international harmony and love.

Is such karmically nullifying energy being directed by any nation at this time? Does it not seem to you that the discord is only increasing?

In divine friendship,

*Excerpts from a letter and statement
written from Swami Kriyananda to
Ananda after the 9/11 terrorist attacks*

3

September 13, 2001

The tragedy in New York and Washington was, and of course still is, appalling. I only hope it has affected none of you personally, through friends and relatives. That it affects all of us in some way is, however, inevitable.

I am proud of America for talking more of prevention of future terrorist disasters than of revenge. For whereas I agree with those who have said we must take preventive measures, any desire for revenge would be motivated by hatred. May our nation's actions ever be on the side of truth, and wisdom, not of destruction and *adharmic* action. . . .

America, as the great Indian yoga master Paramhansa Yogananda often said, has aligned itself with the forces of light, and for this reason is, with its great power, the hope of the whole world. May this country never forsake this divine true role by embracing material greed and forgetting God. . . . As he also promised, God will watch over us, and will be able to do so ever more fully if we cling consciously and lovingly to Him.

The arrogance in the photos shown of bin Laden, and the glee of people in Palestine dancing and laughing in the streets in a victory mood, are despicable. Never have Americans wanted, what to speak of rejoiced in, the sufferings of their enemies. Rather, we've stooped to help the very enemies who first attacked us, after we'd won the wars they themselves launched against us.

These hijackings are manifestations of satanic consciousness. I see no point in pretending spiritual love by showing tolerance for them. Evil is not tolerant of Good.... Good cannot excuse evil in the name of spirituality.... The one clear thing is that weakness in the face of evil simply extends a clear invitation to evil to be even more evil. Thus, action of some kind is unavoidable. Let us pray that it be the right action. Even the best-intended actions, however, can be misinterpreted—as we know very well from many of our own life experiences....

We owe it to ourselves, and to all humanity, to do what we can. Our duty is to act firmly, even sternly—as, during a forest fire, a swath of trees may need to be cut down to prevent the fire from spreading. No world scripture counsels spinelessness. It is sufficient that we not be drawn into hating others. Our concern must be the threat posed by their actions to the rest of humanity. . . . There is no need, spiritually, to love those terrorists. It is enough that we love God. We may love them as His children, but their pardon and salvation lies between their souls and God. Our concern must be for those who are suffering. . . . and the threat posed by their actions to the rest of humanity. . . .

～～～～～

In all sincerity our first concern can only be for those whose suffering is right now. I cannot honestly spare my heart's love for the people who perpetrated this suffering. Nor can I love them for the hatred and anger by which they define themselves. Yes, I love their souls, but I must leave their salvation to God. Within my own limited scope of feeling, my love must go primarily to those who are now suffering.

Surely, in an abstract sense I can love those enemies also, but they have invited God's retribution for their crime. They have lessons to learn if they are ever to become receptive to God's grace. While I've no desire to see them suffer, I leave the state of their souls to God; my present energy is for those whom they have made to suffer.

We as human beings owe it to our nation and to humanity to try—not in anger or hatred, but most assuredly with sternness—to prevent such evils from being perpetrated again. There can be no wrong, spiritually, in using punitive force to whatever extent is necessary to forestall a repetition of Tuesday's tragedy. We cannot simply refrain from acting with the excuse that God wants us to love. This, under the circumstances, would be a non-response, and would be a proof of spineless cowardice—an attitude no scripture in the world has ever counseled. The important thing is not to be drawn into reflecting others' negative emotions.

What, then, do I pray for? I pray for myself, that I become a clear channel for God's grace. My prayer goes to my fellow human beings, too, that as many be strengthened as I can reach in the divine light....

An ocean consists of countless little drops of water. If each of us, like those drops, offers himself and herself up to God, praying, "Lord, use me as You will. Give me the strength to channel Your kindness and love to all—impersonally, not with personal pride or desire"—I think we will have done the most we can possibly do. Thus only may we help most greatly our poor, belabored earth, beset as it is by hatred and ignorance. If we understand that, by loving, it is God's love we express, He will surely flow through any barrier we erect of ego and self-interest, and uplift significantly the consciousness of the world.

One raindrop adds but a little moisture to the earth. Once, however, it unites with enough other raindrops, they become a mighty torrent of water flowing down to the sea. So also we, by uniting our energy and directing it toward the ocean of divine consciousness, can participate in the great drama that is being waged between the forces of light and of darkness.

What should we pray for? We should pray that God use us, and everyone whose life we are able to touch—that He use us not as we may will, but in ever-greater attunement to His will.

In Master's love,

September 23, 2001

Dear _____:

There are a few points in your letter that show misunderstanding. I favor containment, not punishment. This world, as Sri Yukteswar pointed out to Master, is inconveniently arranged for a literal practice of *ahimsa*. I think my image of cutting a swath of trees to save a whole forest is a good one. I've no desire to cause suffering to the terrorists—only a hope that we can keep them from causing much more suffering to other, innocent people.

Values in this world cannot be defined absolutely. The universe is under the sway of relativity. Sometimes a lesser wrong must be accepted in order to defend against a much greater wrong. Even Gandhi, who was not always realistic in this regard, urged that India be kept as one nation instead of divided, even if the result meant many inter-religious deaths (which happened in any case).

America doesn't deserve the criticism it often receives of wanting hegemony. It is the only country in history that has helped the enemies who first attacked it. I don't know what America plans, but certainly they don't want to kill innocent civilians.

I think no master would tell a country to cleanse itself and not bother about others, as you suggest. That would be unrealistic. Krishna himself said there is a need, sometimes, for defensive war. Arjuna chose Krishna in preference to Krishna's whole army without him, but he accepted, in the end, the need to fight.

For individual devotees the matter is different. I had to bear great injustice from SRF, and took it as my karma instead of attacking them. Only after forty years of persecution, and SRF's attempts to destroy me and Ananda by lawsuits, have I accepted that I had to speak out. But I've no wish to harm them; only to prevent them from destroying Ananda.

Your view of these things will undergo change as life brings you greater maturity. Meanwhile, keep in mind that the scriptures themselves teach what I have said: to act, not with the desire to harm anyone, but to prevent harm to many more people. Not to act because of fear, however, would be karmically wrong. Of course no one wants war. Even war, however, is preferable to not standing up for what is right.

In divine friendship,

September 12, 2001

Dear _____ :

Thank you so very much for your concern. From Ananda, there doesn't seem to be any news as yet. I know of no one who has been touched personally by this tragedy.

The whole world is, and has been for some time, in a state of war between the forces of light and of darkness. The war is not between one religion and another, or between one political system and another, but between that aspect of human consciousness which tends upward, toward God, and that other, which tends downward, away from Him and toward material fulfillment and all that is born of matter-consciousness: hatred, greed, intolerance, and the desire to destroy as opposed to the life-giving desire to serve, build, and create.

America, obviously, is at fault for its material greed, which it must learn to refine, and fortunately *is* refining, gradually, by its innate spirit of generosity. Morally and spiritually, however, the whole world is in a state of great confusion. Above all, what it needs is love.

Let us pray that we ourselves be given the grace to be instruments for the divine light, that it may flood ever more strongly and clearly into the world.

A tragedy like the one that just happened will likely inflame anger, which will be to some extent righteous, but which also, unfortunately, will be unrighteous in its demand that suffering be inflicted on the perpetrators. They must, realistically, be prevented from inflicting further harm, but their very suffering, in punishment, could inflame nations beyond all bounds of reason and charity.

It is a time for placing human problems more determinedly in God's hands. I wish there were less talk of the righteousness of democracy (which God knows has its faults, too), and more talk of a determined dedication and submission to God's will, and God's love.

Hard times. I can't help thinking that much, much more suffering lies ahead before humanity will learn its needed lessons.

Thank you for writing.

In divine friendship,

On responding to the terrorist attacks | 6

September 19, 2001

Dear _____:

This issue wasn't easy for me to address, for of course we should look for the cause, but how much are people *actually* able to introspect? I got a letter from _____ saying we should "love, love, love" the terrorists. Beautiful, but do you suppose anyone really does—including _____? I don't think so!

The important thing is to be real, not hypocritical. The truth is that if anyone gave that much energy to the evildoers he would not only be depriving the sufferers but also tuning in to the evil—no wholesome exercise for anyone who is seeking truth and God! I get impatient with such lack of genuine sincerity.

That was a good article from the Dalai Lama. He told the truth. I'd have liked, however, for him to be more specific. I noted he fell into the trap of rhetoric and repetition that I had to try repeatedly to avoid. (And even so I find, on re-reading my article, that I've repeated myself unnecessarily.) Still, his statement is the clearest, wisest, and most genuine of those I've seen on this event so far.

Love,

September 13, 2002

Dear _____ :

I am not willing to appear on _____'s program. My reason is not that I haven't what may be useful thoughts on the subjects raised, but that I am not willing to fight over them, which is what a talk show would be likely to be. My reasons are twofold:

1. I am hard of hearing, and might very well miss key statements in the caller's questions or comments.

2. I have not made these issues a life commitment.

3. I believe deeply in certain principles, and would feel duty-bound to defend them in certain contexts. These, however, are facts, not principles. I think there should be room for different points of view concerning them.

That much said, here are my thoughts on his questions:

Responding to Our Aggressors

I think we should respond *usefully*. I don't think it would be useful to send love to people who hate us in this way. They are God's children. They are not *my* children. My job is to love God. Being human, however, my ability to love is not cosmic. I consider it more important to love God, and in that way to do my little part in opening a channel for His love to this world.

We should send out love *generally* to the world, in His name, but our own love should be directed to those who can be united in working for world harmony and peace. Osama bin Laden is more than I can take on, with my limited powers. I don't wish him ill. I simply feel that the best I can do is wish all well who want to work for God's light and love.

Had I been on that plane from Pennsylvania that was flying to Washington, I would have joined the attackers of the terrorists. It would have meant my death. I wouldn't have hated the terrorists. But I feel we must stand by truth. Life and death are not important before such issues. We must all die someday. I'd rather die for truth than try to live for untruths.

Non-violence

I think we must be practical. A non-violent movement would not be practical at this time, and is not the way to bring about a cessation of violence on earth. Were I a Jesus Christ, I might have the power to win evil with love—though he was crucified, wasn't he? No, I don't think violence is the answer, but if I am attacked I think it is my duty to *win* in some way for the truth. If I can win with love, all the better. If I haven't that power, then I must fight—not with hatred, but with love *for truth*, not for those who are in error.

Creating Peace

Work *for* peace. Don't work *against* violence.

Leadership Style and Philosophies

History teaches the need to learn cooperation, not competition and violence. We should work *for* the good, not *against* evil. The evil will always be there. We aren't going to eradicate it. But we *can* strengthen the side of good. Leadership that seeks to advance a cause, not a person, is what is needed today.

Advice for World Leaders

I would say what I just said, that there is no way we can eradicate terrorism. If God hasn't been able to do it, I don't see how man can hope to. He, however, who created this world, surely knows how to run it. Terrorists, like everyone else, have lessons to learn. In their case, they need to learn to respect other points of view from their own, and to learn that they cannot force others to think just the way they themselves think. We, too, must reach that understanding.

My thought is, we should work with those who are in agreement with our ideals, and let God's love take care, in *His* way, of those who don't agree.

If and when others see that harmony works, they will decide *of their own will* to behave likewise. Otherwise, the only way I can make them behave as I think they ought to is to *force* them to my point of view. If I did that, in what way, essentially, would I be any different from them?

Intentional Communities

I think for the world that communities are the best way of working out questions of how to relate to others, to life, and to God. In large social experiments, people have been *coerced* to abide by the theories of a few. The best solution is if small groups can work these things out, set a good example, and let others decide whether that example appeals to them.

In our Ananda communities we *have* shown that people can live by high ideals, love all, and have communal harmony. *That* is a useful lesson. In that way, we may be of practical service to those who feel in harmony with what we've done.

Yes, I think that small, intentional, cooperative communities are the *best* answer to today's needs. For one thing, they work. For another, they *invite* imitation rather than demanding it. I've gone into this question in depth in my book, *Hope for a Better World!* I don't think in a quick interview that I could express myself at sufficient length to give a clear idea of what I mean.

"All suffering is in the last analysis self-generated. God doesn't will it on us.

SUFFERING AND DEATH

It comes as a result of the misuse of our own will, whether recently or in the distant past. Suffering can be banished by the right use of will."

Circa 1974

Dear _____ :

I was happy to hear from you, though sorry for the trials you have been undergoing. Please remember that all suffering is in the last analysis self-generated. God doesn't will it on us. It comes as a result of the misuse of our own will, whether recently or in the distant past. Suffering can be banished by the right use of will. As Sri Yukteswar said, "Forget the past. The vanished lives of all men are dark with many shames. Everything in future will improve if you are making a spiritual effort now."

Don't think in terms of doing one thing big enough to lift you out of your present state. Think rather in terms of taking one step at a time. Commit yourself to *some* positive act, however small, and carry that act through to completion. Finish whatever you start.

When you make the right effort, and then invoke God's power to sustain you in that effort, you will find Him reinforcing you and giving you the strength gradually to win out over all obstacles. But you must make the right effort first. God cannot help you until you, yourself, first try your best.

Make the attraction you feel to spiritual people and ideals your main focus in life—not in the sense of wishful thinking, but as your inspiration to do your best to become like that. Remember, the same God that sustains the saints is in you, and loves you equally. He is our common Father.

In divine friendship,

May 29, 2001

Dear _____ :

I've been so sorry to hear how unwell you've been. You are dear to me, and I want very much not only to hear that you are physically stronger, but in better spirits, spiritually. Please, _____ , remember Master's words to us:

"God doesn't mind your faults. What He minds is your indifference to Him." Forget yourself in love for God. All suffering begins with self-involvement.

I want very much to see you well—spiritually well, above all. Don't hold negative images of the past. The Divine Mother in you could do no wrong. As Swami Shankaracharya said, "Bad sons there are many, but *never* a bad Mother." He was speaking of the Divine Mother in relation to Her human children. As Sri Yukteswar said, "The vanished lives of all men are dark with many shames. Everything in future will improve if you are making a spiritual effort now."

I think the best thing for you would be to try to give of yourself to others in the community. For starters, *allow* them to help you. They *want* to do so. You will be helping them if you let yourself be open to them in that way.

Next—and this may be more difficult for you—come out a little bit; mix with people. They (we) all love you, and want your welfare. Forget everything but the fact that we are all children of our one Divine Mother. Seek Her love in their eyes. Feel Her love in the energy they want to give you.

Don't let self-involvement betray your soul's desire for self-expansion.

With eternal love,

Give all your pains to God | 3

1988

Dear _____:

I urge you to give all your pains to God. Don't cling to them, for in that way they only increase, and you won't resolve anything. What happens between you and others is unimportant compared to your eternal relationship with God. Let every human pain deepen you in that most important reality: your love for God.

The less you think about yourself and your personal needs, and give yourself wholly to God, the more you will find Him fulfilling your every desire, and in the most beautiful way imaginable! Remember, He wants only the best for you. Trust in Him. Suffering comes from self-love and self-affirmation. Joy comes from self-forgetfulness in the contemplation of high spiritual realities. Try to live more in God.

You have my prayers and blessings.

Love,

Asked about the reality of hell and eternal damnation | 4

May 30, 2001

Dear _____:

The subject of hell demands longer treatment than I'm likely to feel up to devoting to a letter. However, I've dealt with the subject in my books, *The Path*, and *The Promise of Immortality* (which I'm told will be out by the end of June, and is available already on the internet).

Hell, of course, is primarily a state of consciousness, not merely a place. As a place it exists, too, but no damnation can be eternal. It only seems so, to the sufferer. A preacher once shouted angrily at Yogananda, because he didn't subscribe to his entire belief system, "You will go to HELL!" Yogananda, looking at him calmly, observed the anger contorting the man's features. "My friend," he replied, kindly, "I may get there by and by, but *you* are there already!"

Hell and heaven, both, begin with where we are, in our consciousness. Thomas Merton described two old ladies in Harlem—surely an earthly hell, if any be described as such—as saints. It isn't *where* we are physically, but what we make of ourselves: our inner state of awareness. I remember St. Therese of Lisieux wanting to go to hell so that God would have someone to love Him there. What a beautiful thought!

No, I don't believe in eternal hell. But it is true that when people suffer, their suffering often seems forever.

Love,

September 20, 1999

Dear _____ :

I want very deeply to see you come out of all mental anxiety. And I'm concerned about your being alone in Hawaii because I've seen you before, and see you now, tending, when you're off "vacationing," to go into a downward spiral spin of thoughts, thoughts, and more thoughts. One can't come to a resolution of one's problems in that way. Rather, they only increase in size, in number, and in the power they have over us.

Again and again I've seen in my own life that the best thing is simply to redirect my thoughts and energy, and to stop thinking about problems that don't seem to have a clear solution. They'll disappear, if you don't give them energy.

Please engage your mind in work, so it doesn't spin on while you think of all the things you must "process." The best way to process things, I've found, is to drown one's self in work for God, and in loving Him. That's what our lives are all about. Nothing else really matters.

In Master's love,

Late 1980s

Dear _____ :

Don't allow yourself to be swept up on an emotional high. Let the joy you feel well up from deep inside you. Let it be calm, and internalized. In that way it won't set you up for the opposite state, depression, but will remain steadily and increasingly yours.

I pray deeply for you.

Love,

May 30, 1983

Dear ———— :

I don't know you by your fuller name, so can't address you more formally. Our dear mutual friend, ————, sent me a portion of one of your letters to her, along with a plea for suggestions as to what she might say to you to help you extricate yourself from your present bitterness toward life and toward God.

I know you feel you are being simply honest in the bitterness of your appraisal of life, and that any effort to change this attitude could only involve wishful thinking on your part, or sentimentality and delusion on the part of others.

Still, you seem like a reasonable man, and on that basis I would like to offer you these few thoughts. I offer them as ————'s friend, and, through her, as your friend. And I offer them also as one who has known suffering in life—not *your* suffering, to be sure; but then, neither has your suffering been mine. Who is to say whose has been the greater? For each of us, I think, what we have tasted has seemed as much as the heart could bear.

My faith, too, in God was severely shaken—faith not in His existence, nor even in His love for others, but certainly in His love for *me*, a lack that seemed to me the more painful for the selectivity of its focus.

There was a thought that helped me at that time, one that I hope you won't take amiss if I share it with you. For I, too, am a reasonable man, but during that trial I remembered the many times in my life when my ability to reason honestly had been affected by my feelings—even to the extent of becoming totally clouded, when my feelings were distorted. The logic on those occasions had seemed so transparent, so ineluctable, that I hadn't imagined that it might be wrong. Yet, when the upset in my feelings subsided, the logic changed with them, giving me finally a calmer, more balanced perspective on matters that at first had seemed to me chaotic.

Looking back on those occasions, what I resolved to do during my time of severe testing was *to suspend judgment for the time being*, and wait for a time when I might view my experience without the intense aversion which, I knew, was affecting my reason. In fact, a clear, positive outlook did come at last, though only after some years. The marvelous thing was that, when it came at last, I felt nothing but *grateful* for what I had experienced.

I'm not going to ask you even to imagine gratitude for what you've been suffering, and for what you've seen others suffer. But I do ask you to consider suspending judgment for the time being. I might even put it to you this way: Why suffer twice? You are experiencing physical pain: Why add to that mental torture? Indeed, if God be really the sadist you make him out to be, why give him the satisfaction of seeing you broken at last!

I've tried this simple technique many times since those dark days in my own life: Whenever things have gone wrong, and I've been tempted to get upset about them, I've told myself, "This isn't the time for me to pass judgment. For now, let me try to accept things as they are, without trying to understand what they mean. If in fact they do have a meaning for me, perhaps that meaning will come clear later on."

So far, it always *has* come clear, in the end.

_____, if this weren't a letter I'd probably end with that thought. But who knows whether I'll ever be writing to you again? So let me add one or two further points.

First, an interesting statistic: Of all the people—in all countries, in all periods of history, and in all religions—who seem in some way to have known God, *not one* has expressed bitterness toward Him, though in fact not a few of them passed through bitterness to reach Him. Knowing Him, their vision has become one of underlying Goodness—indeed, of perfect Love—spurned by man, who willfully keeps his back turned toward Him.

Second, their bitterness, fanned by suffering, sometimes proved to be the very emotion they needed to turn toward God, for only in their bitterness against Him did they begin to think of Him seriously. Previously, in forgetfulness of Him, they may not have known intense pain, but neither had they known joy, and freedom from those errors of living that had resulted in pain in the first place. In thinking of Him, even with bitterness, the time came at last, through their resulting attunement with Him, when joy drove out all other thoughts, leaving them as I became, finally: grateful.

The history of pain itself makes a fascinating study. Again and again one finds stories of people who, having emerged from the darkness of suffering, have exclaimed with full hearts, "I see now why I had to go through it all! In no other way could I have gained what I've gained, or learned what I learned and know now."

A final thought. My spiritual teacher used to say, "Conditions are always neutral. They appear happy or sad, beneficial or harmful, according to the positive or negative attitudes of the mind." Please think about that statement; on first reading it would be so easy to toss it aside. But I've tested it for nearly thirty-five years now, and I've never known it to fail.

Joy to you. I am perfectly certain, much more so than I could possibly convey in a letter, that under the veil of your present suffering there *is* joy, and that even the suffering is a part—albeit difficult to understand now—of a larger and very important plan for your highest, soul welfare.

In divine friendship,

On humility and grace | 8

February 12, 1991

Dear _____ :

I'm sorry you've had to accept chemotherapy, but at the same time I'm deeply relieved to hear that it isn't as unbearable as you feared (and as it was, two years ago), and above all that it is helping you. Keep at the work of getting well! At the same time, however, concentrate above all on living close to God. I pray for you.

Yes, to echo your words, be humble. It is so easy to think we are the doers, because in a sense we really are. It is our right attitudes and thoughts that draw divine healing power and guidance into our lives. The more we pride ourselves on what we've done, however, the less open we find ourselves to that power. So, remain sweet and humble. I am praying for you.

Love,

October 31, 2006

Dear _____:

I am so sorry. At the same time, you will find this, too, a great blessing, if you take it in the right way. Master does want you to resist this disease with faith and with will. At the same time, he wants you to offer the fruits of even this battle to God.

Don't think of your body as your own. It is God's body, from which at least the consciousness of illness must be banished. Through this sincere, courageous effort, think always of becoming a *jivan mukta* in this life: freed from all identity with body, personality, and ego: with anything, in other words, that defines you as a separate, human entity rather than solely as a manifestation of God.

I have felt more spiritual maturity growing in you, dearest _____. Be strong in Him. Remember, giving your ego to God doesn't mean becoming a non-entity! What happens is that, the more you not only step out of the way mentally but offer your every thought, feeling, and action to God, the more you feel increasingly blessed by an ever-stronger flow of His love, joy, and inspiration pouring through you.

As Jesus said, you must lose your life in God to find true life; lose yourself to find your true Self. The supreme incentive for doing so is that, in clinging to the little self, one clings to limitation, suffering, and misery.

In Master's love,

July 20, 1972

Dear _____:

Thank you for your sweet, touching letter. It is good to have a heart soft enough to feel the sufferings of others. But now ask yourself: Does God suffer? His nature is pure bliss. Is He then callous and unfeeling towards human suffering? Is he perhaps unaware that people suffer?

Don't you see? Bliss is the *answer* to suffering, not merely something we feel when suffering has been temporarily forgotten. It is not by jumping into the water and drowning with the drowning man that we help him, but by standing on dry ground and rescuing him. (Or by swimming if we are strong enough, but certainly not by voluntarily drowning, too.)

Suffering is a result of delusion, not of outward circumstances. There have been people in the darkest dungeons (Benvenuto Cellini was a good example, as he relates in his interesting autobiography), and people suffering from the worst diseases (consider Ramakrishna, St. Teresa, and countless others) who have known only joy. There have been people living in palaces, surrounded by wealth, fame, and all the goods of this world, whose suffering was constant because *in their minds* they knew no peace, were selfish, and did not care for others.

Joy and suffering depend *entirely* on attitudes of the mind. The poorest beggar has found bliss when his attitude was right. The richest king has found only misery when his attitude was wrong. Cellini actually prayed for the grace to be thrown into a dungeon again, so much joy did he find there because his mind was on God. And he was a worldly man, not a saint. People also found God in concentration camps.

So the more we feel of people's suffering, the more we should give them, or long to give them, the healing touch of joy, and not only join them in their suffering. This is true Christlike compassion.

When we ourselves know suffering, it is because of wrong actions of the past that have created these thoughts in our minds. We strengthen those karmas when we give into them.

Dear friend, try to live more in your higher Self, and with others who, too, have joy in that Self. Meditate more. Thank God for the blessing of loving Him, and even for the blessing of every test He sends you. Truly, it is all His grace.

In divine friendship,

June 24, 2001

Dear _____:

Your appeals have deeply touched me. I've been praying for your dear sister, and am praying now that she pull through her operation. Please know that I am no miracle worker, but my prayers sometimes are answered, and I would not deny prayer in your sister's case because of lack of confidence in my own power. After all, God's alone is the power.

Remember always that this is all a play of God's. As Divine Mother said to Master once, when he was going through a severe test, "Dance of life and dance of death, know that these come from Me and as such, rejoice!" Joy comes only when we understand to our depths that this is all Her play.

In divine friendship,

"She died serving God.
What better way to go?" | 12

February 12, 1991

Dear _____:

Thank you for your interesting letter, and for the copy of the speech given about our friend. If indeed she is liberated, what does her death matter? Death comes to all, but liberation to very few.

Do I really accept that she is liberated? It is not for me to judge. Certainly her God-centered life brought great divine blessings to her. And she died serving God. What better way to go?

Still, she was dear to me. I am also sorry that she had to die so young. Her life was a blessing to many people.

In divine friendship,

October 24, 2003

Dear _____ :

I've heard you are feeling a bit low. It's understandable. But I know you don't like that feeling, so may I suggest something? Make a greater effort to meditate longer, and deeper. Don't seek, instead, to distract the mind.

The power to rise comes from within, from superconscious contact, not from pretending everything's all right and just "soldiering" on. Devote yourself more, now, to making God your companion.

Love,

September 24, 1975

Dear _____ :

I am so happy to hear that your feelings are so much more at peace on the subject of your husband's death. Remember, death doesn't really exist. Have faith that he is with you, and that you will be together again some day. A man of his spiritual sensitivity is surely in a much better place now, and able also to send you his love and to help you.

Don't hold him down with sadness, but share with him your joy in mutually loving God and Truth. In this way you will be able to help each other.

As to why your husband should have left so young. It is not really helpful to ask that question. Remember, karma rules us all. Ask rather, "What can I do about it, now?" You can do much by your love, by your loyalty to him, by your support spiritually, and by your prayers. Be joyful above all. This is the best thing you can do for him.

May God bless you always.

In divine friendship,

June 9, 2006

Dear _____ :

I'm sorry I've been unable to stop by to see you in person. This body can no longer get around as much as I might wish.

I understand that the time for your passing may now be very near. I wanted you to know that though I'm not with you in body, I'm very much there by your side in spirit, and in consciousness.

Don't be afraid of what's to come. As you'll soon see for yourself, death is nothing to fear. Illness has its challenges (as well you know). At the moment of death itself, though, there is no pain at all. Rather, what you'll experience is a great release from all the pain and worries you've been dragging along.

These next days are a wonderful opportunity for you. Enjoy them! Leave those burdens behind you: Relax away from them all. Absorb yourself in thoughts of the freedom and light that will soon be yours. You're very blessed to have lived the life you did. Those who have meditated and lived for God go to higher and beautiful realms when they depart this earth.

I know that many friends have been coming to be with you. There will be many more angels waiting to receive you and bless you on the other side. We're a spiritual family who've been doing this together for many lifetimes!

I'm praying for you, _____ : sending you my love, my blessings, my best wishes, and my support in the new adventure that's about to begin for you. I pray especially for your realization in God. Please pray for us, too. We'll miss you. But we'll also be together again soon.

God bless you.

In divine friendship,

May 9, 1998

Dearest Paula:

What a blessing your life has been for us all! Your sweet temper and unfailing cheerfulness have been a constant inspiration. And your selflessness in thinking of others, more than of yourself, has been a perfect lesson in the attitude of a true devotee.

I meditated after hearing that you'd left us. I felt your sweet consciousness: your humility, goodness, and angelic nature. I feel also your strength: both great and inspiring. It is great, because it comes from divine attunement and not from egoic will; it is inspiring, because it channels Divine Mother to others. I know She blesses you, and I know Master blesses you. So also do we all, your brothers and sisters in God.

Thank you for your life. And thank you even more especially for the manner in which you left this world. If they give grades in heaven for the final exam of earthly passing, I'm sure you received an A-plus!

We'll miss you, dearest one.

In Master's and Divine Mother's love, your friend forever,

*"We are here for
God alone.*

SEEK YE FIRST
THE KINGDOM
OF HEAVEN

---

*Everything else
is just fillers."*

May 2, 1996

Dear _____:

It was a joy to meet you. I hope you will be able to find what you are seeking by serving Master's work. I would not want to make up your mind for you on the choice of how to pay back your debts, but I am glad you chose as you did. "Seek ye the kingdom of God first, and all these things will be added unto you."

Since you have made God, and His service, your priority, everything must fall into place accordingly on the material plane also. I've seen this to be true again and again in the lives of hundreds who live at Ananda and have had to face just the choice you've faced. With so many examples, it is easy to see principles at work, both for and against the ideal of serving God first. That is to say, when people put Him second in their lives He kept receding from them while, at the same time, nothing ever seemed to go for them the way they planned.

You are a soul bent on finding, whether late or soon, your own salvation. In the process you want to help others find their salvation. *That* is what life is really all about. Nothing else really matters! You have my prayers and best wishes. God bless you.

In divine friendship,

2003

Dear _____:

I was touched by your letter. Thank you for taking the trouble to write it.

Wealth means much more than money: It means abundance, which in turn means joy, love, and fulfillment on all levels. It is good also, therefore, to realize that a person can be wealthy even if he has little material abundance.

And I'd like to add, finally, something I've learned in life: When I don't seek primarily for myself, but seek to please God and to serve Him in others, I am always provided for.

I also believe in the rule, "Live comfortably within your means." For I've seen many people who somehow seem never to "get it together." No matter how much they earn, they are always in debt. A solid guideline to happiness is not to have too many desires.

I wish you every good.

Sincerely yours,

Desire to return to your true Self | 3

September 11, 1990

Dear _____:

Desires are wrong because they are limiting. It is not wrong, however, to desire liberation, or God, who bestows liberation. Worldly desires take us out of ourselves. Good desires, including above all the desire for God, take us back to our true Self.

In divine friendship,

The deeper message of two dreams | 4

February 28, 1990

Dear _____:

Your dreams are significant. They show that you need to get back to basics: to make a greater effort to put God first in your life. "Seek ye first the kingdom of God, and His righteousness, and all these things shall be added unto you."

Why was Mother Teresa part of your dream? It doesn't mean you need to seek her out or become part of her work. It means that her life represents a dedication to service, and that is what needs strengthening in your life.

The roses in the dream represent your devotion, which has been wilting. Revive them in your heart with more meditation, more service, and more attunement with God, Guru, and your *gurubhais*.

Don't nurse hurts needlessly in your heart. If others seem less generous toward you than you would like them to be, be *twice* as generous toward them! That is the way to victory. Indeed, I know that everyone wishes you well, and wants the very best for you.

The pains God sends us are for our welfare. Take them as His blessings, for they are as much signs of His love for us as His more gratifying gifts.

I pray for your spiritual growth and happiness in God.

In Master's love,

God's grace surrounds you | 5

1975

Dear _____ :

Do not feel discouraged, but continue to meditate and practice Kriya. Master always taught us to affirm success and in that affirmation we become stronger in our realization too. God's grace surrounds you. Try to share your every thought and feeling with Him. It is amazing how one's consciousness changes in this practice.

It's true that it is difficult work to try for a goal and live wholly in the present, but the *Bhagavad Gita* gives us the clue: *Nishkam Karma*, "To act without desire for the fruits of action and only to please God." Indeed, we cannot do our best unless in our hearts we are free. Do everything joyfully, remembering that God is a God of joy.

God bless you.

Love,

January 14, 2002

Dear _____ :

I'm sorry about your mother's slow decline. Try to keep your mind on God when you are with her. This will help her as she approaches the end of life.

In the Bible story of Mary and Martha, Martha still gained spiritually from her service to Jesus. She simply could have gained more if, while serving, she had kept her mind on God.

This you can do while you assist your mother. Serve with joy. Think of being a channel for God's joy.

Love,

August 2, 2001

Dear _____ :

As devotees, our first question should be, "How can I come closer to God?" not, "Why is my work not being appreciated?" As I've said through this whole episode, I'm perfectly willing for my music to be forgotten by everybody, but I am NOT willing that anyone lose spiritually by serving in the cause of reaching people with it.

My concern has been for _____'s attitudes. Every time he replies to anything, it is always on a worldly level of things planned, done, etc. My concern is centered in the fact that I never hear him speak like a devotee. I don't want a "business." I want a *service* to the God in others.

Attitude is everything to me, not what people do or how well they do it. We're here for God alone. Everything else is just fillers. If the spirit isn't right, it's better to drop everything into the ocean and meditate.

Love,

February 5, 1983

Dear _____:

I was saddened to hear of your many trials. Please know that I am praying deeply for you, that you feel God's strength flowing into you and through you.

There are times when we may not even be able to meditate. God can still help us, but we must help ourselves, too, by putting out as much energy as we can to rise above our problems of the moment, and to feel that God is, indeed, shaping our lives in the best possible way for our growth. Even when we think that we are at the end of our strength, God never challenges us beyond our ability.

Sometimes, when we allow ourselves to become too attached to family and to the things of this world, God takes them away from us. It is to teach us to seek only His love in all things. When we love Him to the best of our ability, He gives us everything that we need in life. May you ever feel His love for you.

In divine friendship,

January 25, 2007

Dear _____:

I'll be glad to try to answer your questions.

> *1. What exactly do we mean by saying man has been given free will? If all actions are done by God, how is man free?*

First, soul freedom is a reality, but it must be understood on a deeper level than that of the ego.

Freedom, to begin with, is true only of the soul. Limitation of all kinds is the meaning of bondage, and ego-consciousness is the greatest limitation of all, from which all others proceed. Ego makes us think we have a separate, individual reality.

As waves on the sea appear individual, yet have no lasting reality except as manifestations of that one great body of water, so we ourselves, in ego-consciousness, rise and fall, wavelike, on the ocean of God's consciousness, success followed by failure, happiness followed by sorrow, fulfillment followed by frustration, ever subject to the contrasting states of duality. Our separateness from the ocean, however, and even from one another is a mere appearance. Man may be described as simply a bundle of self-definitions.

Yogananda described divine consciousness as "center everywhere, circumference nowhere." Man's limited existence is the "circumference" formed by his egoic self-definitions. When those limiting self-definitions are removed or dissolved, nothing remains to prevent his consciousness from merging into and becoming one with God. In that stage it is not that we lose all identity; rather, we expand our identity to infinity.

Being omniscient, it must be added that we retain the memory of having been, each one of us, a separate ego. In this way, Yogananda explained, nothing is lost in the Infinite—not even the ego. We can revive that memory of individual existence again, if ever the Divine wills that we return to earth to uplift and save other wandering souls.

Man cannot be free in ego-consciousness, except in the sense that his soul-consciousness within him can impel him to direct his energies and aspirations toward God, or toward *maya*. Everything man does in his egoic state is conditioned by his own past actions, and by the countless outside influences to which he is subject. For man is integrally a part of the great Web of Existence. Egoic individuality is an illusion.

Man has only this much freedom: his soul, being a part of God, is not separate from Infinity. Thus, all of us in our souls have the power either to turn toward God or to reject Him; to love Him, or to spurn Him. This, in essence, is man's only true freedom. Since karma and worldly influences prevent him from expressing that freedom, it must be added that man is free also to the extent that he can free his mind from all habits and separative samskars.

In other words, if he is self-controlled he has greater freedom than someone who is completely bound by habits. Good qualities, which are the attributes of *Sattwa guna*, cannot in themselves bring release from ego. All qualities however noble, being born of ego-consciousness, conceal the inner soul. The *Gita* tells us they hide it as smoke hides a fire: A little puff of wind, and the fire becomes fully visible.

Sattwa guna is like a thin veil covering soul-consciousness and concealing it. A little meditative effort is all that is needed in order to blow away the last delusions of egoic separateness.

The darkening qualities of *Tamo guna*, on the other hand, form a thick covering which conceals the soul within them as if in deep darkness. The *Gita* compares *Tamo guna* to an embryo in the womb: Time alone will enable the embryo to emerge into the clear light of day.

God does indeed do everything, but He also created delusion, and operates through the three *gunas* to bring about His cosmic magic show. We cannot operate through the ego without becoming intrinsic parts of the cosmic illusion. Hence, in our egos we are free only to the extent that we turn back, even with great effort, toward God. Only as we shed ego-consciousness can we reclaim our divine freedom, which means becoming one with God again.

> 2. *How will a person know whether his meditation is proper or not—i.e., whether or not he is making good progress?*

The more deeply you enjoy the peace of meditation, the more satisfactory will be your progress.

Spiritual advancement can be judged also by how free you feel from the constant goading of egoic individuality: the hurts, whether large or small; the pains of life, both physical and mental; the desire for recognition, fame, or worldly power and importance; by how little you refer your painful or pleasant experiences back to yourself, thinking, "I am the one suffering or exulting."

It can be judged also by your inner freedom from desires of all kinds except the longing for God; by how free you feel from every test, including those of blame, opposition, and calumny on the one hand, or praise, popularity, and fame on the other; by your inner freedom from identification with success or failure, in the recognition that, in cosmic reality, all human experiences are essentially equal.

You are advancing when you see all others as allied to your own Self, and your sense of identity expands to include everything. All the above are signs that one is advancing spiritually.

The most important sign is this: that your love for God is growing ever deeper, and you feel selfless joy in the thought of Him—or, better still—in the actual perception of Him.

3. How can a person know how much merit he has already accumulated in past lives, and how far he actually is from Self-realization?

Self-realization comes not as a result of merit—which is to say, of good karma—but by the grace—the *kripa*— of God. God, my Guru used to say, has disappointed many saints who thought in terms of their own personal gain, instead of surrendering themselves completely to His will.

In the last analysis, no one can know when God will come. God is no merchant, to be bought with good works. The less we focus on ourselves, and lose ourselves, instead, in the thought of Him, the more we find that we have Him already, and that we have had Him always!

I hope these answers prove helpful.

In divine friendship,

Index

About the Author

A prolific author, accomplished composer, playwright, and artist, and a world-renowned spiritual teacher, Swami Kriyananda refers to himself simply as "a humble disciple" of the great God-realized master, Paramhansa Yogananda. He met his guru at the young age of twenty-two, and served him during the last four years of the Master's life. And he has done so continuously ever since.

Kriyananda was born in Rumania of American parents, and educated in Europe, England, and the United States. Philosophically and artistically inclined from youth, he soon came to question life's meaning and society's values. During a period of intense inward reflection, he discovered Yogananda's *Autobiography of a Yogi*, and immediately traveled 3,000 miles from New York to California to meet the Master, who accepted him as a monastic disciple. Yogananda appointed him as the head of the monastery, authorized him to teach in his name and to give initiation into Kriya Yoga, and entrusted him with the missions of writing and developing what he called "world brotherhood colonies."

Recognized as the "father of the spiritual communities movement" in the United States, Swami Kriyananda founded Ananda World Brotherhood Community in 1968. It has served as a model for a number of communities founded subsequently in the United States and Europe.

In 2003 Swami Kriyananda, then in his seventy-eighth year, moved to India with a small international group of disciples, to dedicate his remaining years to making his guru's teachings better known. To this end he appears daily on Indian national television with his program, A Way of Awakening. He has established Ananda Sangha, which publishes many of his eighty-six literary works and spreads the teachings of Kriya Yoga throughout India. His vision for the next years includes founding cooperative spiritual communities in India, a temple of all religions dedicated to Paramhansa Yogananda, a retreat center, a school system, and a monastery, as well as a university-level Yoga Institute of Living Wisdom.

Timeless Books of Truth

When you're seeking a book on practical spiritual living, you want to know that it is based on an authentic tradition of timeless teachings and resonates with integrity.

This is the goal of Crystal Clarity Publishers: to offer you books of practical wisdom filled with true spiritual principles that have not only been tested through the ages but also through personal experience.

Started in 1968, Crystal Clarity is the publishing house of Ananda, a spiritual community dedicated to meditation and living by true values, as shared by Paramhansa Yogananda, and his direct disciple Swami Kriyananda, the founder of Ananda. The members of our staff and each of our authors live by these principles. Our work touches thousands around the world whose lives have been enriched by these universal teachings.

We publish only books that combine creative thinking, universal principles, and a timeless message. Crystal Clarity books will open doors to help you discover more fulfillment and joy by living and acting from the center of peace within you.

In this collection of nearly two hundred stories, the remarkable qualities are revealed with breathtaking clarity. The stories cover a diverse range of spiritual practices and topics, presented in an enjoyable, easy-to-read format.

Swami Kriyananda As We Have Known Him | *Asha Praver*

The greatness of a spiritual teacher is only partially revealed by the work of his own hands. The rest of the story is one he cannot tell for himself. It is the influence of his consciousness on those who come in contact with him—whether for a brief moment, or for a lifetime of spiritual training. In this unusual biography, the remarkable qualities of Swami Kriyananda himself are revealed with breathtaking clarity .

Swami Kriyananda, a foremost disciple of Paramhansa Yogananda (author of *Autobiography of a Yogi*) has been prodigious in his service to his Guru. His books and music are available in 28 languages and 100 countries. In India, millions of people watch his daily television show. He has founded schools, retreats, and communities on three continents. He has circled the globe lecturing and teaching.

If you'd like a succinct, easy-to-understand overview of Yogananda's teachings and their place within ancient and contemporary spiritual thought and practices, we suggest:

God Is for Everyone | *Inspired by Paramhansa Yogananda,*
written by Swami Kriyananda

This book outlines the core of Yogananda's teachings. *God Is for Everyone* presents a concept of God and spiritual meaning that will appeal to everyone, from the most uncertain agnostic to the most fervent believer. Clearly and simply written, thoroughly nonsectarian and non-dogmatic in its approach, with a strong emphasis on the underlying unity of all religions, this is the perfect introduction to the spiritual path.

"This book makes accessible the inspired pursuit of Bliss in simple, understandable ways. Written as an introduction for those just starting on the spiritual path, it is also a re-juvenating and inspiring boost for experienced seekers. Clear, practical techniques are offered to enhance personal spiritual practices. The author maintains that "everyone in the world is on the spiritual path" whether they know it or not, even if they are temporarily merely seeking pleasure and avoiding pain. Sooner or later, "They will want to experience Him (God)." Experiencing God—and specifically experiencing God as Bliss—is that underlying goal of this work, based on the teachings of a self-realized teacher. It hits the mark for contemporary spirituality."
—*ForeWord* Magazine

~~~~~

Yogananda has many direct disciples, individuals that he personally trained to carry on various aspects of his mission after his passing. One of the best known of these disciples is Swami Kriyananda, the founder of Ananda and Crystal Clarity Publishers. Kriyananda's autobiography, a sequel of sorts to *Autobiography of a Yogi*, contains hundreds of stories about Yogananda, culled from the nearly four years that Kriyananda lived with and was trained by Yogananda. It offers the unique perspective of a disciple reflecting on his time with a great Master:

The Path: Autobiography of a Western Yogi | *Swami Kriyananda (J. Donald Walters)*

The Path is the moving story of Kriyananda's years with Paramhansa Yogananda. *The Path* completes Yogananda's life story and includes more than 400 never-before-published stories about Yogananda, India's emissary to the West and the first yoga master to spend the greater part of his life in America.

The Path is a deeply moving revelation of one man's poignant search for truth. With this book, Walters provides us with a rarely seen portrait of the joys and the problems of the spiritual path. *The Path* is filled with profound insight and practical advice for the novice and the more advanced seeker. I cannot conceive of anyone not deriving value from reading Walters' life story."—*Michael Toms, Founder and President, New Dimensions Radio*

"This book let me see inside the life and teaching of a great modern saint. Yogananda has found a worthy Boswell to convey not only the man but the spirit of the man." —*James Fadiman, author of* Unlimiting Your Life *and* Essential Sufism

Crystal Clarity also offers two additional biographical resources about Swami Kriyananda. These are:

Faith Is My Armor: The Life of Swami Kriyananda | *Devi Novak*

Faith Is My Armor tells the complete story of Swami Kriyananda's life: from his childhood in Rumania, to his desperate search for meaning in life, and to his training under his great Guru, the Indian Master, Paramhansa Yogananda. As a youth of 22, he first met and pledged his discipleship to Yogananda, entering the monastery Yogananda had founded in Southern California.

~~~~~~

If you would like to learn more about the spiritual heritage of India, the highest meaning of Hinduism, Yoga, and Christianity, including the deeper, underlying unity between Eastern and Western spirituality, you will enjoy reading:

The Promise of Immortality: The True Teaching of the Bible and the Bhagavad Gita | *J. Donald Walters (Swami Kriyananda)*

Destined to become a classic, *The Promise of Immortality* is the most complete commentary available on the parallel passages in the Bible and the Bhagavad Gita, India's ancient scripture. Compellingly written, this groundbreaking book illuminates the similarities between these two great scriptures in a way that vibrantly brings them to life. Mr. Walters sheds light on famous passages from both texts, showing their practical relevance for the modern day, and their potential to help us achieve lasting spiritual transformation.

Praise for *The Promise of Immortality*
"While Walters' study speaks to an urgent need for understanding and compassion, his book also brings both the Bible and The Bhagavad Gita vibrantly to life. The Promise of Immortality is the most complete commentary available on the parallel passages in these two texts." —*Bodhi Tree Book Review*

"The Promise of Immortality takes us on a meticulously researched and lucidly explicated journey through two of humanity's precious scriptures, the Bible and the Bhagavad Gita. Walters shows us how the deep and profound truths within each wisdom tradition align beautifully with each other, and with our inborn creative gifts."—*Mary Manin Morrissey, author of* Building Your Field of Dreams

~~~~~~

If you would like to learn how to begin your own practice of yoga postures, meditation, Kriya Yoga, and more, as taught by Yogananda and Kriyananda, we strongly recommend the following:

The Art and Science of Raja Yoga | *Swami Kriyananda*

Contains fourteen lessons in which the original yoga science emerges in all its glory—a proven system for realizing one's spiritual destiny. This is the most comprehensive course available on yoga and meditation today. Over 450 pages of text and photos give you a complete and detailed presentation of yoga postures, yoga philosophy, affirmations, meditation instruction, and breathing techniques. Also included are suggestions for daily yoga routines, information on proper diet, recipes, and alternative healing techniques. The book also comes with an audio CD that contains: a guided yoga postures sessions, a guided meditation, and an inspiring talk on how you can use these techniques to solve many of the problems of daily life.

Praise for *The Art and Science of Raja Yoga*

"It's tough to do a good yoga book, because a number of variables have to converge: substantive integrity, clarity in how-to explanations and quality visuals. By those measures, this book succeeds. Walters' long teaching record shows his ability to discuss key yogic concepts and practices in simple terms. . . . This comprehensive guide has an extra medium to distinguish it on the crowded yoga bookshelf: an accompanying audio CD that contains a vague lecture as well as more helpful sections of guided meditation and posture instruction. All things considered, it's superior to books that reduce yoga to a series of physical exercises taught by this year's guru."—*Publishers Weekly*

Meditation for Starters | *J. Donald Walters (Swami Kriyananda)*

Meditation brings balance into our lives, providing an oasis of profound rest and renewal. Doctors are prescribing it for a variety of stress-related diseases. This award-winning book offers simple but powerful guidelines for attaining inner peace. Learn to prepare the body and mind for meditation with special breathing techniques and ways to focus and "let go"; develop superconscious awareness; strengthen your willpower; improve your intuition and increase your calmness.

Awaken to Superconsciousness, Meditation for Inner Peace,
Intuitive Guidance, and Greater Awareness | *Swami Kriyananda*

This popular guide includes everything you need to know about the philosophy and practice of meditation, and how to apply the meditative mind to resolving common daily conflicts in uncommon, superconscious ways. Superconsciousness is the hidden mechanism at work behind intuition, spiritual and physical healing, successful problem solving, and finding deep, and lasting, joy.

Praise for *Awaken to Superconsciousness*
"A brilliant, thoroughly enjoyable guide to the art and science of meditation. [Swami Kriyananda] entertains, informs, and inspires—his enthusiasm for the subject is contagious. This book is a joy to read from beginning to end."
—*Yoga International*

~~~~~~~

Affirmations for Self-Healing | *J. Donald Walters (Swami Kriyananda)*

This inspirational book contains 52 affirmations and prayers, each pair devoted to improving a quality in ourselves. Strengthen your will power; cultivate forgiveness, patience, health, and enthusiasm. A powerful tool for self-transformation.

Spiritual Philosophy

Swami Kriyananda has also written extensively on philosophy, science, and the humanities:

Out of the Labyrinth, For Those Who Want to
Believe, But Can't | *J. Donald Walters (Swami Kriyananda)*

Modern scientific and philosophical claims that life is meaningless and merely mechanistic are refuted by Kriyananda with his fresh approach to evolution and directional relativity. Hailed by scientists and religious leaders alike, this book is essential for everyone who is struggling to find answers to existential dilemmas.

~~~~~~~

Hope for a Better World!: The Small Communities Solution

Swami Kriyananda (J. Donald Walters)

In proposing what he calls "the small communities solution," the author expands Yogananda's vision of "world brotherhood colonies," which offer hope and promise for building a better world by example, rather than mere precept.

Praise for *Hope for a Better World!*

"Walters takes us on a fascinating journey backward in time in order to explore the future of human relationships. He guides us through the history of Western thought to arrive at a deep understanding of our evolutionary moment—the expansion of human consciousness. Like a good storyteller, Walters keeps us waiting breathlessly to hear more, and how we can put ourselves on this path to a better world."—*Louise Diamond*

Arts and Education

Art as a Hidden Message | *Swami Kriyananda (J. Donald Walters)*

With insightful commentary on the great musicians, artists, and creative thinkers of our time, this book offers a blueprint for the future of art, one that views both artistic expression and artistic appreciation as creative communication.

"Kriyananda's predictions for Art's future are enlightening. They include a return to simplicity and a renascence of beautiful melodies. This book is, I believe, the most important book of our time on this vitally important subject."—*Derek Bell*

Space, Light, and Harmony: The Story of Crystal Hermitage

J. Donald Walters (Swami Kriyananda)

Space, Light, and Harmony—containing 70 beautiful color photographs—is an adventure in design, building, and living. It is the true story of the evolution of a home—from initial planning to interior decorating—that serves as a powerful metaphor for personal development.

Education for Life: Preparing Children
to Meet the Challenges | *Swami Kriyananda*

This book offers a constructive and brilliant alternative to what has been called the disaster of modern education, which, according to the author, derives from an emphasis on technological competence at the expense of spiritual values. Based on the pioneering educational work in India by Paramhansa Yogananda, the *Education for Life* system has been tested and proven for over three decades at the many *Living Wisdom* schools located throughout the United States, and will provide the basis for *The Yoga Institute of Living Wisdom* in India.

Praise for *Education for Life*
"The author makes clear that 'education for life' begins in the home. The moment people become parents, they become the primary teachers. Through reading this book, parents will be learning more simple and effective methods of leading their children into becoming happier and more successful human beings. They will also be learning from their off-spring. The author's techniques will help produce a much less stressful home-life for all."
—*Jim Doran, Education Consultant,* Joyful Child Journal

Higher Consciousness in the Workplace

The Art of Supportive Leadership: A Practical Guide
for People in Positions of Responsibility | *Swami Kriyananda*

Here is a new approach, one that views leadership in terms of shared accomplishment rather than personal advancement. Drawn from timeless Eastern wisdom, this book is clear, concise, and practical—designed from the start to quickly produce results even for those who don't have huge amounts of time to spare.

Used in training seminars in the United States, Europe, and India, this book gives practical advice for leaders and emerging leaders to help them increase effectiveness, creativity, and team building. Individual entrepreneurs, corporations such as Kellogg, military and police personnel, and non-profit organizations are using this approach.

Praise for *The Art of Supportive Leadership*
"We've been looking for something like this for a long time. We use it in our Managers Training Workshop. This book is very practical, very readable, and concise. Highly recommended!"—*Kellogg Corporation*

Money Magnetism: How to Attract What You Need When You Need It | *Swami Kriyananda*

This book can change your life by changing how you think and feel about money. According to the author, anyone can attract wealth: "There need be no limits to the flow of your abundance." Through numerous stories and examples from his own life and others', Swami Kriyananda vividly—sometimes humorously—shows you how and why the principles of money magnetism work, and how you can immediately start applying them to achieve greater success in your material and your spiritual life.

Praise for *Money Magnetism*
"A thoughtful, spiritual guide to financial and personal prosperity. This book has timeless wisdom and practical solutions."—*Maria Nemeth, author of* The Energy of Money

Books by Paramhansa Yogananda

Crystal Clarity publishes the original, unedited edition of Paramhansa Yogananda's spiritual masterpiece:

Autobiography of a Yogi | *Paramhansa Yogananda*

This is a new edition, featuring previously unavailable material, of a true spiritual classic, *Autobiography of a Yogi:* one of the best-selling Eastern philosophy titles of all-time, with millions of copies sold, named one of the best and most influential books of the 20th century.

This highly prized verbatim reprinting of the original 1946 edition is the ONLY one available free from textual changes made after Yogananda's death.

This updated edition contains bonus materials, including a last chapter that Yogananda himself wrote in 1951, five years after the publication of the first edition. It is the only version of this chapter available without posthumous changes.

Yogananda was the first yoga master of India whose mission it was to live and teach in the West. His first-hand account of his life experiences includes childhood revelations, stories of his visits to saints and masters in India, and long-secret teachings of Self-realization that he made available to the Western reader.

"In the original edition, published during Yogananda's life, one is more in contact with Yogananda himself. While Yogananda founded centers and organizations, his concern was more with guiding individuals to direct communion with Divinity rather than with promoting any one church as opposed to another. This spirit is easier to grasp in the original edition of this great spiritual and yogic classic."—*David Frawley, Director, American Institute of Vedic Studies*

~~~~~~~

In addition to *Autobiography of a Yogi*, one of Yogananda's other best-known and most profound masterpieces is his commentary on the Bhagavad Gita. Recently, Swami Kriyananda, direct disciple of Yogananda, published an edition of Yogananda's Gita commentaries:

Revelations of Christ | *Proclaimed by Paramhansa Yogananda, Presented by his disciple, Swami Kriyananda*

Over the past years, out faith has been severely shaken by a growing series of attacks, including: the breakdown of church authority, the repeated discovery of ancient texts that supposedly contradict long-held beliefs, and the sometimes outlandish historical analyses of Scripture by academics. Together, these forces have helped create a spiritual vacuum filled with substantial confusion and uncertainty about the true teachings and meanings of Christ's life. The rising tide of alternative beliefs proves that now, more than ever, people are yearning for a clear-minded, convincing, yet uplifting understanding of the life and teachings of Jesus Christ.

This galvanizing book, presenting the teachings of Christ from the experience and perspective of Paramhansa Yogananda, one of the greatest spiritual masters of the twentieth century, finally offers the fresh perspective on Christ's teachings for which the world has been waiting. This book presents us with an opportunity to understand and apply the Scriptures in a more reliable way than any other: by studying under those saints who have communed directly, in deep ecstasy, with Christ and God.

"Reading *Revelations of Christ* is like having a dialog with our Creator about the meaning of Jesus' life, actions and teaching. . . . The closing sentence of the book says it all: 'The more you tune into his deep message, the more you will know that only one thing matters in life: selfless, divine love, like that of an eternal child for his Heavenly Father, and for his Divine Friend.'" –*Bernie Siegel, MD author of* 365 Prescriptions For The Soul

The Essence of the Bhagavad Gita | *Explained by*
Paramhansa Yogananda, As Remembered by his disciple, Swami Kriyananda

Rarely in a lifetime does a new spiritual classic appear that has the power to change people's lives and transform future generations. This is such a book. *The Essence of the Bhagavad Gita Explained by Paramhansa Yogananda* shares the profound insights of Paramhansa Yogananda, as remembered by one of his few remaining direct disciples, Swami Kriyananda.

This revelation of India's best-loved scripture approaches it from an entirely fresh perspective, showing its deep allegorical meaning and also its down-to-earth practicality. The themes presented are universal: how to achieve victory in life in union with the divine; how to prepare for life's "final exam," death, and what happens afterward; how to triumph over all pain and suffering.

Swami Kriyananda worked with Paramhansa Yogananda in 1950 while the Master completed his commentary. At that time Yogananda commissioned him to disseminate his teachings world-wide. Kriyananda declares, "Yogananda's insights into the Gita are the most amazing, thrilling, and helpful of any I have ever read."

Praise for *The Essence of the Bhagavad Gita*

"*The Essence of the Bhagavad Gita* is a brilliant text that will greatly enhance the spiritual life of every reader."—*Caroline Myss, author of* Anatomy of the Spirit *and* Sacred Contracts

"It is doubtful that there has been a more important spiritual writing in the last 50 years then this soul-stirring, monumental work. What a gift! What a treasure!"—*Neale Donald Walsch, author of* Conversations with God

~~~~~~~~~

There are two different collections of the sayings, stories, and wisdom of Yogananda, each covering a diverse range of spiritual practices and topics, presented in an enjoyable, easy-to-read format.

Conversations with Yogananda
Edited with commentary by Swami Kriyananda

This is an unparalleled, first-hand account of the teachings of Paramhansa Yogananda. Featuring nearly 500 never-before-released stories, sayings, and insights, this is an extensive, yet eminently accessible treasure trove of wisdom from one of the 20th century's most famous yoga masters. Compiled and edited with commentary, by Swami Kriyananda, one of Yogananda's closest direct disciples.

~~~~~~~~

The Essence of Self-Realization | *Edited and compiled by Swami Kriyananda*

A fantastic volume of the stories, sayings, and wisdom of Paramhansa Yogananda, this book covers more than 20 essential topics about the spiritual path and practices. Subjects covered include: the true purpose of life, the folly of materialism, the essential unity of all religions, the laws of karma and reincarnation, grace vs. self-effort, the need for a guru, how to pray effectively, meditation, and many more.

~~~~~~~~

How to Be Happy All the Time: The Wisdom of
Yogananda Series, Volume 1 | *Paramhansa Yogananda*

The human drive for happiness is one of our most far-reaching and fundamental needs. Yet, despite our desperate search for happiness, according to a recent Gallup Poll, only a minority of North Americans describe themselves as "very happy." It seems that very few of us have truly unlocked the secrets of lasting joy and inner peace.

In this book Yogananda playfully and powerfully explains virtually everything needed to lead a happier, more fulfilling life. Topics covered include: looking for happiness in the right places; choosing to be happy; tools and techniques for achieving happiness; sharing happiness with others; balancing success and happiness, and many more.

Praise for *How to Be Happy All the Time*

"The most important condition for happiness is even-mindedness, and here the author of Autobiography of a Yogi brings some of this sense to a treatise on how to be happy under virtually any condition. From identifying habits, thoughts, and practices which steal from happiness to understanding simplicity is the key and sharing happiness with others, How to Be Happy All The Time: The Wisdom of Yogananda, V. 1 is a fine starting point for reaching contentment."—Bookwatch

Karma and Reincarnation: The Wisdom of
Yogananda Series, Volume 2 | *Paramhansa Yogananda*

The interrelated ideas of karma and reincarnation have intrigued us for millennia. In today's post-modern culture, the idea of "karma" has become mainstream while belief in reincarnation is now at an all-time high in the West. Yet, for all of the burgeoning interest, very few of us truly understand what these terms mean and how these laws work.

Here, Paramhansa Yogananda definitively reveals the truth behind karma, death, reincarnation, and the afterlife. With clarity and simplicity, Yogananda makes the mysterious understandable. Topics covered include: how karma works; how we can change our karma; the relationship between karma and reincarnation; what we can learn from our past lives; how to overcome karmic obstacles; how to die with uplifted consciousness; what happens after death; the true purpose of life, and much more.

Spiritual Relationships: The Wisdom of
Yogananda Series, Volume 3 | *Paramhansa Yogananda*

Discover how to express your own highest potential in relationships of friendship, love, marriage, and family. Selfless love is the essential key to happiness in all our relationships, but how do we practice it?

Yogananda shares fresh inspiration and practical guidance on: friendship: broadening your sympathies and expanding the boundaries of your love; how to cure bad habits that spell the death of true friendship: judgment, jealousy, over-sensitivity, unkindness, and more; how to choose the right partner and create a lasting marriage; sex in marriage and how to conceive a spiritual child; problems that arise in marriage and what to do about them; the divine plan uniting parents and children; the Universal Love behind all your relationships.

Few people have viewed their fellow human beings with as much fondness, compassion, and true insight as Yogananda. Both humorous and down-to-earth in his description of human foibles, Yogananda also holds out the highest, divine potential within us and gives practical, sometimes surprising, steps to reach it.

How to Be a Success: The Wisdom of
Yogananda Series, Volume 4 | *Paramhansa Yogananda*

Is there a power that can reveal hidden veins of riches and uncover treasures of which we never dreamed? Is there a force that we can call upon to give success, health, happiness, and spiritual enlightenment? The saints and sages of India taught that there is such a power.

Now, Yogananda shares how we can achieve the highest success of material and spiritual efficiency.

~~~~~~~~~~

Crystal Clarity also makes available many music and spoken word audio resources. Here are some that you might find helpful:

Kriyananda Chants Yogananda | *Swami Kriyananda*

This CD offers a rare treat: hear Swami Kriyananda chant the spiritualized songs of his guru, Paramhansa Yogananda, in a unique and deeply inward way. Throughout the ages, chanting has been a means to achieve deeper meditation. Kriyananda's devotional chanting is certain to uplift your spirit.

~~~~~~~~

AUM: Mantra of Eternity | *Swami Kriyananda*

This recording features nearly 70 minutes of continuous vocal chanting of AUM, the Sanskrit word meaning peace and oneness of spirit. AUM, the cosmic creative vibration, is extensively discussed by Yogananda in *Autobiography of a Yogi*. Chanted here by his disciple, Kriyananda, this recording is a stirring way to tune into this cosmic power.

Gayatri Mantra | *Swami Kriyananda*

This Mantra is one of the most revered of all Vedic mantras. The mantra helps bring about a Divine awakening of the mind and soul. Chanting the mantra deepens the understanding, and helps the practitioner to attain the highest states of consciousness and realization.

~~~~~~~~

Mahamrityunjaya Mantra | *Swami Kriyananda*

The Mahamrityunjaya mantra reflects the soul's call for enlightenment through the practice of purifying ones karma—and soul. Considered beneficial for mental, emotional, and physical health, it is said that whoever recites this mantra everyday will not die an early death.

Metaphysical Meditations | *Swami Kriyananda (J. Donald Walters)*

Kriyananda's soothing voice leads you in thirteen guided meditations based on the soul-inspiring, mystical poetry of Paramhansa Yogananda. Each meditation is accompanied by beautiful classical music to help you quiet your thoughts and prepare you for deep states of meditation. Includes a full recitation of Yogananda's poem, *Samadhi,* which appears in *Autobiography of a Yogi.* A great aid to the serious meditator, as well as those just beginning their practice.

Also available as an audio book:

Autobiography of a Yogi | *by Paramhansa Yogananda*
Audio book read by Swami Kriyananda, selected chapters, 10 hours

This is a recording of the original, unedited 1946 edition of *Autobiography of a Yogi,* presented on six cassettes. Read by Swami Kriyananda, this is the only audio edition that is read by one of Yogananda's direct disciples—someone who both knew him and was directly trained by him. This abridged reading focuses on the key chapters and most thrilling sections of this spiritual classic.

Ananda Worldwide

Ananda Sangha, a worldwide organization founded by Swami Kriyananda, offers spiritual support and resources based on the teachings of Paramhansa Yogananda. There are Ananda spiritual communities in Nevada City, Sacramento, and Palo Alto (CA), Seattle, Portland (OR), and Hopkinton, RI, as well as a retreat center and European community in Assisi, Italy and a center and community near New Delhi, India. Ananda supports more than 75 meditation groups worldwide.

For more information about Ananda Sangha, communities, or meditation groups near you, please contact:

mail:	14618 Tyler Foote Road
	Nevada City, CA 95959
phone:	530.478.7560
online:	www.ananda.org
email:	sanghainfo@ananda.org

The Expanding Light

Ananda's guest retreat, The Expanding Light, offers a varied, year round schedule of classes and workshops on yoga, meditation, and spiritual practice. You may also come for a relaxed personal renewal, participating in ongoing activities as much or as little as you wish.

The beautiful serene mountain setting, supportive staff, and delicious vegetarian food provide an ideal environment for a truly meaningful, spiritual vacation.

For more information, please contact:

phone:	800.346.5350
online:	www.expandinglight.org

Crystal Clarity Publishers

Crystal Clarity Publishers offers many additional resources to assist you in your spiritual journey including many other books, a wide variety of inspirational and relaxation music composed by Swami Kriyananda, and yoga and meditation videos.

To request a catalog, place an order for the above products, or to find out more information, please contact us at:

mail:	Crystal Clarity Publishers
	14618 Tyler Foote Rd.
	Nevada City, CA 95959
phone:	800.424.1055 or 530.478.7600
fax:	530.478.7610
online:	www.crystalclarity.com
email:	clarity@crystalclarity.com